The Stones Will
Cry Out

Recent Titles in
Contributions to the Study of Religion

The Star of Return: Judaism after the Holocaust
Dow Marmur

Just War and Jihad: Historical and Theoretical Perspectives on War and Peace in
Western and Islamic Traditions
John Kelsay and James Turner Johnson, editors

Sacred Places and Profane Spaces: Essays in the Geographics of Judaism,
Christianity, and Islam
Jamie Scott and Paul Simpson-Housley, editors

Choosing the Dream: The Future of Religion in American Public Life
Frederick Mark Gedicks and Roger Hendrix

Death and Afterlife: Perspectives of World Religions
Hiroshi Obayashi, editor

Buddhist Ethics and Modern Society: An International Symposium
Charles Wei-hsun Fu and Sandra A. Wawrytko, editors

Religion and Political Conflict in South Asia
Douglas Allen, editor

Popular Religion in America: The Evangelical Voice
Erling Jorstad

Politics and Religious Authority: American Catholics Since the Second
Vatican Council
Richard J. Gelm

Drums of Redemption: An Introduction to African Christianity
Harvey J. Sindima

Being Religious, American Style: A History of Popular Religiosity in the
United States
Charles H. Lippy

Buddhist Behavioral Codes and the Modern World: An International Symposium
Charles Wei-hsun Fu and Sandra A. Wawrytko, editors

THE STONES WILL CRY OUT

Pastoral Reflections on the Shoah
(With Liturgical Resources)

DOUGLAS K. HUNEKE

Contributions to the Study of Religion, Number 39
Christianity and the Holocaust—Core Issues
Carol Rittner and John Roth, Series Editors

GREENWOOD PRESS
Westport, Connecticut • London

Library of Congress Cataloging-in-Publication Data

Huneke, Douglas K.
 The stones will cry out : pastoral reflections on the Shoah (with liturgical resources) / Douglas K. Huneke.
  p. cm.—(Contributions to the study of religion, ISSN 0196–7053 ; no. 39. Christianity and the Holocaust—Core Issues)
 Includes bibliographical references and index.
 ISBN 0–313–29216–7 (alk. paper)
 1. Holocaust (Christian theology) I. Title. II. Series: Contributions to the study of religion ; no. 39. III. Series: Contributions to the study of religion. Christianity and the Holocaust.
BT93.H86 1995
231.7′6—dc20 95–2094

British Library Cataloguing in Publication Data is available.

Library of Congress Catalog Card Number: 95–2094
ISBN: 0–313–29216–7
ISSN: 0196–7053

First published in 1995

Greenwood Press, 88 Post Road West, Westport, CT 06881
An imprint of Greenwood Publishing Group, Inc.

Printed in the United States of America

The paper used in this book complies with the Permanent Paper Standard issued by the National Information Standards Organization (Z39.48–1984).

10 9 8 7 6 5 4 3 2 1

For Elie Wiesel,
whose witness restored faith and hope;
Rabbi Harold M. Schulweis,
whose vision preserved the memory of goodness; and
Jane Huneke,
whose love, goodness, patience, and perseverance sustained me,
the antidote for the evils I seek to comprehend and address

A religious person is one who holds God and humanity
in one thought at one time, at all times,
who suffers in himself [herself] harms done to others,
whose greatest passion is compassion,
whose greatest strength is love and defiance of despair.

Abraham Heschel

Contents

Editors' Foreword

The Holocaust did not end when the Allies liberated the Jewish survivors from Nazi Germany's killing centers and concentration camps in 1945. The consequences of that catastrophic event still shadow the world's moral, political, and religious life.

This Greenwood Press series entitled *Christianity and the Holocaust—Core Issues* explores Christian complicity, indifference, resistance, rescue, and other responses to the Holocaust. Concentrating on core issues such as the Christian roots of anti-Semitism, the roles played by Christian individuals and groups during the Holocaust, and the institutional reactions of Christians after Auschwitz, the series' focus is historical, but it addresses current concerns as well.

While many of the series' authors are well-known, established Holocaust scholars, the series also features young writers who will become leaders in the next generation of Holocaust scholarship. As all of the authors study the Holocaust's history, they also assess the Holocaust's impact on Christianity and its implications for the future of the Christian tradition.

In the first book of this series, *The Stones Will Cry Out: Pastoral Reflections on the Shoah*, Douglas K. Huneke, a Holocaust scholar who is also a parish minister and a university chaplain, explains how encounters with the Holocaust have reformed his theology and radically informed his approaches to teaching, preaching, counseling, and social justice. As he tells his story, Huneke combines historical and theological insights with practical suggestions that show Christians how to respond to the Holocaust in ways that can mend the world.

Carol Rittner and John Roth

Acknowledgments

Once again my family, Jane and Jason, Karen and Tim, has graciously supported me during this extended time of reflection and writing on the Nazi destruction of European Jewry, the Shoah.

I am also grateful to the members and friends of Westminster Presbyterian Church of Belvedere-Tiburon. For fourteen years they have listened to my stories and shared their own; we have joined our struggles and united in a journey to be faithful, just, and compassionate Christian people. Their kindness and generosity afforded me the sabbatical leave in which to write this volume. They have helped me reclaim my trust in the possibility of the institutional church to be an agent for justice, altruism, and the common good. Sadly, there were not thousands of such churches and people of faith in central and eastern Europe between 1933 and 1945.

I owe special thanks to colleagues who encouraged me to write this book and who have offered support and inspiration: Barbara Daniel Rowe, Michael Barenbaum, Linda Compton, Sheldon Lewis, Rebecca Kuiken, Art Mills, James Noel, William M. Perdue, Donald R. Purkey, Ted Scott, Mary Lynn Tobin, Karl and Rebecca Travis, John Turpin, and Deborah Wright. I am particularly grateful to John Roth and Carol Rittner for guiding this much-needed series and for leading the Christian and academic communities in responding to the evils of the Shoah. To my friend and editor, Pamela Wight, thank you for your tireless watchfulness and invaluable encouragement.

The Stones Will Cry Out

I

REFLECTIONS

Chapter One

Preliminary Reflections, Transforming Encounters

We do not see things as they are, we see them as we are.

Talmud

There is a story, set at the end of the eighteenth century, of two Hasidic Jews who had been traveling for a very long time. They arrived in a certain town and sought a place to rest for the night. Walking the streets, they began to tremble and their hearts were filled with fear. So great was their terror that they left the town without resting. The town was Oświęcim. Years later the occupation forces of the Reich arrived in this Polish town and renamed it Auschwitz.

Unlike the Hasidim, I journeyed to that town in 1977, knowing its German name and with a historical understanding of the horrors that the name had come to represent in the centuries between our respective visits. After five years as a minister to college and high school students in a suburban Presbyterian church and four years as Presbyterian University Pastor at the University of Oregon, where I was also a member of the Honors College faculty teaching courses on the Shoah and the writings of Elie Wiesel, I began a spiritual and intellectual pilgrimage into the universe of the death camps.[1] I carried with me the personal agonies of the war in Vietnam and the searing scenes from the massacre at Kent State University. I was burdened with the trials of my times and the more recently acquired struggles with the Nazi era.

As a result of this pilgrimage to Poland, East Germany, and Israel, I intended to complete a Christian response to the Shoah for its victims and survivors, something that was, for the most part, absent from the library of Christian theology. I studied in archives; visited memorials; toured the remnants of the death camps, museums, and forested mass graves; and listened to the stories of witnesses and survivors.

My first day in Kraków, Poland, fell on a public holiday, so I could not present my papers at the Auschwitz archives. I decided instead to make a personal, spiritual visit to the former death camp. I would find a quiet place to continue reading André Schwarz-Bart's novel *The Last of the Just* and Elie Wiesel's memoir *Night* in the places where the events occurred, to write in my journal, and to reflect and pray.

I found an English-speaking taxi driver to take me to my destination. As we drove, he asked to converse so that he could practice his English. In several months, he would retire and be allowed to leave the country for a reunion with his family who had fled wartime Kraków, resettled in London with the Polish government in exile, and now lived in Chicago. Along the way, he asked about my reasons for traveling a great distance to visit such a terrible place. I explained as best I could that I felt a certain responsibility to compose and offer a Christian response to the profound evils perpetuated against Jews, evils that found both genesis and sustenance in the history, theology, and ministry of the church. The remainder of the drive we both sat in silence. Was he a secret anti-Semite or neo-Nazi, testing my resolve? What thoughts did his silence mask? As he came to a stop in a spacious parking area the nagging questions were satisfied as he turned, took my arm in his strong hand, and said, "No one should enter this place alone the first time. I will go with you."

I perused the books and memorabilia at a small kiosk near the entrance to the auditorium and mused about his intense and sincere words. Why did this taxi driver choose those words? And where was he in 1944 when this camp was gassing and cremating 10,000 Jews each day? What would it have meant if hundreds of Poles or just their national leaders had made the same statement to the Nazis and their collaborators, or engaged the same risk of escorting a stranger into the world of death?

The taxi driver went off to secure passes for a film about the death camp. As we sat together viewing three distinct sequences of historical footage (the first, by Nazi cinematographers of the camp in action; the second and third sequences, by Soviet and Allied liberation forces, respectively), the driver began to cry. By the time the film was over, his body was racked with sobs. He had never seen the films—indeed, he had never before entered the camp—but he knew firsthand why Oświęcim, renamed Auschwitz, was a place of profound evil. We joined the crowd exiting the theater and read the large sign that admonished visitors in a half dozen languages to leave in silence. For whatever reasons, a small group of people five rows in front of us began to speak excitedly in German. My companion was outraged. He raced ahead, cursed them in German, Polish, and English, and disappeared for the remainder of the day.

I wandered through the barracks, offices, and warehouses, and past plaques, posters, and narrative renderings that recounted the history of Auschwitz but that deftly omitted any reference to Jews or Judaism (that offense and the failure to offer any translations in Hebrew or Yiddish were subsequently corrected by the national government). On a shaded railroad loading dock, I found my quiet place to read and reflect. To sit at Auschwitz and read Wiesel's memoir and Schwarz-Bart's novel was to be drawn into an evil that belied the tranquillity of the setting. My reading at that dock personalized the abstract statues, brought to life the horrific photographs, and helped me to confront the deliberate failure to mention that Auschwitz was built to exterminate Jews and obliterate the memory of Judaism. In this setting, I struggled with how a Protestant, American pastor could respond to such an evil era.

Where in this tortured hell were the places that Elie Wiesel described with such staggering simplicity in his memoir? I never found the one location, but I felt the presence of the place where Wiesel's faith in God and life was tested. He wrote:

Not far from us, flames were leaping up from a ditch, gigantic flames. They were burning something. A lorry drew up at the pit and delivered its load—little children. Babies! Yes, I saw it—saw it with my own eyes . . . those children in the flames. (Is it surprising that I could not sleep after that? Sleep had fled from my eyes.)[2]

I looked up to the skies that once carried away the ashen remains of thousands of Jewish children, women, and men. I looked to the clouds, as Schwarz-Bart demanded, for itinerant images of the murdered, for the watery drops where history's tears and my own merged.

As the afternoon shadows lengthened over the camp and as different shadows eclipsed my own spirit, I numbly wandered in the direction of the parking area. I was completely preoccupied with the readings; by my feelings of actually being in the place where it all had happened; by the premonition that had frightened the Hasidim and later became an enduring presence, and by the visions evoked at the archway proclaiming the lie: *Arbeit Macht Frei*. Seventeen years later I still do not have words to adequately describe what I was feeling, the dark forces at work on me in that moment.

Lost in thought and gripped by a nameless fear, I rounded the corner of block number sixteen. The sign said it had been a men's barrack. Suddenly, out of the corner of my eye, I saw a figure move inside the window. With my heart awash in adrenaline, I turned to look at the man staring out at me through the hazy, darkened pane. My eyes adjusted, focused, centered. It was my own reflection. In that encounter, I faced the most personally demanding questions of the Shoah. Thirty-three years earlier, what would I have seen in the window? On which side of the glass would I have stood? What uniform would I have worn? Given my German-Dutch ancestry, would I have cast my lot with the Reich or the Resistance? Would I have worn the executioner's brown uniform, or would I have been a beaten, deteriorated man in a dingy gray-and-blue-striped uniform? Had I been an inmate of Auschwitz, would it have been because I resisted the rise of National Socialism or because I gave aid and comfort to desperate Jews endangered by the fury of the Reich?

If I had been an inmate, what internal sources would I have found to preserve my integrity, what strength to resist the torture and dehumanization of this place? If I had worn the Nazi uniform, what aspects of my humanity, faith, education, and theology would have failed to save me from becoming an executioner? What values, ethics, and stories would I have ignored, denied, or rejected?

The souls of the millions of Jews who died at Auschwitz and a thousand similar places cried out from the ground, as the Bible says Abel's voice cried out for justice from the soil he tilled. The voices did not demand justice of me but, rather, cried out for remembrance and for an answer: Who will I be in response to what I have seen and learned? Who will we be and what will we do because we have heard their testimony? As I broke away from the mirrored image in the window of block sixteen, I felt a sharp pain in my heel. I picked up the pointed pebble and put it in my pocket. I stopped by the execution wall, composed a prayer, and wrapped the stone in the piece of paper containing the prayer, just as I had done at Treblinka and Majdanek, in Warsaw and Lublin. These were the last prayers I would compose or offer for a very long time.

ORIGINS AND DISRUPTIONS

My introduction to Judaism and Hebrew Scripture came late in my schooling. It was a marked contrast to my exclusively Protestant upbringing and to the mild anti-Semitism that I had experienced in my family and church. In my first year of seminary, Professor James Muilenburg introduced me to the compelling and contemporary nature of Hebrew narrative, to the power of the Hebrew prophets, and to the rich and evocative spirituality of biblical poetry. He made the stories and characters live. His respect for the tradition and for Judaism was clear and contagious, but he only once spoke to us directly of the Shoah. In a small weekly gathering where we read the Hebrew text and he commented on the Book of Jeremiah, he referred to that "terrible time in Germany" and its threat to the theological enterprise that was his whole existence, noting that Jeremiah would certainly have confronted the Reich and died at the hands of Hitler.

At the same time, theologian Benjamin Reist formally introduced me to the writings of Dietrich Bonhoeffer and the struggles of the German church. As we studied the drafts of the Presbyterian denomination's social-political Confession of 1967, we had to return to the church-state struggle of the Theological Declaration of Barmen, written and subscribed in 1934 at the General Synod of Barmen. At the very core of the Barmen confession was the confrontation between the comparatively few German church leaders who resisted the Reich's attempt to control and ultimately supplant the churches and the many pastors and theologians who conformed to the dictates and philosophy of National Socialist ideology. That confrontation led to the imposition of a Reich's bishop and to the arrest and imprisonment or execution of clergy who refused to profess allegiance to the Reich. The German church struggles severely challenged my emerging ecclesiology. I found William Shirer's conclusion about the fate of the church to be a stinging indictment and a profound disruption of my sense of Christian community and the calling of the church:

It would be misleading to give the impression that the persecution of Protestants and Catholics by the Nazi State tore the German people asunder or even greatly aroused the vast majority of them. It did not. A people who had so lightly given up their political and cultural and economic freedoms were not, except for a relatively few, going to die or even risk imprisonment to preserve freedom of worship. What really aroused the Germans in the Thirties were the glittering successes of Hitler in providing jobs, creating prosperity, restoring Germany's military might, and moving from one triumph to another in his foreign policy. Not many Germans lost much sleep over the arrests of a few thousand pastors and priests. . . . And even fewer paused to reflect that under the leadership of Rosenberg, Bormann and Himmler, who were backed by Hitler, the Nazi regime intended eventually to destroy Christianity in Germany.[3]

Because of what I learned about Christianity in the Nazi era, I have sought, throughout my service to the church, to use the moral prerogatives of the ministry to remove barriers and to build bridges between religious traditions in the hope that the hatreds and ignorance of the past would not take root in the present. Widespread suspicion and ignorance created tremendous impediments for both sides in those attempts. During my first tenure in parish ministry, the Shoah and its antecedents did not play a dominant role. I intentionally sought a constructive relationship and dialogue with the rabbi and Jewish students at the nearby synagogue because I felt a responsibility to build bonds where my theological ancestors had built excluding fortifications. Concerns about proselytizing and secular observances of Christian holy days took precedence over weightier matters. Later, while serving as the Presbyterian University Pastor in the Campus Christian Ministry at the University of Oregon, I labored to create an environment of respect and cooperation that eventually led to the inclusion of the rabbi on the staff and to a significant name change to Campus Interfaith Ministry. The issues focused on authentic dialogue, the integrity of our respective faith traditions, and an acknowledgment of the primacy of the Shoah. Protestants, Jews, Catholics, and eventually Muslims studied and served together but prayed according to their own traditions.

With my campus ministry colleagues, I spent considerable time counseling Vietnam-era draft resisters and conscientious objectors. The work was intensely demanding because of the urgency felt by the students who faced immediate choices about their role in the war. Campus confrontations and violence, the challenge of the Kent State murders, the general social malaise, and the pressure to keep people talking escalated the stresses. Everywhere around me reason quickly gave way to anger, tolerance to demands, and after the Christmas bombing of Hanoi, rage was easier. A good friend came to talk about the stresses and my state of mind. As we ended our conversation, he said, "You must read an important book—*Night*, by Elie Wiesel."

I had only heard of Wiesel and read one of his essays and a review of one of his books. That very evening I read *Night* and read it again in the morning. Outraged, I sought my friend and demanded an explanation of how he could drag me into the Nazi era and the horrors of the Shoah when I was already overwhelmed by a war that none of us seemed able to successfully resist. He responded simply, "Read it again and see what it can teach you." I reread it and suddenly realized that the entire basis of my work was founded on resistance to those I perceived to be the perpetrators of the war in Vietnam (John Kennedy, Lyndon Johnson, Richard Nixon, Lewis Hershey, Robert McNamara, and William Westmoreland). But I had not taken the side of the victims (the Vietnamese civilians; American soldiers, who were in my estimate pawns or fodder; and American youth who awaited or resisted such a fate).

Elie Wiesel's writings sensitized me to the plight and opened before me the perspective of the victims. His words disrupted my angle of vision, made the most severe demands on my faith, and transformed my worldview. It may seem a subtle thing, but that one memoir was enough to change my motives and expand my definition of who were the victims of the war in Southeast Asia. I poured over every book I could find by Wiesel, and I also started to search out and study the works of witnesses to and victims of the war in Vietnam. Somewhere, Albert Schweitzer wrote, "Sometimes our light goes out but is blown again into flame by an encounter with another human being. Each of us owes the deepest thanks to those who have rekindled this inner light." At a time when all that remained of my inner light was a tiny ember, I read this memoir of a pious, sheltered young Jewish boy whose life had been changed by eight words. Wiesel wrote, "Spoken quietly, indifferently, without emotion. Eight short simple words . . . 'Men to the left! Women to the right! . . .' "[4]

To dispel the darkness of my era, I had to let Wiesel's experience and that of other survivors of the "kingdom of night" pull me into its darkness. The disruptions were wrenching: enter the horrors of Auschwitz while tormented over Christmas bombings and My Lai, confront the seemingly inconsistent presence of God in history, abandon a primary angle of vision for one that was at once more demanding and yet central for a person of faith, and eventually undertake a pilgrimage into the universe of the concentration camps. My deepest thanks to the one who admonished me to read Wiesel, and especially to Elie Wiesel.

ANOTHER DISRUPTION: THE RETURN OF THE TAXI DRIVER

> What is to one man a coincidence is to another a miracle.
>
> Richard Selzer[5]

From the Shoah, humanity derived a frightening and distorted self-perception. A cadre of Shoah-era scholars, students, novelists, and theologians devote most of their writings and studies to reflections on or reports about the overwhelming violence, the unconscionable indifference, and the profound inhumanity that characterized the Shoah. Considering the magnitude and pervasiveness of this evil, and the threat that perhaps worse events lurk beyond the horizon of modern history, they are called to probe every darkened recess in order to understand its origins and to search for some evidence, some quirk, that helps to explain, justify, or excuse. All understandings and explanations are inadequate in the face of Hitlerian genocide, and no justifications or excuses will stand the scrutiny of the victims and survivors of ghettos, mass graves, and death camps.

The taxi driver found me as I walked away from block sixteen, beset by the voices of the millions who died in or suffered Auschwitz, reeling with the struggles, feelings, and fearful thoughts that flooded over me. We had to leave at once, he told me. He had to tell me a story to explain his emotional outburst at the beginning of the day, but he would not speak inside the camp. The story was holy, the camp profane!

The driver talked without pause as he alternately drove and pulled to the side of the road in order to excitedly underscore a point, telling me that his was an old Kraków family and that his sister, like the other family members, was a devout Roman Catholic. She once hoped to become a nun but later studied the modern equivalent of public health nursing. She devoted her life to this work, choosing not to marry or raise children. When the Nazis established first a regional government and then a Jewish ghetto in Kraków, his sister was ordered by the German commander to make daily rounds in the ghetto. She was to determine who was sick, the degree of the illness, and the likelihood of any epidemics that might decimate what she was told would eventually become a labor column working on the rail lines.

At first, because her family was decidedly opposed to what the representatives of the Reich were imposing on the residents of Kraków, she requested medicines but strategically failed to identify the sick. Later, she began completing her reports after a stern rebuke and the assurance that there were no medicines to spare and the sick would be transported to distant clinics, rehabilitated, and returned to Kraków. Each day she first passed through a guard station and, farther along, a check post, both staffed by Ukrainian Militia under the command of a Nazi officer. As she departed she gave a list of the ill and their addresses to the German clerk. From time to time she was able to find a little milk, some potatoes, or sugar; once she even had a medication. All of it she secreted into the ghetto. Otherwise, there was little more she could do than offer comfort and the assurance that the sickest would soon be taken to clinics.

One day in the late fall a neighbor pounded on her door and demanded that she bring first aid immediately. They went a distance outside of Kraków, to a forest adjacent to a railroad spur. Hundreds of bodies were piled beside several cattle cars, awaiting machines that would dig a mass grave. Most of the dead had been shot, and a few were badly wounded—all were Jews. Among the dead and dying she recognized a number of people whom she had identified in the previous week as being sick and in need of hospitalization. Still others she recognized from her visits. Immediately she knew the true use and outcome of her lists. She dared not risk confronting the commandant with her discovery, but neither could she continue naming people or stand idly by as they were murdered.

The nurse devised a plan. She had to save as many of the Jews as possible. Her plan was simple common sense. Her brother explained that his sister was about my height (six foot two inches) and wore as part of her uniform a large hoop skirt. Her plan was to remove small children from the ghetto hidden between her legs by the dress. The nurse told her family what she planned to do and recruited both family and closest friends in the farming area outside Kraków. She asked them to receive the Jewish children as their own or as the offspring of relatives who wanted their children to be safe from the advancing armies. Everyone agreed to participate in her plan. She also understood that people needed papers in order to survive raids and casual discovery. She went to her priest, told him the plan, and asked for baptismal papers that she would complete later. He refused to help, saying that it was neither wise nor safe to defy the Nazis. He would not, however, betray her. Undeterred, she set her plan in motion.

She had identified the first small child and convinced the parents of both her sincerity and the external dangers posed by the Reich and militia. Next, she spent several weeks practicing walking with the child hidden between her legs, his arms wrapped around her thighs, the better to anticipate her every move and to provide a measure of stability on the rutted cobblestone streets leading out of the ghetto. When she was certain that the child could follow her lead without verbal commands, she walked out of the home with her charge well hidden. By the side of the road somewhere between Oświęcim and Kraków, her distraught brother shook as he recalled the fear that gripped her on the morning of the first mission and the terror that kept his entire family at home until after the mission was over. At the first post, she stopped and filed her report: Once again, there was no illness in the ghetto! Then she walked to the next station, waved, and went to a nearby park. She sat down, the child slipped out from under the dress, and the two of them practically ran to the farm that would become the boy's home.

Weeks passed before she found the strength to begin again. But she did. Over the next months, she evacuated numerous children from the Kraków Jewish ghetto (the exact count was uncertain, but her brother thought the number to be a dozen or more). Then one day she decided to take out a child she believed to be sick with tuberculosis. All day they practiced walking in the special way. To save his life she must have felt compelled to take him out that same day. As they approached the guard post, the child began to cough. Without a command, a Ukrainian guard hit the nurse in the head with the butt of his rifle, and as she fell the child was exposed. With no command, other militia held the terror-struck child by the ankles and others shot him to death. Still without a command from the German officer, they turned their rifles and summarily shot the nurse. The only command from the officer was that the two bodies should lie where they were for three days, a warning to anyone else who might dare to defy the edicts of the representatives of the "Master Race" by giving aid or comfort to the Jews of the Kraków ghetto.

Few Jews are thought to have survived these deportations from the Kraków ghetto to the death camps. Did these children survive? Did they reclaim their heritage and traditions? Where are they today? What do they remember? The taxi driver refused to give me his name for fear that he would be kept from the reunion with his extended family, nor would he share the name of his sister for fear of reprisals against family members who remained in Poland.

I always tell her story, primarily because it started me on a new path of understanding and also because I believe her courage and compassion must be remembered, even if anonymously.

Given my state of mind and soul in front of block sixteen, I was ill prepared for another abrupt, invasive disruption, just as I had not been ready for the introduction to the writings and person of Elie Wiesel six years earlier. Suddenly I carried within me the story of a person whose behavior was the antithesis of murder, silence, indifference, and complicity. I was uncomprehending, unprepared for the dislocations that carried me from the "valley of the shadow of death" to the mountaintop of trust, hope, and goodness. While I remained loyal to the central purpose of my pilgrimage, this deeply moving story became a haunting counterpoint to the inhumanity of the Shoah and was the genesis of what would later become a full study of the morality and spirituality, the courage and compassion, of Christians who selflessly defied the Reich in order to save Jewish lives and their own humanity.

WHERE FROM HERE?

Rabbi Harold Schulweis, the originator of all rescuer studies and the patron of rescuers who live at the economic margins of their societies, correctly notes that there could not have been great courage and compassion without corresponding evil and inhumanity. Of the millions of people in central and eastern Europe who should have been expected to respond to the plight of the Jews, only a faithful remnant met the challenge of evil with altruistic interventions. But then it is most often the few, the remnant, who maintain the faith and act according to the dictates of their belief systems, thereby providing the foundation for the reformation of traditions lost to the uncaring majority. Rabbi Schulweis also wisely counsels that if humanity knows the names and the deeds of the likes of Adolf Eichmann, Heinrich Himmler, and Adolf Hitler, then it must balance the fragile spiritual ecology and know the names and celebrate the deeds of Nazi-era rescuers such as

Herman Graebe, Irene Opdyke, Oskar Schindler, and André and Magdala Trocmé.

Professor James Muilenburg taught his students the perspective that the Hebrew conception of human beings in the midst of time was not linear but rather sequences of highs and lows, with long stretches of routine, even banal periods, all of which were disrupted by explosive intrusions of the holy, the breaking in of grace. Human beings, he said, lived between the highs and lows, in the sustaining movements of grace. The truth and power of that lesson was proved for me in the encounters at Auschwitz.

Exploding into the midst of the anxiety and pain that I experienced outside of block sixteen, and in the readings and reflections that were hammering at my soul, was a moment of grace unleashed through the excited, fearful, and liberating story of goodness told from the searing, vindicating memory and in the tremulous voice of a taxi driver from Kraków. The Dutch Calvinist in me is quite certain that this was not a matter of serendipitous coincidence but, rather, in the least likely moment, of the Holy One breaking into the lostness and alienation that pilgrims to Auschwitz feel so acutely. It is the movement of grace that can transform the darkest encounter into a sacred journey, the memory of incredible evil into a life of blessing and hope. The profound difficulty of the Shoah is that it does not easily afford its sojourners the means of locating the balance between evil and goodness, of communicating the emergent blessings and hope. Also, the goodness of rescuers dares not precede the evil or dominate the true nature of the Shoah. If it does, one cannot adequately face either the inhumanity or the compassion that the Shoah gave rise to.

For many years, I felt a certain isolation from most of my professional peers. There was something about my involvement in and responses to the Shoah that separated us. A large measure of the distance was due to the mandate I felt to address the evil before integrating the compassion. It was also a matter of my urgent need to re-form my theology and construct new paradigms. In retrospect, I had not been able to create a harmonious balance between the horrors and the grace. For the longest time, I could not find adequate words and images to speak of the Shoah and tell of my experiences. It was a painful time, and it remains a painful memory. I could not understand why others did not feel the urgency I felt to understand, to respond as Christians, to be versed in and somehow radically different because of the Shoah. Too often, it seemed that many of my colleagues were not even searching for a way of knowing and responding. Were they listening to the voices? When would they face the implications, probe the lessons, and commence a reformation of denominational traditions and theologies that were the fertile soil of the Shoah? At the beginning, I

interpreted the isolation as a moral judgment and imposed my own judgments, thereby widening the gulf that divided us.

In my study of the Shoah, listening to the survivors, making the pilgrimage to the former death camps, responding as a Christian, and pursuing the
research on Nazi-era rescuers, I had felt the need to fully immerse myself.
It would not be enough to view it from a distance or to read about it in a
detached way. It was, in a Christian sense, like an adult baptism in which
one "dies" to a way of living and emerges from that Jordan River reborn to
a new being and way of thinking.

In 1978, at a teach-in honoring Wiesel, Irving Greenberg delivered a
paper in which he addressed the "Holocaust shattered paradigms." The
shattered paradigm metaphor fit perfectly, expressing my experience of the
nothingness and providing me a baptismal mode for speaking about the
effect of the Shoah on my life and thinking. The paradigms of a faith that
had once seemed fixed and certain no longer satisfied when the questions
focused on a "lorry drawing up at the pit and delivering its load—little
children. Babies!" The paradigm shattered on unthinkable evils set against
the questions of God's presence, power, and promises, and on Christian
persons and denominations that acted arbitrarily and conformed rather than
offering a faithful witness of resistance. My faith was adrift in the dark
turbulence of the Shoah, in spite of the courage and goodness of a Roman
Catholic public health nurse in Kraków.

The encounters and the specific shattered paradigms, which I will address
more fully in subsequent chapters, forced me to ask about the uniform I
would have worn at Auschwitz. But moving tsunami-like beneath the
surface was another question: Who would I have become without the taxi
driver's story? At about the same time as Greenberg spoke of shattered
paradigms, a dear friend and colleague, Donald Purkey, penned the following verse that captured my struggle:

> The ad suggests
> that this magic epoxy
> will increase
> the tensile strength
> of broken fragments.
> What graceful glue
> will bind
> the fracture lines
> of my shatteredness?
> And knit the fragments
> of my jagged edges
> into a rainbow prism?

Indeed, "What graceful glue will bind . . .?" How shall we find the harmony and build from the shattered paradigms? Ultimately, that which is shattered is never again the same—for the sake of memory and the future, it dare not be unchanged.

The challenge of this volume is to share reformations and paradigms that advance the delicate spiritual ecology of post-Shoah Christianity by maintaining the tension between the suffering of the victims, the offense of the killers, and the goodness of the rescuers. And yet the edge must be given to the faithful remnant who saved and sanctified life, rather than to those who chose to ally themselves with the forces of death. It is a demanding but essential balance.

My purpose is to provide my colleagues, clergy and laity, in seminaries, synagogues, and churches, with a way of appropriating essential elements of the history of the Shoah in order to respond to both the evils and the grace that came from it. For those who cannot devote themselves to a long-term study of the Shoah or who fear being consumed by it, I intend to provide entry points that will employ our professional knowledge and facilitate pastoral responses that have integrity and authenticity. In recent years, I had an important awakening as I listened to my colleagues discuss their struggles to read about the Shoah, to view documentary and commercial films, to reflect theologically on its meaning from an American angle of vision in the waning hours of the twentieth century, and to find ways to speak constructively of it in sermons and classes to congregants who for many reasons feel that neither they nor their nation were responsible or accountable for what the Nazis did. With all respect to the survivors and victims, not everyone can or even must immerse themselves in the Shoah in order to take its lessons to heart and respond. They can know its history, they can read and speak of it, and be different because of it, without devoting their lives to understanding it. Having written that, it must also be said that there will be no reformation of the pastoral and theological enterprise unless we listen to the voices of those who perished, the witness of those who survived, appropriate the model of compassion of those who rescued, and extend the lessons of those who resisted.

By reflecting on the Shoah in the context of pastoral ministry and by presenting liturgical, homiletical, and educational resources, I will offer readers the opportunity to draw on the universal lessons and implications of the Shoah without diminishing or ignoring the uniqueness of this Jewish experience. The challenge is to find ways to share the stories that will enable us to stand in pulpits and before classes to speak an authentic word of hope in an increasingly violent and alienating time and, paradoxically, in an era when peace among the nations is growing.

There is an oft-told Hasidic story of Israel Baal Shem Tov (1700–1760). He would go to a specific place in the forest where he would light a fire and offer a special prayer, and God would respond. Before his death he instructed his disciples to do the same, and the first of them complied. But later, a disciple went to the forest and offered the prayer without knowing how to light the fire. Still, God was present. Much later, with the fire forgotten, the place lost to memory, and the prayer gone, a disciple remembered and told the story, as did succeeding generations, and they knew God's presence in the transmission of the tale. One possible interpretation of this legend is that we are entrusted with all manner of stories and with the responsibility of passing them from generation to generation. Along with the work of repairing shattered paradigms, we must also enlarge our collections of stories that will move us and our people to greater faithfulness, to hope, to acts of goodness; that will keep us from averting our eyes when we are in the presence of evil and death; from acts of complicity; and from ignoring the cries of the human family.

Every story and resource in this volume is shared with the hope that readers will freely transmit them and encourage others to do the same.

Chapter Two

Shattered Paradigms, Healing Affirmations

When you remember me, it means that you have carried something of
who I am with you, that I have left some mark of who I am on who you
are. . . . It means that even after I die, you can still see my face and hear
my voice and speak to me in your heart. For as long as you remember
me, I am never entirely lost.

Frederick Buechner[1]

As I review my journals, notes, and commentaries spanning nearly twenty
years of listening to, studying about, and teaching the Shoah, what strikes
me is the relentless intrusions of holiness and grace into the formidable
darkness. At times, the intrusions were only thinly scattered glimpses of
light, but they pierced the darkness as surely as the darkness had shattered
my foundations. Those rays of light guided and sustained me. How is it that
the remembrances of such overwhelming evil and death can also be so full
of life? Something in the confrontations with the horrors of the Nazi era
heightened my yearning for hope and peace and added an urgency to my
desire to know that justice prevailed and had a future. In the midst of a bleak
landscape came the craving for beauty and love. As all that had earlier
seemed certain and secure became capricious and unstable, I found myself
searching for symbols and affirmations that would stand against the constantly encroaching void. I could not—I did not—search for saving graces;
they found me.

The experience of life and blessing piercing and, even in their diminutive
stature, balancing the oppression and suffering is the model for the reflections that follow. A compensatory equilibrium, between shattered paradigms

and healing affirmations, is essential if we are to empower faithful responses
to and meaningful preaching and teaching about the Shoah. The end result
is most likely to be a vested passion that is communicated with people in
the pews who hunger for worship that sustains, comforts, and sends them
back into their daily worlds to be faithful, just, and compassionate people.
The stories set in the global context of the Shoah and the tales of bravery
and goodness (footnotes rather than volumes in the global context) become
the moral role models and the ethical compass for both pulpit and pew. I
would go so far as to say that an authentic encounter with the Shoah gives
an empowering sense of meaning that in turn makes it possible to get out
of bed each morning and meet a new day with all of its challenges and
demoralizing headlines, that transforms the numbness and assaults into life
and blessing, and that gives mere existence a sense of mission and wholeness rather than banality and stale routine!

Philosopher and theologian John Roth, in an essay on the impact of Elie
Wiesel's writings on his life, offers an insight that speaks of the tone I intend
for this book and the purpose of a pastoral and theological engagement with
the Shoah:

What [Wiesel] seeks . . . is the understanding that lives in friendship—understanding that includes tentativeness, fallibility, comprehension that looks for error
and revises judgment when error is found, realization that knowing is not a matter
of fixed conviction but of continuing dialogue.

Elie Wiesel's lessons about understanding urge one not to draw hasty or final
conclusions. Rather his emphasis is on exploration and inquiry. It might be objected
that such an outlook tends to encourage indecision and even indifference. To the
contrary, however, one of Wiesel's most significant contributions runs in just the
opposite direction. . . . Dialogue leads not to indecision but to an informed decisiveness. . . . Openness results not in indifference but in the loyalty of which
friendship is made and on which it depends.[2]

For post-Shoah American clergy, the dialogue between ministry, theology, and the Shoah is indeed a search for historical awareness and listening
posts where the stories and encounters can safely be shared. Flowing from
the encounters and dialogue is the reformation of ecclesiastical paradigms
and the birth of fresh models for engagement with a broken world. There
are two vital conditions under which this dialogue must take place. First, it
must be a dialogue based on friendship between the student of the Shoah
and the world. The dialogue must be built on a foundation that affirms life
and moves toward people in friendship rather than against them as enemies.
Moses spoke to the people of Israel about a choice as they were poised to
enter the Promised Land, a sacred geography that Moses would only see

from a distance but never touch. In the Book of Deuteronomy, on God's behalf, Moses said, "Today I set before you life and blessing, death and curse. Choose life, then" (30:29b). Our dialogue with the Shoah begins and ends with an affirmation of life and blessing, with the rejection of the forces of division and death.

As Roth suggests, the essence of the choice is a matter of approaching the Shoah and the brokenness of the modern world, and also the Creator of the Universe, as a friend. I include God in the act of friendship because I believe we must exercise empathy for the One whose intentions for the entire creation are routinely routed by ill will, carelessness, apathy, and detachment. The One whose ultimate sympathy embraces all of humankind must be the object of our compassionate understanding. In his fourth novel, *The Gates of the Forest*, Elie Wiesel's protagonist is Gregor, a young Jewish survivor of the death camps. He struggles with the troubling and elusive presence (or absence) of God in a world dominated by the effects of Nazi annihilations. What is his alternative if God has abandoned creation and no longer honors the covenant? If that is not the question, then Gregor labors to find a meaningful concept of God.

In his prior novel, *Town Beyond the Wall*, Wiesel used his characters to establish that respectful and liberating human relationships are the primary response to the Shoah, the only way of living in the human community after Auschwitz. But in *The Gates of the Forest*, Gregor protects himself by pretending to be mute. Later, he is forced to be Judas in a Passion Play. With his youth ripped from him by the Nazis, Gregor befriended (or was it that he was himself befriended?) by a mystical character named Gavriel. As their relationship bonds, Gavriel and Gregor speak first of a friend of Gavriel's who was murdered because of his words, and then they enter into a dialogue about friendship.

Gregor asked, "Who was he?" "I told you. A friend." "A shadow?" "No. He was the opposite, he was the enemy of night. . . . And what is a friend? More than a father, more than a brother: a traveling companion, with him, you can conquer the impossible, even if you must lose it later. Friendship marks a life even more deeply than love. Love risks degenerating into obsession, friendship is never anything but sharing. It is to a friend that you communicate the awakening of a desire, the birth of a vision or a terror, the anguish of seeing the sun disappear or of finding that order and justice are no more. . . . What is a friend? Someone who for the first time makes you aware of your loneliness and his, and helps you to escape so you in turn can help him. Thanks to him you can hold your tongue without shame and talk freely without risk. That's it."[3]

To adopt a position of friendship with survivors, witnesses, and rescuers, to let the Shoah tell us of the "birth of [its] terror" or of the anguish of "seeing the sun disappear or of finding that order and justice are no more," is the beginning of a liberating act. In this dialogue the survivor, in the act of telling the story, and the student, in the act of listening to the story, together liberate one another from the rapidly descending spirals of violence, through the act of being changed because of what is shared and learned. The troubled world is the beneficiary of that friendship and the consequences of truthful disclosure, authentic hearing, and genuine transformation. In the dialogue between friends, the choice is made for life and blessing rather than death and curse.

For Gregor, in an encounter with a Rebbe, friendship took on a theological component. Gregor speaks to the spiritual leader:

"Has nothing changed?" "Nothing." "What about me?" "You haven't changed either." "And Auschwitz? What do you make of Auschwitz?" "Auschwitz proves that nothing has changed, that the primeval war goes on. Man is capable of love and hate, murder and sacrifice. He is Abraham and Isaac together. God himself hasn't changed." Gregor was angry. "After what happened to us, how can you believe in God?" With an understanding smile on his lips the Rebbe answered, "How can you *not* believe in God after what has happened?"[4]

Faith continues in spite of and often because of what is experienced, remembered, or encountered later. The liberating power of friendship, personal and theological, comes a few lines later when the infant son of Gregor's work colleague, Mendel, dies. Gregor said, "No one can fight the night by himself and conquer it, Mendel. Victory would be meaningless even if he won. For two persons together victory is possible."[5] Gregor, the tested and still unsettled survivor-pilgrim, persisted as Mendel resisted. One night, as the two walked home, Gregor finally began to talk about himself and his childhood; he remembered the Hasidic world of his youth, "generous and full of love."[6]

In Christian Scripture, friendship is the defining character of the relationship between believers and the Messenger of God. The writer of John's gospel radically changes the relationship between Jesus and his followers from vertical to horizontal, from removed to intimate, when he quotes Jesus as saying in his farewell discourse:

A person can have no greater love than to lay down his [her] life for his [her] friends. You are my friends, if you do what I command you. I shall not call you servants any more, because a servant does not know the master's business; I call you friends, because I have made known to you everything I have learned from my Father. (John 15:13–15)

At the end of the pericope, Jesus identified the single condition for friend-ship as following his commandment "to love one another." Love is the defining character of God's relationship with humanity, and the example of God's love is to be the defining character of all human relationships. To believe in God, because of and in spite of the Shoah, is to believe in love as the defining quality, the final word, the redemptive force responding to evil, suffering, and death.

This friendship is a way of life, a posture toward creation and the human family, and the ground of any relationship with God. Friendship and love are the pathway to passion and a means by which to prevent the destructive forces of the Shoah, and for that matter, every force of death, from having the final word over life. We enter and emerge from the Shoah with a word of hope, an affirmation to cast against the negations, an articulated and enfleshed choice of life and blessing, and the sustaining power of love.

The second condition of the dialogue addresses the angle of vision from which we prepare the words that we offer from our pulpits and the spirit in which we speak them. Pulpit clergy, theologians, and teachers enjoy the privilege of regularly giving expression to their concerns, reflections, and commentaries. For many, the privilege is understood to be such and is generally honored by thoughtful, creative presentations of carefully crafted words, insightful metaphors, contemporary applications, and probing ques-tions. A core aspect of the post-Shoah reformation of my practice of ministry has been to find a careful measure to test the integrity and credibility of each of these qualities. In 1974, Irving Greenberg postulated what he called a "working principle" that has become a personal standard to judge the spoken and written word or, for that matter, the liturgical arts generally. He writes, "Let us offer, then, as a working principle the following: no statement, theological or otherwise, should be made that would not be credible in the presence of burning children."[7]

Post-Shoah Christian preaching, teaching, and theology must have a radical and sustained point of origin and be weighed by one of the most demanding standards imaginable. The point of origin must be at the ledge of a filling mass grave, below the hose disguised as a shower head in a gas chamber, beside a wall that bears the bloodstained mark of an infant's skull. It must begin in the presence of burning children. The standard demands to know: Can you speak that word, offer that reflection, use that metaphor, or rely on that perspective in "the presence of burning children"? It must know if our words will unite or divide the human family, move peoples closer together, rather than apart or against each other.

Greenberg's working principle, our standard, is also an ultimatum: Do you see in the burning children of memory the starving child in the sub-Sahara, the impoverished child of the ghetto, the lost child of affluence, the brutalized child of Bosnia, the throwaway child of an urban shelter, the shunned and alienated homosexual youth, the languid children of fetal alcohol syndrome or abuse or neglect or torture? A critical caution is necessary, however: The burning children of memory must not be compared to the other children. We invoke the memory of the past in order to engage in moral discourse that confronts and challenges the evil of the present hour. We invoke the past because we have committed to the persons of its memory that we will do everything in our power not to let their suffering be repeated.

From radical friendship and presence, we take seriously the memory of those who died and survived. Through us, they have being and substance; it is as if they live on. On behalf of memory, we proclaim our willingness to be changed and never silent in the face of inhumanity or indifference. We carry in us the stories of the burning children of memory and covenant to tell of their experiences from one generation to the next. They are the foundation of our choice for life and blessing, the alarm that will alert us to what we must say and do if the specter of some mutation of Auschwitz crests the distant horizon of history. Our ordination vows demand nothing less of us than that those children determine the vantage point from which we will speak our words of hope and affirmation.

SNAPSHOTS

Nazi-era rescuer Herman Graebe transformed my "book knowledge" of the Reich's mobile killing units (*Einsatzgruppen*—literally "Special Action Groups") with his eyewitness stories of their atrocities. In 1942, the Reich Security Service commissioned four battalion-sized (approximately 3,000 men in each unit) mobile killing units. These groups moved rapidly through Poland, the Ukraine, and parts of the then-Soviet Union. They were virtually autonomous, always free of the usual military constraints and wartime protocols, and they never had historically legitimated military objectives. Usually the units followed behind the German army, but they were free to conduct lightning raids, or "Actions" as they came to be called, well ahead of advancing forces. Their mission was to round up and kill Jews, whom they referred to as "undesirables."

As the preliminary hunt of an Action progressed, Jews were beaten, shot on sight, or victimized by whatever whim struck a soldier's fancy. Graebe, assigned by the Reich Railroad Administration to manage large labor columns preparing rail services for the advancing German army, watched one group of soldiers in a subunit of *Einsatzgruppe* C rip small children and infants from their mothers' arms and smash them into door posts and pillars.

He once saw one of the men throw a screaming infant into the air and catch it on his bayonet. The Actions that Herman Graebe witnessed usually ended on the ledges of mass graves, away from the towns and villages where they had commenced. Naked Jews of every age waited under heavy guard for the order to take their place on the narrow ledge, to be shot, and left to die on a mound of bodies. At one such massacre in the Ukraine, Graebe listened as the shooters ordered women to hold their small children in front of themselves so that two persons could be murdered with one bullet. A perverse economy of death!

Ernest Biberstein had two identities. He was a student of theology and for nearly eleven years a parish minister. He also commanded *Einsatzcommando* 6, a unit of *Einsatzgruppe* C, a barbaric and proficient force that carried out deeds similar to those witnessed by Herman Graebe in Rovno, Dubno, and Sdolbonov. How does one move from ministerial leadership in the worlds of theological discourse, pastoral care, and spiritual practices to a position of authority in the Nazi universe of brutality and genocide? By what twists of logic and corruption of the Gospels does a minister detach himself from the ethical and compassionate mandates of Scripture and place himself in the service of the opposite of what his faith teaches?

It was one thing, understandable but not excusable, for countless Protestant clergy, indeed the majority, to acquiesce, with the largest portion of the civilian population, to the social ideology and political propaganda of the National Socialist movement. It was altogether different to craft for Hitler the thirty-point agenda for the pagan National Reich Church. Worse still, to act in complicity with the Nazi death machine as Biberstein did. We can understand how the humiliating defeats of the past and the seemingly glorious promises of Hitler's Reich could win the early favor of a patriotic World War I submarine skipper like Pastor Martin Niemöller. But the initial support of Niemöller and some of the eventual dissidents in the evangelical churches quickly waned as they began to see the realities of the movement and contemplated taking an oath to "One People, One Reich, One Faith." Fervor paled before the demand to ascribe one's assent to points seven and nineteen of the agenda,which read, respectively, "The National Church has no scribes, pastors, chaplains or priests, but National Reich orators are to speak in them" and "On the altars there must be nothing but *Mein Kampf* (to the German nation and therefore to God the most sacred book) and to the left of the altar a sword."

As Pastor Biberstein allied himself with the forces of death, Niemöller joined forces with the anti-Nazi clergy and the synods of dissent. While Biberstein's homicidal activities earned him the accolades of those who crafted Hitler's genocide, Niemöller and his marginalized colleagues were quickly isolated and imprisoned. In many cases, these clergy vanished into the darkness of the concentration camps. Helmut Gollwitzer, in *Dying We Live*, collected a remarkable witness to their courage, recorded in letters and diaries written in Reich prisons. One can only guess what words filled the diaries of a man such as Ernest Biberstein. Biberstein's entries might have included a self-congratulatory acknowledgment for 5,000 Jews dispatched to mass graves in one town in a week or recorded the successful "elimination" of hundreds more of those people Hitler alternatively referred to as a superior race and as infectious "vermin." We know Pastor Niemöller's courageous wartime witness as a leading strategist of the anti-Nazi resistance, and we remember his celebrated postwar admonition:

In Germany they came first for the Communists and I did not speak out because I was not a Communist. Then they came for the Jews, and I did not speak out because I was not a Jew. Then they came for the trade unionists, and I did not speak out because I was not a trade unionist. Then they came for the Catholics, and I did not speak up because I was a Protestant. Then they came for me, and by that time no one was left to speak up.[8]

The striking dissonance of Biberstein's and Niemöller's lives raises the potent question of each person's accountability for what is done with his or her knowledge. To the service of what ends do we give our intellectual, spiritual, and moral being? For five years, while a member of the Honors College Faculty at the University of Oregon, I probed that question with students who examined their academic pursuits and intended vocations in light of readings by Elie Wiesel and from the history and literature of the Nazi era. Once again, the question returns from my mirrored image the window of block sixteen: Who would you have been, and what would you have done, then? More urgently, who will you be today because of the stories you have heard and the lessons you have acquired? How can we be certain that postsecondary higher education and advanced seminary education prepare students to address these two fundamental questions in a humane and humanitarian fashion?

That the National Socialist movement found its earliest strengths in the hallowed halls of academia is not new information. But we may personalize that distant, abstract truth. One of my students, grappling with the magnitude of 6 million dead Jewish human beings, wrote, "Such a number is well beyond my grasp. What I can grasp is the picture of my great-grandfather, a German Jew who brought a Nobel Prize home to his country, and by all accounts I have heard, a great man, being made to flee Germany as a rabbit before the jaws of a cruel and sadistic dog. Then there were the Hitler Youth who entered my great-grandfather's classroom stomping their jackboots and shouting anti-Jewish slurs." In class, he asked the haunting question: Is the university or college education offered in America capable of empowering its graduates to withstand tyrannical acts of inhumanity?

Another student,with a pre-med major, entered one of the classes with an exceptionally idealistic interpretation of the "Hippocratic Oath" and the practice of medicine. The purpose of the final paper was to integrate the Shoah and a student's vocational goals. As part of the assignment, she read several volumes of the medical experiments at Auschwitz. The medical experiments conducted by physicians shattered her paradigms and took away her innocence. From the shadow side of her vocational calling, she wrote of her new commitments and perspective: "As a pre-medical student and scientist any future avenue I might take will require that I look closely at how I will apply my knowledge. I must be aware and cautious of possible inhumane uses of my knowledge and research. I hope I will be strong enough to use my knowledge for the benefit of the human community." The challenge she faced was not wasted. She called from a roadside phone one night, en route to an embarkation point where she would deliver the truck and trailer loads of donated medical supplies she had secured from her colleagues, supplies destined for a free clinic serving a community of poor and oppressed *campecinos* in Central America.

It is not merely reasonable, it is essential, given the potentials for violence and oppression in the world, to expect that all students will so examine their vocational aspirations and test their own values against those of the academy and the practitioners of the particular work. In addition to raising these issues in higher education, one of the most appropriate places to initiate and sustain these inquiries is from the pulpit and in the classrooms of churches and synagogues. Using the pulpit and religious education venues to address the questions of the moral use of knowledge attaches a theological importance to work that has the power to transform labor into vocation, aspiration into calling, all the while refining and applying the ethical and humanitarian values of a faith tradition.

A final snapshot of this central issue of callings and values: When Franz Stangl moved from being an Austrian policeman to being the commandant of Treblinka, he exchanged his calling to protect life for a murderous enterprise. British journalist Gitta Sereny has ably told Stangl's story in her book *Into That Darkness: An Examination of Conscience.*[9] When Stangl, a nominal Christian, arrived at Treblinka, he found that extermination was by means of carbon monoxide gas, generated from the exhaust of a submarine engine, pumped into truck trailers that were fully loaded with Jewish children, women, and men.

Often the engine broke down and the victims were forced to remain in the vans without air or room to move. Death by carbon monoxide poisoning is gruesome and slow; the entire process was horrible for the victims and repulsive to the unprofessional soldiers who carried out Stangl's orders and who were near the point of refusing to continue the killings. The commandant was also earning the criticism of Berlin. The fact that his quotas were not being met infuriated the German High Command. Stangl asked Nazi doctors what he could do to expedite the deaths. He inquired of educated engineers how he could make the submarine motor more reliable. The engineers made their suggestions for changes in the design. For their part, the physicians told him to force the intended victims, already weakened by the trip to the camp, to run at full speed a distance of one kilometer. Their reasoning held that people whose rate of respiration was at its peak and whose hearts were pumping fast would rapidly absorb the carbon monoxide and die much faster. Orders could be followed by squeamish troops and quotas would be met.

Later, working in concert, doctors, chemists, architects, engineers, builders, and other learned persons used their knowledge and training to turn cargo trailers into gas chambers, mass graves into crematoria, and carbon monoxide into the vastly superior pesticide Zyklon-B. What characteristics, qualities, and learning distinguish a devout Roman Catholic public health nurse who became a rescuer of small Jewish children in the Kraków Jewish ghetto and those who used their knowledge and training to mastermind the machinery of mass extermination? What experiences and values compelled one German engineer to design and build a successful rescue network in the Ukraine, while countless of his peers plotted the plans that set the death camps into operation? The same questions apply to priests, pastors, and theologians who intervened, resisted, remained indifferent, or were complicit. For that matter, the questions belong to everyone in every field of endeavor.

One of the primary shattered paradigms from the Shoah is the failure of both secular higher education and the educational enterprises of Christianity to provide the majority of people with internal intellectual and spiritual voices of conscience that would give them reason to pause and the basis for questioning the morality of their behavior. Education, in spite of the influence of classical moral inquiry and its positive links to religious ethics and traditions, was inadequate before the task of containing the uses of knowledge.

As the example of Ernest Biberstein, pastor and commander of a Nazi mobile killing unit, dramatically depicts, a commitment to Jesus Christ, a course of formal theological education, public concurrence with and profession of historic credal statements, biblically based ordination vows, spiritual practices, and knowledge of religious values and teachings are not solely adequate to prevent complicity in evil. Each of those, individually and collectively, serves no purpose unless it is translated into values and behaviors that protect, sustain, and sanctify human life.

Parallel to this shattered paradigm is the healing affirmation of Nazi-era rescuers. These faithful, altruistic people are the antithesis of complicity and indifference, and studies of their lives reveal important values, characteristics, traits, and skills that they translated into inclusive, egalitarian worldviews and compassionate actions that in turn protected, sustained, and sanctified life. Clearly, these values, worldviews, and actions led to what Professor Roth referred to as "informed decisiveness." In a later chapter, I will discuss and illustrate in detail the commonalities that made it possible for Nazi-era rescuers to differentiate themselves from those who were either indifferent or complicit. While none of the rescuers reported taking formal classes or remembered hearing many sermons or lessons in which the question of the moral uses of knowledge was discussed, almost to a person, they had thought about their lives and actions during the war years in precisely those terms. Years later, they reported experiencing the essential unity and cohesion of faith, work, values, and behavior and the feeling of being at peace with themselves. They are not smug about any of this; indeed, most live with a tension between knowing that they did their best and all they could and speculating that if they had done something differently or started rescues earlier or only worked at it harder, they could have saved more lives.

FROM ASSERTIONS TO QUESTIONS

For generations, two of the primary tasks of theology have been the preservation and maintenance of doctrinal assertions and the protection of the Christian faith from external challenge and internal dissent. Without doubt, there is an important place for spiritual certainly and a measure of uniformity, though not lockstep conformity, in the midst of what seems an eternal ebb and flow of moral relativism, barely moderated societal chaos, and the vulnerability of the constraints that prevent institutional anarchy. I grew up in churches where dogma, assertions, and a benevolent theological absolutism were common. We knew what we could believe, therefore assert, even if we had not adequately analyzed it, intentionally appropriated it, sufficiently judged its merits and effects, or actively allowed it to inform our lives.

The ideas presented in a seminary course on Scripture were new to me and were taught without any hint of anti-Semitism but also without a disclaimer about their potential to inspire anti-Jewish sentiments. We were introduced to dozens of so-called fulfillment quotations in the Gospel of Matthew—quotations borrowed by the author of the text to apparently establish that Jesus "fulfilled" the "Old Testament's" prophetic anticipations. We were told that the author of the Gospel used them to establish a triangular link between the Hebrew expectation of a messiah, the presence and mission of Jesus, and the northern Palestinian Jewish audience for whom the text was intended. In short, they were used to make Jesus attractive to his audience; the quotes had evangelistic designs. I must say again that the professor never exhibited an anti-Semitic animus. Not until years later, after studying the Christian origins of anti-Semitism and still later after the pilgrimage, did I fully appreciate the potential dangers implicit in teachings that did not include a caveat about their potential abuse.

An additional illustration will help make the point. During the season of Lent, at the parish that considered itself to be the "university church," adjacent to the campus I served, a visiting preacher delivered what should immediately have been recognized as an anti-Semitic sermon. He spoke of Jesus as the "completion" of the Hebrew tradition. He decried his death at the hands of the "Jewish establishment in Jerusalem." He lamented the failure of "the world" to recognize and follow Jesus. (The phrase "the world" could have been understood as a universal reality or as a camouflaged reference to Jews: the latter interpretation seemed more likely, given the flow of the sermon.) The sermon concluded with a soliloquy extolling the spiritual primacy of Jesus and the moral supremacy of Christianity.

Following the service, a professor, who recognized the anti-Jewish bias of the sermon, and I began to dissect the contents and the assumed motives of the preacher. Several people who happened into the discussion simply did not see the improprieties of the sermon or the dangers of the assertions. Too often, people unknowingly practice an uncritical attention to the contents of sermons. They fail to analyze the implications and consequences of a particular line of thinking, and they allow dangerous assertions to passively slip into their theological storehouse, unexamined or unchallenged. When preachers or theologians are uncritical, or fail to judge their words and measure the implications of what they are saying, or fully consider historical settings and remember the antecedents that give rise to contemporary acts of hatred and division, they fall prey to the same problems as people in the pews. Worse, because of their status, they actually perpetuate the dangerous theological assertions.

In spite of its pleasant, occasionally humorous presentation, the sermon in question was an example of triumphalist Christian thinking. The labeling of certain "Old Testament" passages, quoted in a Gospel, as "fulfillment" quotations also implies a triumphalist conclusion. A habituated form of triumphalist usage is to refer to the Hebrew texts as the "Old Testament." Why not simply call it either the Hebrew Testament or the Hebrew texts? In summary, triumphalism contends that the birth, life, ministry, death, and resurrection of Jesus Christ, and the advent of Christianity and the church, supplant Hebrew Scripture, the Temple, synagogues, and Judaism. Carried to various extremes, Christian triumphalism has been the fertile soil for charges of Deicide against all Jews in all times. It has fostered the notion that Judaism is "Old" and Christianity is "New"; that Christianity replaces convenantal Judaism because it is the bearer of a universalized and therefore greater covenant; and that as a result, Christianity is morally and spiritually superior. Christian triumphalism has been the foundation for anti-Semitism that found expression in pogroms, in suspicion and isolation, in division and hatred, and ultimately, in the Shoah.

To be sure, the sermon preached in Eugene, Oregon, would not have inspired the congregation to make rabid Holy Week raids on Temple Beth Israel. It was, rather, part of a pollution system that takes decades, if not centuries, before its damage to the ecology of faith becomes obvious. The sermon dampened any inclination toward critical thinking, and it subtly slid a wedge between Christianity and Judaism that likely would make future dialogue immeasurably more difficult and tedious. There was nothing in the sermon that identified Jesus as a Jew or established him in the religious, social, political, and historical contexts of his times. The sermon left its listeners with the erroneous impression that Jesus was crucified by the "Jewish religious establishment in Jerusalem" rather than by the Roman occupation government; that the followers of Jesus were "Christians" and not Jews; and that through Jesus, Christianity triumphed over and "completed" or "fulfilled" a Judaism that had no further reason to exist. At no point did the sermon challenge the congregation to examine the gaping gorge that divides much of the modern church from the practices and moral vision of its founder. I have heard several variations on this sermon, from Protestant, Orthodox, and Roman Catholic pulpits. Fortunately, the delivery is generally unimpassioned, and, sadly, the sermons consistently fail to challenge the listeners to emulate the sacrificial and inclusive love of Jesus, or to accept the transformative power of his life and teachings in their own lives.

SNAPSHOTS

One day after being accorded the highest honors at the Israeli Holocaust memorial and research center, *Yad Vashem*, the grandmotherly woman sat in a Jerusalem apartment provided by those she had rescued from the Nazi invaders of their former homeland, Poland. As she talked about her ten or so altruistic interventions, she offered her commentary on Nazis, collaborationists, Communists, and the fate of the Jews of Poland and of Judaism, generally. Her motive for rescuing Jews in her community was clear and simple: They would have been murdered, and she could not allow that to happen. She said that to allow the enemy to kill innocent people did not coincide with her faith, though she could not be specific about the elements of her faith that informed her decision. She knew quite certainly, however, that her actions were a result of her Roman Catholic upbringing. She hid people in her attic, in an outbuilding, and in various rooms of her small home. She shared food and clothing and, after the war, kept contact with the rescued, whom she referred to in a protective, if patronizing, way as "my Jews."

As our interview went on, she moved from a narrative description of the individual rescues to another of her unsolicited commentaries. Some random thought set her to reflecting on why the Shoah had been the fate of the Jews. In a kind and reflective tone, she asserted, "If only the Jews had not violated the Ten Commandments, this would not have happened to them." I inquired, "Why do you think that is true?" Her response, "The priest told me that after the war." She continued, without malice or rancor, "If the Jews had honored the Ten Commandments and believed in Jesus Christ, the Virgin Mary, and the Saints, God would not have allowed any of these horrible things to befall the Jewish people." Again, I gently pursued her assertions, "When did you come by that conclusion?" She responded, "I have known this all my life. I have always heard it in church and I believe it is true." With a hint of irritation in her voice and a stern look on her face, she concluded the commentary with the observation, "They killed Christ, you understand, and that was their worst offense—if they had not done that terrible crime, the Nazis would never have bothered with them."

I asked her if she had ever witnessed a pogrom. Once or twice when she was growing up in a small rival village, she remembered how "thugs" beat or tormented Jews and once even burned a Jewish home and a business before Easter. She recalled how most of the Jews boarded up their property. Once again, she understood the attacks to be a result of the murder of Christ and the failure of Jews to honor the Ten Commandments or to convert to Christianity. I asked her if she thought the Jews of her community were responsible for the crucifixion of Jesus. "Yes, they were," she replied, "not because they actually did it, but because they refuse Baptism." As gently as I could, I explained how many in the Reich had held beliefs exactly like hers. I paraphrased the following lines from Adolf Hitler's *Mein Kampf*: "Today I believe that I am acting in accord with the will of the Almighty

Creator: by defending myself against the Jews, I am fighting for the work of the Lord.[10]

I asked her how her beliefs about Jews were different than those of Hitler and the National Socialists, and I wondered out loud why, if she believed such things, were her actions diametrically the opposite of Hitler's actions. She said she had no idea that Hitler and the Nazis held those views—indeed, she thought they were simply a matter of arcane theological reflections amongst priests and, during Passion weeks, the subject of sermons. Deprived of a historical context, critical thinking, and unchecked assertions, this woman had no idea that she stood squarely in the anti-Jewish, Nazi camp. She was quiet and pensive for a time and then, with great animation and conviction, said, "None of that [her anti-Jewish sentiments] matters. Maybe it is true and maybe it is not. What is important is that it is not right to kill people. No matter what I believe about Jews, I could never let them or anyone else be killed and not try to do something."

The story of this compassionate and generous woman's life is infinitely more reliable and memorable than the bad theology she was served in church and that created a crippling discontinuity in her life, a discontinuity that could have turned into complicity in genocide if she had not somehow forged an unpronounceable worldview that had at its heart a spirit of altruism. Because there were so few rescuers in all of central and eastern Europe, we have no choice but to judge the failed theologies that led the majority to complicity or indifference.

IN THE PRESENCE OF BURNING CHILDREN: ASSERTIONS OR QUESTIONS?

Teachings or sermons, no matter how benign or benevolently intended, referring to such things as "fulfillment quotations," Christianity as the "completion of Judaism," the "superiority" of Christianity, or charges of unfaithfulness and Deicide, cannot stand the test of Greenberg's working principle. "No statement, theological or otherwise, should be made that would not be credible in the presence of burning children." At their worst, such teaching and preaching inspire brutality that eventuates in an explosion of hatred like the Shoah, and at its best, they slowly create antagonism, fear, suspicion, and prejudices that isolate and alienate members of the human community. Furthermore, a tradition that builds itself upon triumphalist thinking—the vulnerabilities, assumed inadequacies, and alleged weakness of another tradition—is itself vulnerable and weakened. The alternative is to undertake a thorough examination and a studied reformation as suggested by theologian Paul van Buren:

At least a few Christians have begun to realize that a reconsideration of what Christians have been saying about Judaism and of Christian-Jewish relations must lead to a reconsideration of Christianity itself. . . . Theology can shut its eyes and pretend that the Holocaust never happened and that Israel doesn't exist. Theology has shown itself capable of such blindness before! But if there are prospects for serious theology, for a theology not hopelessly blind to matters that pertain to the heart of its task, then the time has come for a reconsideration of the whole theological and Christian enterprise of the most radical sort.[11]

A revisioning of the manner in which Christians recount and comment upon the Crucifixion provides an example of the reconsideration van Buren calls for or of the examination and reformation I feel is urgently needed. In 1947, the Third Commission of the International Emergency Conference of Christians and Jews meet in Seelisberg, Switzerland, to consider a study paper by French historian Jules Isaac entitled "The Rectification Necessary in Christian Teachings: Eighteen Points." As a result of its deliberations, the commission issued a statement under the title "The Ten Points of Seelisberg." To its credit, the commission membership was composed of Catholics and Protestants, and they solicited the critique of their work by Jewish leaders. The final document, which challenged the prevailing attitudes and theologies that encouraged division and hatred between Christians and Jews, was written in light of the emerging accounts of the fate of Jews in the Shoah—in other words, in the presence of burning children.

The seventh of the ten points directs Christians to "Avoid presenting the Passion in such a way as to bring the odium of the killing of Jesus upon all the Jews or upon the Jews alone."[12] Critical, historical, analytical thinking opened the commission to the awareness that responsibility for Jesus' crucifixion could not truthfully be laid at the door of any one group. Point ten concluded in a reformationist tone, calling for a change in religious education (presumably in church schools, adult education, and seminaries) that would not enflame Christians or lead them into "an undiscriminating hatred of the Jews at all times, including those of our own day." The penultimate point addressed the theology of the Polish rescuer by urging an end to the "superstitious notion that the Jewish people is reprobate, accursed, reserved for a destiny of suffering." Finally, in the commission's study paper, Isaac wrote of those who had Jesus arrested and encouraged his conviction: "[T]he chief priests . . . were representatives of a narrow oligargic caste, subjugated to Rome and detested by the people.

How, then, shall we understand the multitude of varied forces that led to the crucifixion of Jesus? Ellis Rivkin has written arguably the most helpful treatment of this volatile issue. He investigates the political, social, and religious bases for the execution and effectively challenges the charge of Deicide. Examining the convergence of circumstances leading to the Crucifixion, Rivkin writes:

The times were no ordinary times; the tempests, no ordinary tempests, the bedlam no ordinary bedlam; the derangements, no ordinary derangements. The chaos that gave birth to a charismatic like Jesus was the very chaos that rendered clarity of judgment impossible. . . . Everyone was entangled within a web of circumstance from which there was no way out. . . . The emperor sought to govern an empire; the procurator sought to hold anarchy in check; the high priest sought to hold his office; the members of the high priest's Sanhedrin sought to spare the people the dangerous consequences of a charismatic's innocent visions of the kingdom of God, which they themselves believed was really at hand. . . .

It is in this maelstrom of time, place, and circumstance, in tandem with impulse-ridden, tempest-tossed, and blinded sons of men, that the tragedy of Jesus' crucifixion is to be found. It was not the Jewish people who crucified Jesus, and it was not the Roman people—it was the imperial system, a system which victimized the Jews, victimized the Romans, and victimized the Spirit of God.[13]

The execution of Jesus was a profound tragedy for the Jewish followers of the Jewish Jesus and for those who later came to be known as Christians. With tragic consequences, significant numbers of theologians, clergy, and laity misunderstood and misstated the causative events of that fateful experience, perpetuated the distortion that Jews were responsible, timelessly so, for Jesus' death, and based their faith and proclamation on triumphalist ideology. In a conversation with Roman Catholic literary scholar Harry James Cargas, Elie Wiesel reversed the usual line of discourse on who broke faith with Jesus:

Whether he was the Christ is for Christians to decide. As far as the Jews are concerned, he may be retroactively guilty for all the murders and massacres that were done in his name. I believe that the Christians betrayed the Christ more than the Jews did. . . . He knew that they were going to misinterpret his teachings and distort it and make it inhuman.[14]

The betrayers of Jesus willfully imposed their own moral judgments over those of God. They chose to ignore Jesus' final prayer on the cross, "Father, forgive them, for they know not what they do." In all of this, they condemned themselves to remain on the Holy Friday side—the death side—of Christian history while ignoring the emptiness of the tomb and life in spite of death on the Easter side of our history. They turned Christianity into a transhistorical vigilante movement. They completely missed the liberating power of the message that the Resurrection eclipses the Crucifixion as a witness to the love of God, a love that overcomes corrupt power and defeats death, ultimately, and in its myriad manifestations.

There is no rational reason for contemporary theologians and clergy to perpetuate these myths and errors, nor for the laity to fall victim to those who cannot free themselves from that history. The geography of twentieth-century faith finds sensitive Christians simultaneously standing at the foot of Golgotha and in the presence of burning children. From that location, they will be moved, changed, and empowered to find the courage and compassion to resist injustice and suffering. Remembering both, they will derive new lessons and a fresh mandate to resist oppression and evil. From that location, they will find the means to step away from the spiral of violence and to help others do the same.

A parishioner once complained that I asked too many questions and gave too few answers. A premarriage couple called to tell me that they had found a minister who did not ask so many hard questions. A student asked me to identify the core beliefs in my theology. I realized afterward that I framed virtually every affirmation in the form of a question. In spite of, or perhaps because of, my great regard for the Confessional traditions and standards of the Presbyterian denomination, I approach *The Book of Confessions*— and for that matter, all dogma and theology—with questions rather than with unconditional concurrence. If simple, easy answers were the way of my early Christian upbringing, my encounters with and the lessons and implications of the Shoah have drawn me into the intellectual and spiritual power of critical, analytical questions.

Questions opened the way for me to hear the voices of victims and to be moved by their stories. Questions created an environment that welcomed a broader, less possessive and constrained experience of God, made life more intentional (also more complicated and challenging), and moved me toward people rather than away from or against them. Questions asked without accusation or acrimony invite dialogue and the opening of lives and ideas that otherwise would be locked behind suspicion and fear. The urgency to find answers, have absolutes, and create certainties was replaced by the more peaceful, humane, and respectful endeavor of constantly identifying and refining questions.

I actually felt more rudderless and adrift ensconced in the vessel of answers and solutions, assertions and dogma. That boat had limited space, reserved of course for like-minded souls, but its incestuous navigationals and severely limited view of the horizon left it at the mercy of the great and tumultuous sea of human experience. What began as pained and often cynical questioning, the outgrowth of a total frontal assault on the Shoah, was transformed by the idea of friendship and the choice of blessings and life rather than death and curse, discussed earlier in this chapter. Through the art of questioning, cynicism was replaced by constructive suspicion, and the purpose quickly became rebuilding and reformation rather than destruction and burial.

I hold significant affirmations that inform and guide my life and values, but they are always subject to my questions, to new stories and fresh encounters, to nascent insights and experiences of God, and to the demanding voices of those who suffer the movements of history. Questions have not left me adrift; on the contrary, they have sharpened my focus on the horizon of life and blessing, provided a reliable compass, offered security in the tempest, deepened my gratitude, and fortified my resolve.

The practical application of all this is to be found in two arenas: first, the formation and implementation of a style of questioning; and second, in the development of essential disclaimers. After presenting them, I will illustrate an application from the issue of Holy Week and the Crucifixion. In advance of preaching or teaching, I build a stable of questions that emerge from the topic at hand. I try to place myself inside the text or the experience in order to get a feeling for what is happening, to listen for competing and complementary voices that will heighten my empathy and invite new questions from fresh angles of vision. Walter Wink has provided a helpful introductory model for this style of questioning in his book *Transforming Bible Study*.[15] His model, which is directed at enabling students and teachers to interact with a biblical text, can be easily adapted for a variety of pursuits.

A reflection on questions: The art of questioning is not exclusively a matter of composing sentences that end with a question mark. Questioning includes probing meaning, implications, alternative possibilities, and interpretation and visualizing a scene, the cast of characters, the options for dialogue, and various likely outcomes. Empathy and ecstasy as forms of questioning open me to the range of issues and concerns and allow me to experience the text or topic more personally, almost firsthand.

In a sermon or classroom lesson, I am most likely to approach a sensitive or controversial theme by announcing that I have been wrestling with certain questions, and then I identify those that I think are the most salient. I explain where those questions have taken my thinking, and I share any stories or texts that are illustrative. I am likely to invoke silence and invite people to reflect for a few minutes on one or two of the questions, or to recall something in their own lives that is informative or illustrative. Trusting the intellect and spirit of the listeners, I take the risk of admitting that in spite of the fact that I have not exhausted all the questions or found the perfectly suitable vantage point, the questions, illustrative narratives, Scripture, and my own sense of the faith have led me to a specific conclusion. Hubris is avoided, and the congregation has both a clear sense of how I reached my perspective and the freedom to struggle with their own resolutions. Finally, I invite people to take my questions, add their own, and later, to share where they cast their lot.

The effect is refreshingly affirmative. Authority is claimed in a shared pilgrimage rather than by virtue of a removed and lofty pronouncement that fails to invite the concerns, struggles, and questions of thoughtful, faithful persons. For each story and question I share, the return is geometric. For every invitation to reflect and talk, I am gifted with many opportunities for dialogue. In my experience, assertions and dogma are most often met with silence, disinterest, or argumentation. But this model transforms silence into discourse and complacency into action. It leads to the most meaningful and fulfilling pastoral and personal relationships, and to the fulfillment of my calling as a minister.

The second application relates to offering textual disclaimers. When I first started this practice, it felt awkward and intrusive. As I gradually filtered the disclaimers into my style of presentation, they became more comfortable and, like the previous application, surprisingly opened new opportunities for dialogue. Most preachers are taught to identify textual variants and problems. They learn to include these, along with brief summaries and commentary, in their study groups and exegetical sermons. The disclaimer simply takes this practice one step further by alerting listeners to the possible abuses of certain texts or the dangers of careless uncritical understandings of those texts.

There are numerous portions of the Gospels and epistles that quickly and easily lend themselves to anti-Jewish interpretations and uses. Certain obvious texts have inspired and justified all manner of calumny, hatred, and violent acts against Jews. A number of the authors of the Christian Testament had undisguised disdain for Jewish leadership in the time of Jesus and often wrote without discriminating between Jewish leadership, Jewish people, and the Jewish faith. Their carelessness in referring collectively to "Jews" and their thinly veiled frustration with a population that did not universally embrace the teachings of Jesus gave ammunition to succeeding generations that turned their words into warrants for racist hatred, pogroms, and ultimately, mass murder.

Let me combine the two applications, disclaimers and questions, using the example of a portion of the Passion narrative. A disclaimer might read: The tragedy of Holy Friday had been interpreted over the centuries to give the appearance that the arrest, trial, and crucifixion of Jesus reflected the collective will of the majority of Jewish people in Jerusalem or in all of

Israel. The interpretations in question have led to charges of Deicide that have been leveled against all Jews, regardless of distance in time from the actual crucifixion, and without critical study of the specific original historical context. As a result, for centuries hatred and division have been directed against Jews by Christians. In this century alone, during Holy Weeks, Christians in various nations have targeted Jews, their homes, and their businesses for violent, often fatal attacks, known as pogroms. The ultimate expression of that hatred and division was the attempt by the Nazis to destroy European Jewry and to expunge all vestiges and memory of Judaism. When we read the Passion narratives, we do so mindful that the misinterpretation of these accounts has resulted in centuries of violence and, ultimately, in our generations, significantly contributed to the mass extermination of millions of innocent Jews by Christian peoples.

The disclaimer should be offered as the introduction to the reading of the specific biblical narrative or at the beginning of a class. In light of the disclaimer, here are some of the questions that I would wrestle with and raise in the course of a sermon or class session:

1. Is it intellectually accurate or morally correct to blame all Jews, in all times, for what appears to be the actions of a few isolated Jewish leaders in Jerusalem, thousands of years ago?

2. What could be the justification for imposing a collective guilt that has no limits on time or geography?

3. Does the text, which moves from the particularity of "chief priests and Pharisees" to a collective reference to "Jews," justify an interpretation that suggests widespread, common support for or participation in the actions of Jewish leaders and Roman officials?

4. According to certain renderings of the historical context, the chief priests and Pharisees were an isolated caste serving the interests of the Roman government and, largely, serving at the pleasure of the Roman government. Foment that originated in the religious community and in any way threatened the Roman regional government was their responsibility. Put yourself in the place of the chief priest or a Pharisee. In the case of Jesus, what might you have done to protect the integrity of your tradition and the security of your position?

Put yourself in the place of Pilate or Herod. There was great disquiet over the impact of the occupation. It was also Passover, and that meant a surge of people coming into Jerusalem and an open invitation for more acts of dissent and terror that could result in stern repercussions. What thoughts would go through your mind as you considered the charges against Jesus, and would you have responded any differently to them? How might you have resisted both the personal and external pressures to execute him? What forces caused you to take the actions recorded in Scripture?

5. Finally, what points would you make in a Holy Friday sermon that looked from our position in the latter third of the twentieth century, back to the mass graves of the Shoah, beyond to pogroms, and finally to the events at Golgotha? How would each of those experiences influence your message? What do they have to say to the contemporary moment? What words of caution, hope, and alarm do they call forth from you?

The church has been excessively tardy in checking the advance of those individuals or institutions that use Scripture or the assertions of creeds and dogmas to isolate, condemn, or harm people, and whose textual interpretations are used to maintain the power and superiority of some while diminishing the status of many. There can be no tolerance for institutions, theologians, clergy, or laity who, in the name of God or Jesus or a particular denominational action or confession, seek to exclude, dominate, or harm people whose experience of the Almighty is different than their own.

I shall cast my lot with those who wish to reclaim the integrity of the Christian faith and the vocation of ministry; who are willing to risk listening to victims and making their invisibility become visible on the pages of church history and theology; who sustain the common good, speaking the truth and speaking truth to power. I understand the vocation of preaching, teaching, and ministry in terms of posing and constantly refining critical questions that are asked publicly in the service of securing a just and peaceful world, of resisting expressions of evil, of opening people to the beauty and goodness of an inclusive and egalitarian community.

MEMORY

Herman Graebe did not want immortality; he only wanted people to know and to remember. The publication of his biography was as much an act of vindication as it was an act of testimony and memory for the sake of history. He had been slandered in the postwar German press and finally forced to flee his homeland because of his testimony in the Crimes Against Humanity portion of the Nuremberg Trials. Later, charges and innuendo challenged his motives and actions. Even when the story of his bravery and compassion were carefully documented and internationally known, the son of the prosecutor who read Graebe's sworn testimony into the Nuremberg record ignorantly published a portrayal of Graebe as a do-nothing German. Graebe also knew of ill-willed revisionists who were growing in numbers in the United States and in both West and East Germany. At a panel presentation in San Francisco, one such denier of the Shoah publicly challenged the accuracy of the figure that 6 million Jews died and suggested non-genocide-related causes for the deaths that did occur.

In his early eighties, plagued by a worsening heart condition and physically frail but in full command mentally, Graebe interrupted the challenger by pushing himself to his feet and leaning over the table. In a firm voice and with his finger shaking its accusations at the man, Graebe asked, "Are you calling me a liar? How dare you tell me that I did not see all the things I witnessed during the war, that I lied under oath at Nuremberg! I saw it all and I will never forget. You, sir, are the liar."[16] The rescuer of Jews in the Ukraine defined himself as the living memory of those whose fate he resisted and witnessed. Through his meticulous record keeping, his thorough memory, and his unambiguous conscience, Herman Graebe gave being and substance to the living and the dead of the Shoah.

A cautionary note regarding memory: The memory I have in mind is not a passive recollection of historical curiosities. For centuries past and for centuries to come, believers have and will continue to regularly remember Jesus Christ in the Eucharistic sacrament. Granted, it can become a banal ritual, but the highest essence of it is to reclaim presence and rekindle memory, to participate in the being of Jesus Christ, and to draw strength in order to live faithfully. Like Judaism, Christianity is a religion of active, meaningful memory. To remember the Shoah as a Christian and as a Jew—though I believe it is far more complex for Jews—is not just to master a catalogue of facts, figures, and dates; it is to remember the insanity of evil on behalf of the past and for the sake of the future. Understanding the memory of the Shoah must be as central to Christianity as binding ourselves to the memory of Pharoah's oppression; the escape from Egypt; the apocalyptic terror of Shadrach, Mechsach, and Abednego; the mystery of the Last Supper; the tragedy of the cross; and the power of the empty tomb. Just as we gather at the table to remember and be different, so also we gather in the presence of burning children and remember in order to be different!

Joining their memories to those of the Jewish survivors of the Shoah, Graebe and other rescuers, liberators, and members of the Resistance embodied Frederick Buechner's sensitive and insightful words quoted at the opening of this chapter. In the voice of victim and survivor, "When you remember me, it means that you have carried something of who I am with you, that I have left some mark of who I am on who you are. . . . It means that even after I die, you can still see my face and hear my voice and speak to me in your heart. For as long as you remember me, I am never entirely lost."

The memory of the Shoah contains three imperatives for believers and their institutions. First, the victims and survivors must know that they and their experience have left the marks of meaning and challenge on who we are and how we fulfill our callings and that after they have died, their words will continue to speak to us and have presence in our lives. Second, because the various institutional expressions of the church generally have not confronted the implications and lessons of the Shoah, changed because of it, or given full voice to its victims, we must continue to remember in order to extend the memory and knowledge of it. Third, in remembering and searching the recesses of the Shoah, we will likely find the spiritual, moral, theological, and humanitarian resources and the communal will to resist the contemporary provocations created by the evils that spiral off of the Shoah.

My encounter with the Shoah began in waves of jolting, shattering revelations that gave way to despair, doubt, outrage, and protest. Today, when I remember or speak of the Shoah, it is an act of hope and trust. The theological antecedents of the Shoah in Christian anti-Jewish teachings and generations of despicable anti-Jewish behaviors had the power to rob me of the will to faith. The actions of people like Commander-Pastor Ernest Biberstein, the Reich Bishop, the collaborationists in the German churches, and the complicity of ministers, priests, and laity throughout Europe despoiled the sanctity of ordination vows and cheapened the call to the offices of ministry. But do they deserve the final word, the power to eclipse my memory of and commitment to the Galilean's healing goodness, his witness to the justice, grace, mercy, and love of God, and the beckoning call of his Spirit to serve?

When Emil Fackenheim admonished Jews not to do Hitler's work for him or hand him a posthumous victory by abandoning their faith, he also inadvertently challenged me to examine what the Shoah was doing to my faith and calling. Why the Shoah? How does a North American minister's total frontal engagement with the memory of the Shoah lead him to faith and hope? The willful distortions and compromises of trained and common believers led to the failure of institutions, creeds, dogma, and assertions; but Christianity did not fail. I had no choice but to wrest my faith, my experience of Christianity, from the death grip of Hitler's Shoah. I would be both a Christian and a pastor, minister of Word and Sacrament, a teaching elder. I could not hand Hitler a posthumous victory or do his work for him by abandoning the faith, the church, or the call. I could not contribute to the work of those who sought to deconstruct the faith, corrupt the office, and replace them with a reign of pagan totalitarianism and fascistic leadership.

As we continue exploring the intersections of shattered paradigms and healing affirmations, I turn to a dialogue with Philippe de Saint-Cheron in which Elie Wiesel captures the essence of the struggle to remain faithful when the memories are so tragic and at once compelling and repulsive:

I would say that, in our epoch, nothing is as whole as a shattered faith. Faith has to be tested, but then it must not remain a rupture or a laceration. One must continue while facing what is happening in the world today and what has happened yesterday. We can no longer accept faith just as it is. We must pass through a period of anguish and then a period of respite in order that in the end we may find the faith of our Masters. Because, without faith, we could not survive. Without faith, our world would be empty.[17]

Chapter Three

In Pursuit of a Theodicy

There are three kinds of souls, three kinds of prayers.
One: I am a bow in your hands, Lord. Draw me lest I rot.
Two: Do not overdraw me, Lord. I shall break.
Three: Overdraw me, and who cares if I break! Choose!

Nikos Kazantzakis[1]

To be present in the moments before death, to stand watch at the instant of death, and to share with the living the hours after death are among the most sacred experiences in the life of a minister or rabbi. Each appointment with death contains its own burden and liberation, each carries its unique emotional and spiritual freight. Paradoxically, every encounter with death has heightened my will to live and to be a blessing. The power of death fades and there is an equilibrium when presence and acts of compassion bring their unique degree of meaning and healing, when listening and sharing endow their special gifts, and when memories begin to regenerate and encourage commitments beyond grief. Surprisingly, many clergy feel inclined, if not obligated, to mask death with pious euphemisms or to diminish a person's sense of loss with premature words of encouragement or hope. But our vocation is to unmask, name, and face death, to diminish its power by being present. Presence lessens the chill of isolation and abandonment. Presence enables the mourner and comforter to find at the center of their intuitive souls the words and reflective questions that spark healing memories, the healing of memories, and that turn grief into a certain kind of meaning and despair into hope.

Those who mask and diminish the power of death become its unwitting colleagues. They want to foreshorten the tears, to have all eyes averted from death, and to hush the feelings of those who suffer the loss of another. Pastors and rabbis know well the colleagues' formula words, most often directed at mourners in the early hours of their grief, "You'll get over this. You must move on with your life." In their unwillingness to confront death, to return its gaze, they usually intensify and lengthen the anguish of another by drawing them into the charade.

There are also those who seek to mask or diminish the work of evil and death in the Shoah. Numerous times I have had people, even clergy, say such things as, "After so many years, shouldn't you let this be a thing of the past?" Or, "The Jews should not dwell on the Holocaust. They should forgive and forget." Are these not variant forms of Shoah denial, "polite," whispered modifications of the revisionists' shout that "Auschwitz was a lie"? Do they not reflect the familiar difficulty that many people have confronting death? Do the proponents of such thinking realize they are trivializing an immense tragedy whose implications and lessons the Christian community has not yet adequately considered or applied? For survivors, such assertions and questions cause outrage, renew grief, and lead to profound alienation. These are among the human consequences of averting our eyes from death and evil.

Whenever I am present as death is about its work, I feel that I am simultaneously an exile in an alien place and that my liberation from the grasp of death is at last at hand, just beyond the traverse through what the Psalmist envisioned as the uncharted valley of darkness. Both mourners and clergy must travel that valley if they are to have hope for a future they suspect awaits beyond the distant crook on death's corkscrew path. Because death is an end, or because it can be brutally ugly, or perhaps because we have unquestioningly handed over the reins that bridle our fear and loss and rage, death has bullied us into thinking that we must avert our eyes in its presence. It is a matter of the power of grief and the dominion of death. Wearied, brutalized, or indifferent people submit, willingly going along with the deception, eyes averted or closed.

In Scripture it is only God who can direct the faithful not to view the divine countenance. Simply because death remains a mystery whose razor edge lacerates the living with the unsuturable wounds of abandonment and grief, it does not deserve the respectful deference that generations of believers have accorded the Deity. To look away from death is to be robbed of strength and resolve. Nothing of death, neither its presence nor its dispatchers and couriers, can be ignored or viewed in only a hasty, momentary side glance. Those who turn their eyes away acquiesce to those who do the work of death, be they physical malady or masters of a murderous art. Through the Shoah, I crafted the resolve to never again look away from death or the dying, regardless of the circumstances, and to never again give up my power to death's withering gaze.

I no longer despair of finding meaning in death or of probing its vastness for understanding. Meaning and understanding depend not on death but on who I am in the midst of death and after death has finished its work.

Because of the lessons from the Shoah, I retell and celebrate the stories of simple experiences of grace and great acts of courage in which common people muster the fullness of their humanity to resist death as long as they have being.

LIVING IN THE PRESENCE OF THE MEMORY OF EVIL

On the journey toward understanding and meaning, in the quest to find models of goodness and hope, in the struggle to secure the stories that empower the renewal of commitment to life and blessing, encounters occur that enable people to begin to heal the wounds that exist between the memory of the dead and the actions of the living. For me, entering Auschwitz in the morning, burdened with profound fear, unbridled rage, and uncertainty about the future, and leaving the death camp in the evening, flooded anew with the horrors but enveloped in the story of a woman's compassionate courage, is an example of such a healing moment. These fleeting encounters have the power to break the grip of death. Eyes that are averted from death miss these grace-filled rendezvous or cause us to dismiss them as trifling in spite of their potential to contain the spark that can illumine an otherwise lifelong darkness.

Throughout history, depraved and pathological political leaders and military forces inflicted themselves upon the Jewish people, particularly, and on world history, generally, showing no conscience in their treatment of children and women. According to Scripture, in his fearful attempt to squelch the Hebrew passion for freedom, Pharaoh ordered the deaths of all male Jewish infants (certain Egyptian midwives did not obey). Later, Elisha warned the people of Israel that when Hazael became the king, he would smash the Israelite children and disembowel pregnant Jewish women. So it happened. King Herod, perpetually trying to keep his occupation of Israel peaceful and appease the scornful eyes of his superiors in Rome, ordered the execution of male children two years old and younger after his soldiers failed to find Mary and Joseph. Once again, it happened.

SNAPSHOTS

The biblical record of the fate of children and women is pallid compared with that of Hitler and the SS (*Schutzsaffel*). The German rescuer Herman Graebe watched one militiaman throw a baby in the air and impale it on his bayonet as others dashed the heads of infants against pillars and posts. Mothers went mad watching, Nazis laughed, and the militia continued. It is painful, I know, but if we do not avert our eyes now, as if these deaths did not happen, perhaps we can delay or even prevent the forces of death from continuing through history unchallenged, unabated. In reality, because so many have averted their eyes and failed to learn the lessons of the Shoah, children are still dying. Don't look away, not now.

How can a person be in such oppressive exile from his humanity as to exterminate women and children? Had the men who performed these vile acts completely forgotten or utterly repressed what it felt like to cradle a sleeping child, to watch the first steps, to hear the first words, to witness a child's awe? Many of the men who ordered the liquidation of children, women, and men, directed the hanging of a family, or supervised wagons at the edges of burning pits returned home at night to play with their own children. They made love with their wives. What shall we make of the fact that the wife of the commandant of Auschwitz gave birth to two children, one while she resided at Dachau and the other while she lived on the grounds of Auschwitz?

Pre-war Lublin, in central Poland, was the home of a fervent, centuries-old community of Hasidic Jews. By the war's end, it fulfilled Hitler's mandate to be *Judenrein* (literally "free of Jews," Hitler's stated objective in the policies directing the universal extermination of Jews). Majdanek was a primary concentration-extermination camp on the outskirts of Lublin. When I visited it, the town extended to the outer perimeter of the former camp, which is now a frighteningly well preserved memorial. To the traveler passing through Lublin, Majdanek appears suddenly, a surrealistic stain on the map as one rounds a bend in a neighborhood. It is encircled by double rows of barbwire fencing with the original wooden guard posts interspersed every several hundred yards. Crematoria chimneys break the horizon, a massive concrete and boulder memorial dwarfs everything, and beyond the perimeter are rows of apartment houses, a school, a modest high-rise, stores, parks, and an active military encampment.

Just outside the barbwire fence is a long, narrow grassy knoll with benches fastened in place, looking in the direction of the former camp. On a level walkway meandering through the knoll, three women silently pushed small babies in rickety strollers and occasionally paused to look into the camp. Another woman sat in the shade of a tree, on a curved bench, serenely looking into Majdanek as her baby nursed at her fleshy, flaxen breast, releasing its hold long enough to gaze contentedly before turning back to suckle.

The contentment and tranquillity of the four women and their babies belied the universe in whose presence they took repose: the brutality of processing; public nudity for Jews whose modesty was a matter of obedience to God; delousing for those who would work and therefore live a little longer in squalid, fetid barracks; and for those who would live scant minutes or hours, the vicious separation of parents and children. For the latter, the majority, flailing clubs hastened the run to disguised gas chambers and finally to an ashen escape.

Women of Lublin! Who are you? Why are you here, strolling and nursing your babies under this dark cloud of history? Is there no other pastoral park to take the living consummation of your sexual love, the gift of your wombs? Do you knowingly mock the more than 75,000 Jewish mothers and children who died at the hands of Majdanek's Nazis and militia?

As I stood at a discreet distance watching the women with their babies, a quiet dawning came over me. I began to imagine an interpretation of their presence that depended on my intuition of a secret the women and babies never revealed. Was theirs a story of resistance to death, a tale of courage and grace embracing the past and enfolding the living? They did not avert their eyes nor quietly accept the demand of death to forget, ignore, pass by, to neither care nor become involved. Death represented the worst motives for the presence of these people. It pushed me to look away from this inexplicable display at the edge of one of its fearsome citadels.

Choosing life and blessing, I listened in the soft stillness for the voices of life representing the voices of the dead. In my poetic interpretation, she who held the most vulnerable symbol of life close, warm and peacefully suckling, and they who strolled along that path filled with ashen memories proclaimed:

> I am!
> See! Look at my baby—
>   You shall never smash another one against a wall!
> Look! My breasts are full of milk—
>   You will never cause another woman's breast to wither and dry!
>   I am
>   here to declare to you that you
>   shall never again separate children from parents!
> You imposed death, but I gave life—

I live beyond you. Against you!
They were innocent women and children—not a danger to you; now
      I am
  a threat to your memory because I exist,
  I create beyond your life and death.
For the souls of women and children who knew your whips,
  your humiliations, your terrors,
      I am!
For my child and for one million five hundred thousand children
  I offer the warmth and nourishment of my breasts,
  The rich milk of human love and hope.
Do you see me?
  I am here!
  I am nursing!
In spite of you, because of you,
      I am!

A moment of grace, an act of hope at the gateway to death. Were they Jews or Christians? Does it matter? In that encounter, they became for me messengers of God, living embodiments, enfleshing reminders of Paul's words to the church in Rome: "Neither death nor life, no angel, no prince, nothing that exists, nothing still to come, not any power, or height or depth, nor any created thing, can ever come between us and the love of God made visible in Christ Jesus our Lord" (Romans 8:38–39).

Yes! With Moses and the Israelites, we must choose life and blessing. The fury and mayhem of Egypt's Pharaoh, Samaria's Hazael, Rome's Herod, and Hitler with his murdering cohorts all attest to two immutable truths: They did not have the last word; and second, the smallest, most vulnerable human beings are stronger than every sovereignty, especially the anticipated thousand-year Reich that has ceased to be.

A FORAY INTO THEODICY

The questions raised in the pursuit of a theodicy that might begin to address the place of God in the midst of the Shoah may seem, at first reading, to be a solely intellectual foray into the arcane worlds of theology and spirituality. That is, unless the questions are asked "in the presence of burning children" rather than in a scholarly debate. Fundamentally, theodicy is a discipline that seeks to understand the role and the place of God in human tragedy and suffering. Theodicy attempts to derive some explanation for the paradoxical existence of a God who is all powerful and wills only good, and the perpetual existence of evil and suffering in the world. Clergy and rabbis often hear the primal formations of theodicy at times of suffering and death, when someone asks, "Why is God doing this?" or asserts, "God must have a purpose in causing this to happen." Reduced to its most basic universal formulation, theodicy asks, "Where is God when people suffer?" And in its most intimate and personal address, theodicy asks, "Where will God be when I suffer, endure evil, or face death?"

The questions are timeless because suffering and evil have no constraints. The questions take on an urgency because they most often form in the minds of believers whose trust has been forcibly dragged to the very edge of the precipice of faith and life when they are victims of or witnesses to evil. The questions of theodicy and the Shoah are essentially the same for Jews and Christians, but the angle of approach is different. Jews come to the questions as the victims and survivors of genocide, while Christians meet the questions from the perspective of the perpetrators of divisive teachings, pogroms, and mass murder.

What are the questions? Where was God during the Shoah? Did God allow the Shoah to occur or, worse, intentionally will it to happen? If so, for what reasons—why? What was God's role in the Shoah? Where was God in the midst of the brutality, the horrors, and the suffering? Where is God after the Shoah? What is the nature of God's post-Shoah role: How and where is God's presence to be known after the mass graves, burning pits, and gas chambers?

For believers the questions can be intensely personal, because they challenge the nature of faith and the foundation of a life and worldview. Standing in the presence of burning children, how can one have faith in an all-powerful God whose will is justice, love, and goodness? If God is all powerful and wills only good, why did God not save the children and stop the Shoah from happening? Why did God not defeat Hitler's armies, flood the flames, and stanch the flow of poisonous gases? For generations, the faithful have been instructed to believe the core narratives of the Hebrew and Christian Scripture that teach that God parted the Red Sea to liberate the Israelites and closed it over Pharaoh's pursuing troops, and sent an angel to protect the apocalyptic trio—Shadrach, Meschach, and Abednego—from a latter-day Pharaoh's burning, fiery furnace. If the traditions expect believers to accept these stories as literally true, then the questions must be asked. If God saved the Jews from those oppressors, why not from the Nazis? Because the Jews of central and eastern Europe were not saved, shall we believe that God was indifferent or perhaps powerless? The ultimate questions push the limits of faith: Is there no God? Is God dead?

The often-heated argumentation and the near-certain absence of universally acceptable answers to the questions of the presence or absence of God, and the death of God, are best illustrated in an exchange between Shoah survivor Elie Wiesel and American philosopher Richard Rubenstein. It took place in 1969, at the first Wayne State University conference on the German Church Struggle and the Holocaust. Rubenstein, who had previously established himself as a primary proponent of the "death of God" movement, addressed the testimony of Pastor Heinrich Grueber at the trial of Adolf Eichmann in Jerusalem. In the trial, Grueber held that Hitler's ascent to power and attempted extermination of European Jewry was an act of God—in fact, the will of God. Rubenstein wrote in response:

If one takes Covenant Theology seriously, as did Dean Grueber, Auschwitz must be God's way of punishing the Jewish people in order that they might better see the light, the light of Christ if one is a Christian, the light of Torah if one is a traditional Jew. . . . I have had to decide whether to affirm the existence of a God who inflicts Auschwitz on his guilty people or to insist that nothing the Jews did made them more deserving of Auschwitz than any other people, that Auschwitz was in no sense a punishment, and that a God who could or would inflict such punishment does not exist. . . . I have elected to accept what Camus has rightly called the courage of the absurd, the courage to live in a meaningless, purposeless Cosmos rather than believe in a God who inflicts Auschwitz on his people.[2]

Elie Wiesel, who was to speak after Rubenstein, adjusted the theme of his lecture in order to respond to the rabbi-philosopher who popularized the phrase "the death of God." Wiesel noted that none of those who originated this viewpoint had been survivors of the death camps. Wiesel went further in his challenge to Rubenstein, asserting that it was the intellectuals, liberals, and humanists who collaborated in order to save their lives, and did so because they had no foundational moral or spiritual supports in their lives. He went on to tell of studying Talmud while in a Nazi labor column with a *Rosh Yeshiva* from a school in Galicia. Finally, Wiesel respectfully put the questions of theodicy and Rubenstein's challenges into his own unique experience. Speaking of the survivors, Wiesel said,

And here I will tell you, Dick, that you don't understand *them* when you say that it is more difficult to live today in a world without God. NO! If you want difficulties, choose to live *with* God. Can you compare today the tragedy of the believer to that of the non-believer?! The real tragedy, the real drama, is the drama of the believer.[3] (Emphasis Wiesel's)

Throughout his response to Rubenstein, Wiesel's arguments ranged between theology and anthropology. Struggling with the issues of theodicy from a faith perspective and the imposition of suffering and evil by humankind, Wiesel said, "I have my problems with God, believe me. I have my anger and I have my quarrels and I have my nightmares. But my dispute, my bewilderment, my astonishment is with men. I didn't understand how men could be so 'barbarian,' as you called it, Dick. I still don't understand it."[4] Clearly, certainly, the questions of theodicy must be appropriately reformulated, refined, expanded, and addressed also to the roles of humanity. In the next two chapters, I shall attempt to address the theodicy questions in terms of humanity and to reflect on the mandate to "do justice" in a post-Shoah world.

SNAPSHOTS

I sat with a nine-year-old youth whose father was about to die of a virulent, fast-moving cancer that had only recently been diagnosed. Knowing that the boy was a prayerful person, I asked him if he was saying prayers for his father. He said he was but offered no details. So I asked, "How do you pray for your dad?" "He's very sick and may die today or tomorrow," came the response. "I asked God to help him be strong and brave, and to have peace." The child's maturity was at once frightening (did he expect little of God and therefore did not ask God to save his father's life?) and assuring (did he understand both the limitations and sympathies of God?). Within forty-eight hours his father had died, with dignity and at peace. A few weeks later, without particular invitation, the lad said, "I'm not sure about God right now."

In his memoir, Elie Wiesel recounts the hanging of two men and a boy, for alleged sabotage, in front of the entire camp. As their necks were placed in the nooses, the men shouted, "Long live liberty!" The child was silent. Behind him, Wiesel heard a voice ask, "Where is God? Where is He?" The boy did not die immediately, and everyone was forced to witness a slow, agonizing death. As the entire camp paraded past the gallows, Wiesel again heard the voice: "Where is God now?" And I heard a voice within me answer him: "Where is He? Here He is—He is hanging here on this gallows."[5]

Did the fourteen-year-old announce the death of God? Were his words the sad but reliant recognition that God suffers the same fate as God's people, that God was present in the midst of the suffering and death?

After concluding my work at the Buchenwald archives, the state-run memorial to "patriotic anti-fascists," I traveled directly to Jerusalem and contacted my friend Rabbi Pinchas Peli. The Pelis invited me to their home for the Sabbath, two days hence. Having put significant geographical but not spiritual-psychological distance between myself and the death camps, I must have relaxed my subconscious guard, and for the two intervening nights, my sleep was wracked by dreadful nightmares and terrors.

With great sensitivity to the despair I felt from my encounters with the universe of former extermination camps, both of the Pelis drew me out and gently offered perspectives that might tip the scales. In the sanctity of Sabbath time, in holy space, and illumined by the light of Shabbat candles, we struggled with the questions of the Shoah and God. We discussed the complicity of the church and professing Christians at length. After I related my experience outside block sixteen at Auschwitz, Peli shared an insight from his mentor, Rabbi Joseph Soloveitchik.

According to Peli, two approaches to the problem of suffering and evil existed in Soloveitchik's model. In the first, a person who thinks about suffering and evil without finding meaning or understanding is rendered immobile and powerless. This person will likely be silent, indifferent, or complicit as well as faithless when confronted by suffering or evil in the future. In the second, the suffering and evil are confronted, and whether or not meaning and understanding are found, the person makes very certain decisions about what values will direct the priorities of his or her life.

The encounter with the mirrored image in the window of block sixteen began to make sense. The belief, strengthened by each succeeding experience, returned: Meaning and understanding depend not on death but on who I am in the midst of death and after death has finished its work.

SHATTERED PARADIGMS AND HEALING AFFIRMATIONS

In 1973 Elie Wiesel published a cantata based on the twelfth of Maimonides' thirteen Articles of Faith. The penultimate article states, "I believe in the coming of the Messiah, even though he tarries, I still believe." The Cantata, entitled *Ani Maamin: A Song Lost and Found Again*, features Abraham, Isaac, and Jacob, the Narrator, a chorus, and an unidentified being (perhaps, suggests the text, "an angel") named simply Voice. The plot has the Patriarchs return to the Creation to determine how the Covenant is being honored and to assess, record, and report. Their arrival coincides with the Shoah, and what they witness is the worst of it, recounted in restrained, dignified verses that make the atrocities that much more horrible. In the course of the drama the three elders return to speak with the Creator of the Universe, to report what they have seen, and to make demands on behalf of those who remained behind. For Abraham, the journey to Canaan follows the road to Treblinka. For Isaac, the ascent to Mount Moriah only gives him a view of Majdanek. For Jacob, the struggle to bring his descendants home finds that every road leads to Auschwitz.

Words and songs, protests and affirmations, grapple with the essential questions and issues of theodicy. Each in their turn, the Patriarchs address their complaints and charges to God. Theology and anthropology are virtually inseparable for Wiesel. The Voice interrupts the grievous indictments to ask the questions that search for some basis for the vindication of humankind, more than for God:

> What do you want?
> What do you seek to prove?
> Accomplish?
> What right have you to speak thus?
> Does God owe you an accounting?
> All this—
> His sole responsibility?
> What about man?
> What about his role?
> Does God not have the right
> To question you, in turn,
> To ask of man:
> What have you done with my creation?
> *Narrator:* Suddenly, Abraham, Isaac, and Jacob are at a loss, conscious of
> the futility of their efforts. God chooses to be question. The answer is not
> known. Nor will it be. Know it only those who, from Babi-Yar to
> Treblinka, fled the earth, fled from life—and they are mute. Like God.[6]

In despair, having imposed their own interpretations on what they experienced as God's silence, the Patriarchs decide to return to the Shoah-plagued Creation and tell the people. Before they depart, each of them recounts, to God or perhaps to the Voice or maybe to the chorus, the horrors that they have witnessed, and significantly, each recounting ends with a form of the affirmation "I believe." Indictment and affirmation frame and balance the testimony of each. Abraham speaks. His words sear. And in a stunning response to the questions of theodicy, the narrator interrupts, "Having spoken, Abraham . . . does not, cannot, see that God for the first time, permits a tear to cloud his eyes."[7]

Next, Isaac proclaims his staggering witness and then his affirmation. Again, the Narrator interrupts: "Having spoken, Isaac . . . does not, cannot see that for the second time a tear streams down God's somber countenance, a countenance more somber than before."[8]

At the end, Jacob's charges cascade ahead of his affirmation. The chorus, as it has between each recitation of indictment and affirmation, sings its faith, but this time its words contain a statement of hope that is one possible response to the struggles with the questions and issues posed by theodicy:

Chorus: . . . Auschwitz has killed Jews by not their expectation.

Narrator: Having spoken, Jacob . . . does not, cannot, see that God, surprised by his people, weeps for the third time—and this time without restraint, and with—yes—love.[9]

The end of one traverse through the "valley of the shadow of death" is at hand, and another journey is about to begin with an unprecedented revelation about God's place when human beings suffer or are victimized by evil. Each Patriarch speaks a final soliloquy, and the Narrator intrudes one last time, followed by a final chorus:

Narrator: Abraham, Isaac and Jacob . . . leave heaven and do not, cannot, see that they are no longer alone: God accompanies them, weeping, smiling, whispering. . . . The word of God continues to be heard. So does the silence of his dead children.

Chorus: Ani maamin. . . .
         Pray . . .
         Pray to God,
         Against God,
         For God.
         Ani maamin. . . .[10]

SNAPSHOT

Recall the lad whose father died of cancer and who said to me a few weeks after the memorial service, "I am not sure about God right now." As we stood there, I asked him what he thought God was feeling when his dad died and how he thought God felt about his grief. I asked him to picture God in his mind as he thought about how God felt. "God is sad," he said after a time. I asked him where God was in the picture. "Looking down at my family and me." No other images emerged, so I coached him. How would you feel if you looked over and saw that God's eyes were filled with tears? What would you feel if tears ran down God's cheeks? Thoughtful silence. What would you feel if God was not "up there" looking down but rather walking with you, beside you, and sharing your sadness? Following what seemed an interminable pause and some youthful fidgeting, the boy asked, "Is that what you think God would do?" Yes! "Then I guess I'd feel the peace I asked God to give my dad."

AN ALTERNATIVE APPROACH TO THEODICY

Regrettably, in spite of ample scriptural indications, the idea that God would be moved to love, shed tears, share grief, and somehow be present in the midst of suffering and evil has not developed as a universal image or popular teaching in Christianity. Certainly an abstract theological concept exists of the God who knows and shares the grief and burdens of believers and responds with compassion and love. Isaiah (53:3b) sings of the Servant of God who is a "Man of sorrows, and acquainted with grief" (many Christians arguably contend that the prophet's words describe and anticipate Jesus). John 3:16–17 is a classic Christian summary of God's presence, compassion, and love. The summary speaks from a time of an oppressive occupation by the Roman government, not a period of catastrophe: "For God so loved the world that God gave the only-begotten Son, so that whoever believes in Him should not perish, but have everlasting life. For God did not send the Son into the world to condemn the world but to have the world saved through Him." Still, this potentially powerful and liberating view of God languishes in an essentially unexplored theological archive.

One primary reformation of theology, fraught with multiple dangers, is the liberation of God from the imposed trait of being all powerful and both subjective and selective in delivering people from suffering and evil. In place of that absolutely impossible and insoluble quandary is a theology of a God whose empathy is expressed in a face flooded with tears of grief and whose love is expressed in unconditional presence. This is the God who accompanies the faithful throughout life and into death, and whose power is the ability to inspire believers to choose life and blessing in the face of death and curse and to transform their suffering into acts of justice and hope, faith and compassion. This is the image of the God attested to in the experiences of multitudes who have lived in the very company of evil and of those who have endured every manner of suffering.

The choice that is to be made is the subordination of a theology of power to a theology of presence. What will likely be abandoned, and in that reformation become a threat to established traditions, is the notion of a God who has the power to stop evil, suffering, and death but does not. The church would do well to jettison an ecclesiology of power that has traditionally offered up a God who randomly intervenes for some while ignoring the equally honorable and compelling supplications of others. In this regard, many will mourn the passing of the conception of a God with whom people can barter for privileges and favors, if not for life itself. Both parallel and antithetical to perpetual existence of evil, suffering, and death shall be the God who embodies goodness and righteousness; who summons believers to lives of faithfulness and compassion; to blessing, life, and affirmation; and to acts of justice. If it wishes, theology will still wrestle with the arcane and debatably relevant issues of God's power, but in terms of praxis, in the settings of pastoral ministry, the struggle will be more beneficial and applicable to believers if it shifts from the questions of God's power to intervene to the nature of God's presence in suffering, a presence that inspires people to turn their suffering into blessing.

Where was God during the Shoah? Where is God in the midst of any experience of evil, suffering, and death? We shall continue to hear this commanding question of the Shoah and its universalized plea, "Where is God now?" The answer will likely be different depending on the circumstances and the angle of vision of the questioner. Rubenstein's death of God theology concluded that God was incinerated in the ovens of the death camps, dying with millions of Jews who perished in the Shoah. Wiesel's answer to the commanding question of God's presence, posed from behind him in the camp, "He is hanging here on the gallows," cannot be legitimately understood exclusively in terms of the death of God. If the response to Rubenstein's challenge, Wiesel's assertion, and the questions of theodicy is a declaration of God's empathic presence, then God must attend the dying, in every instance, in their deaths. God is the accompanying presence through death and transcending death. In dying and death, the commanding question "Where is God?" can only be answered: On that gallows, in that crematorium, in the cancer ward—always present with those who suffer and die.

SNAPSHOT

An encounter by the rescuer Herman Graebe illustrates one expression of God's presence. Graebe stood beside a rapidly filling mass grave in the Ukraine, watching hundreds of Jews undressing, stacking their clothing, and waiting under heavy guard to be called to the edge of the grave. He watched as an "old, naked Jewish man" comforted his naked, weeping "twelve year old son," pointed to heaven, and whispered inaudible words that evoked a fragile smile amidst the fearful tears. The German officer in charge of the *Einsatzcommando* bellowed, "Next ten! Quickly! Quickly!" More than forty years later, Graebe's memory of that scene was perfectly vivid when he said, "I know precisely what I would say to my [twelve-year-old] son in that moment. I would point to heaven, comfort him, and say, 'Do not be afraid, where we are going there are no SS or mass graves.' "[11] Seconds later, the man, his son, and their family descended to the ledge of the mass grave and died. It would seem in a father's whispered words and a gesture toward heaven, and a son's tentative smile of recognition, that God became present to them, eclipsed their fear, and accompanied them, in the powerful image of David's Twenty-third Psalm, "through the valley of the shadow of death" on the ledge of a mass grave to a heavenly "banquet set in the presence of their enemies."

The Nazis quite literally tried to substitute themselves for the God of the Covenant and their ideology for the faith of Judaism. But the Nazi table was set with only a banquet of death. In Nazi hands, heads were crushed against pillars, not anointed with oil. All of Nazi geography was traversed on the highway of evil, not on paths of righteousness. A theology of empathic, accompanying presence and a theology of transformative grace are consistent with Scripture and the opposite of the Nazi paganism. At present, a theology of empathic, accompanying presence is the only credible response to the challenges presented by the issues and questions of theodicy, and the presence of burning children.

Whether a Jew died or survived the evils of Nazism, or entered the universe of the camps with faith or found faith there, in the theology of Wiesel's cantata God was their sustaining and accompanying presence. Those who survived and sanctified life and affirmed the future understand that the true nature of God is the inspiration and strength to choose life and blessing in spite and because of the Shoah. Victims and survivors often recognized God beside the dying, or were reunited with God in the study of Talmud during forced labor, or knew God in an act of kindness or in a courageous intervention, or found in their trust the unexplainable strength to persevere. Is this not what the Psalmist had in mind with the timeless words in the Twenty-third Psalm: "If I should walk in the valley of deepest darkness no evil would I fear. You are there with your rod and your staff; with these you give me comfort"? Is not the challenge faced by the believer to recognize and take strength from the "goodness and mercy" of God, regardless of the circumstances, "all the days of their lives"?

These responses to theodicy, either empathic presence with the dying or sustaining accompaniment with the surviving, are not neatly conclusive. Many victims of Nazism, both Jewish and Christian, felt the abandonment of God, but also many found faith for the first time. The tragedy of the Shoah was that a theology of God's empathic presence and sustaining accompaniment was overshadowed by centuries-old teachings that led believers in both traditions to expect either God's beneficent interventions in times of catastrophe or the unbridled vengeance of a tyrannical, despotic divinity. Tragically, the presumed silence and inactivity of God led Nazis to believe that God ordained their work and led their victims to feel abandoned by God for reasons beyond their ken. We perpetuate those time-bound and constricted teachings by failing to tell the personal stories and encounters that focus on the reality of God's presence more than on the magical thinking associated with the imagined power to intervene or the contrived intention to inflict suffering, pain, and grief.

What would be the theological and lifestyle consequences for believers who began to embrace the idea that we are responsible for what we do with our suffering, that rights and privileges do not accrue from suffering but, to the contrary, magnify and intensify our calling to transform evil, suffering, and death into life and blessing and affirmation? What will become of a lay theology that begins at the threshold of suffering (in the presence of burning children) and there discovers not a distant, disinterested, or absent God but precisely the opposite? For those who might succumb and become victim-izers, there would be the resounding deterrent warning, absent in previous generations, that God is never present with them nor in their enterprise. And for those who are the victims of history or some other manner of trauma, there would be the assurance that they do not face their circumstances alone but rather in the presence of an empathic, sustaining God.

The chorus concludes Wiesel's cantata with the admonition, "Pray, men. Pray to God, Against God, For God. Ani maamin." Absent the essential reformation of theology and the human expectations of God's location in the midst of evil, suffering, and death, we are compelled to pray—even though the circumstances command us to be silent. We "pray to God" because God is present, not dead; we pray that we might know the presence of God. We "pray against God" because evil, suffering, and death will always rip at the human spirit. Why? Because we are almost always pitifully powerless before it. We "pray against God" in order to be truthful with God, to honestly confess that we have not resolved the powerful grip of the paradox of an all-powerful and good God and the perpetual existence of evil and suffering. We will "pray against God" because we easily and often lose sight of God's presence with us when we find ourselves in the midst of evil, suffering, and death. We "pray for God" because we have both empathy and sympathy for the torment that God endures at the hands of human complicity in evil and injustice.

Sometimes as I think about a reformation that terminates the expectation that God has the power to intervene when humanity suffers evil and death, I wonder if I am diminishing God and expecting too little of God. For twenty-five years of ministry, from death camps to intensive care units, from pastoral care to recording eyewitness accounts, I have listened and felt the struggle of those who suffer and those who offer comfort. The greatest peace and most trustworthy confidence come from the God whose presence is felt and sustains, whose accompaniment lifts the shadows of isolation and abandonment, and in whose tear-stained face human beings see both the mirrored reflection of their grief and agony and the possibility of hope and future.

Presence is more demanding than power. It would be the end of human freedom, responsibility, and moral creativity if God exercised all power. Presence has its risks. What if we do not recognize God's presence in our suffering? What if the presence of the divine is misinterpreted? What if we continue to demand assertions of power and reject presence? Presence presupposes an intimate relationship that would allow us to know that God is present. This perspective of God demands that we reform our expectations by allowing God to be present and accompanying, day by day, rather than by entertaining that illusory resolution or interpretation predicated on strength of arm or will. I expect too little of God when I count on God to be a sorcerer of power with a magic wand. I find the peace and strength when I recognize the divine presence in my life.

Are we, am I, willing to free God from the traditional biblical interpretations and theological constraints of power and willfulness and in their place begin to explore the nature of God who is present? Then, are we willing to free God of responsibility for the Shoah and to assess responsibility to those who were complicit in evil, to those who collaborated or looked away, and to those who betrayed biblical Christianity and Jesus Christ?

REGENERATING PARADIGMS

Remembering Israel's exile by the rivers of Babylon, the Psalmist plaintively beseeched, "How could we sing the Lord's song in an alien land?" (137:4). Not only the people of Israel but also the familiar words, rituals, and songs of Scripture were oppressed and exiled by the captivity. Babylon's brutality, slavery, and the gradual widespread loss of identity through assimilation into the culture and practices of the captors shattered the paradigms of faith. Centuries later, in yet another catastrophe, the central organizing constructs that joined believers to God were shattered by the Shoah. Suffering, evil, and death broke paradigms and bonds and overturned the well-known and trusted sources of meanings and rites of faith.

Rather than submit when the paradigms of faith are shattered by tragedy, the task at hand is to look squarely into the face of the tragedy and then begin to reform the constructs of belief and meaning, replacing those that are irreparable or that proved themselves to be contrived or unhelpful. I use the word *reform* rather than *rebuild* because almost by definition virtually every experience of evil and death takes people out to the extremities of existence, often beyond the boundaries of faith or meaning. At such times, the usually unexamined, untested, and static ways people believe, organize their values and lives, and construct meaning are rarely useful or supportive. They can be reformed, changed, and perhaps have some fleeting resemblance to their past form, but they can no more be rebuilt than a broken Stueben crystal can be seamlessly restored.

If, in the language of a later Psalm, we are to "[s]ing to the Lord a new song, God's praise in the assembly of the faithful" (149:1), then the new song must grow out of the tragedy and from a dynamic, creative, reformed, and renewed engagement with faith and life. Absent such a response, it is questionable if faith will sustain or survive. The task of believers who have encountered suffering, evil, or death is not to deconstruct their faith but, rather, to learn, grow, change, and amend. It is in this manner that persons of faith reclaim their identity and know who they are and whose they are. In this way, they will construct concrete acts of defiant hope and realize the possibility of a faithful future. In this way, we affirm the presence and fidelity of God, and open ourselves to the creative and ever-refreshed work of God's life-giving Spirit.

In the opening lines of the "Mass for the Day of St. Thomas Didymus," poet Denise Levertov articulates the acute tension created by the Shoah, and by faith, theodicy, and reformation:

> God then,
> encompassing all things, is defenseless? Omnipotence
>   has been tossed away, reduced
>   to a wisp of damp wool?
>   And we,
>   frightened, bored, wanting
> only to sleep till catastrophe
> has raged, clashed, seethed and gone by without us,
>   wanting then
> to awaken in quietude without remembrance of agony.[12]

It would seem to be so much easier to construct prayers and offer sermons "without remembrance of agony" or struggles with the nature of God and to respond to pastoral concerns with less compelling and damning paradigms. It would seem to be less painful and frightening to simply explore brokenness in a cursory manner from a safe distance rather than plunge into the chaos of reformation. It would be less consuming to abstractly reflect on one's place in the scheme of suffering and evil than to immerse one's self in a search for identity in the midst of exile. But it would not be in keeping with the origins of Christianity nor an authentic response to Jesus Christ to ignore the agonies of history or deflect the hurtful agendas imposed by the world. Similarly, as Emil Fackenheim has persuasively asserted, it would not be in keeping with the tradition of biblical prophets and the narratives of courageous resistance to cooperate in the completion of the work of Hitler and the Reich after they are gone.

In a letter to his niece at the time of her confirmation, before he was arrested for his role in the conspiracy against Hitler, Dietrich Bonhoeffer reflected on what I understand to be the power of a God of presence rather than the presence of a God of power. His reflection is a beginning point for a post-Shoah reformation:

There are so many experiences and disappointments which drive sensitive people into the paths of nihilism and resignation. For this reason it is good to learn early that suffering and God are not contradictory, but rather form a necessary unit. For me the idea that God himself suffers has always been by far the most convincing piece of Christian teaching.[13]

The pastor, theologian, member of the Resistance to the Reich and to Hitler—Dietrich Bonhoeffer—and the fourteen-year-old surviving victim of the Shoah, author, theologian, Nobelist—Elie Wiesel—helped me to comprehend and appropriate the nature of an empathic, suffering, loving, just, and present God. Their faithful wisdom in the tragic mystery of the Shoah turned me away from exile, indifference, and renunciation and toward freedom, reformation, and renewal.

They also taught me two essential lessons about my relationship with people and with God. First, how can Christians arrive at a sustaining theology of presence, how can Christians know and serve Jesus Christ, if we are not touched by or opened to the suffering or ecstasy, the joy or grief, the despair or hope that inhabit the lives of others? Unless we encounter and resist suffering or evil, unless we stand with those who face the forces of evil and death, whether in the Shoah or at some other intersection of tragedy and human life, we will not reflect the love and service of Jesus Christ. I will more fully explore the implications of empathic compassion and justice in a succeeding chapter.

Second, on the night before his crucifixion on a Roman cross, Jesus prayed in a garden outside the walled city. He asked of his disciples, "How is it that you three were not able to keep watch with me for even one hour?" (Matthew 26:40). It has always been our lot to request that God or Jesus stand watch with or pray for us, but there are times when humanity must be present for God—to offer the support; to wipe the tears; to share the prayers, joys, betrayals, and disappointments of the Creator and Redeemer. Wiesel heightened the awareness of the suffering of God in the world, at the hands of the world. Bonhoeffer's notion that Christians are people for others is extended to being people for God.

Believers choose to live in such a way that they do not contribute to the forces of evil or participate in the works of death, all of which bring suffering and grief to humankind and to God. Ultimately, people of faith make common cause with God and become partners with God in healing and bringing justice to the shattered world. The post-Shoah response to the questions of theodicy is to first proclaim our mutuality with the just and peaceful purposes of God and to recognize God present with us and through us. Somewhere Wiesel summarized an element of this response for Jews, and I would add for Christians, "A Jew can be for God and with God and against God, but not without God." Second, it is to recognize and accept the fact that meaning and understanding depend not on death or evil but on who I am in the midst of death and evil and after they have finished their work.

Chapter Four

Anthropology and Theodicy

Love and death: the two most simple things given to man.
You asked if I understand love.
I understand it because I understand death too.

Elie Wiesel[1]

The Narrator in Wiesel's cantata, *Ani Maamin*, radically readjusts the focal point of theodicy, placing God in the role of the questioner who demands to know what human beings in the twentieth century were doing to one another in Europe and to God's intentions for Creation. In response to the anguished challenges and the disappointed charges of Abraham, Issac, and Jacob, the Narrator asserts, "What right have you to speak thus? Does God owe you an accounting? . . . What about man? What about his role?"[2] Clearly, it was not the Creator but rather the created who conceived of and commanded mobile killing units, used the gifts of thought and knowledge to build gas chambers and crematoria, and plotted the genocidal murder of millions of Jews.

Without a tripartite application (God, the church, and humankind), the questions and issues of theodicy fuel a limited and fruitless academic exercise. While the forms of the questions will vary slightly between them, the three foci are part of a systemic, unified address in which the restoration of one is linked to that of the others. In spite of centuries of teachings about and expectations of God's unlimited power, will, and ability to intervene, and of God's capacity for vengeance, God was neither the architect nor the grand executioner of the Reich. God was not an interventionist or a disinterested bystander, at least not in the usual categories of theodicy. Similarly, the majority of those who read this text will not have played any of these roles in the Shoah. We come to this enterprise to understand the implications and to apply the lessons in a dangerous world where powers and principalities constantly push humanity toward the precipice of world war of genocidal madness. Because humanity has not mastered the art of peaceful coexistence or reached a theological state of perfection or wholeness, it is essential to join with God in asking the questions of human and divine accountability for the Shoah.

There are at least four basic levels of questions about responsibility and accountability that must be confronted with the Shoah. The questions can be generalized to other arenas of suffering, but they must be specifically asked of the Nazi era. In the case of the Shoah, the first questions must be put to the killers and, by extension, to the institutions that were either complicit in the killing or failed to engage and attempt to overturn the destructive powers of the Reich. Victims, survivors, and witnesses demand accountability of those who used their powers for evil or idly stood by: What was your role? How did you justify your complicity in or indifference to mass murder, your wanton acts of inhumanity, your support of the National Socialist agenda, and deeds that ultimately deprived you of your humanity? Why did you not turn aside anti-Semitism and other forms of hatred? Why did you not resist? How could you look away and not try to save the lives of those targeted by the Nazis and their collaborators? How could you let children and babies die without at least trying to hide them?

At the second level, there is a single question that presupposes our appropriation and use of history, a question that will be asked by victims, survivors, and witnesses. They demand to know of succeeding generations of individuals and institutions: Considering what you have learned about what we suffered, who will you be? This question is perhaps most difficult for Christians who were not present, complicit, or involved, neither killers nor bystanders, and who therefore feel no direct or personal responsibility for the acts of those who lived in an earlier time, in distant lands, and who abused their faith by participating in evil.

For theologians, clergy, and church leaders, the second question is difficult because, absent a personal or moral investment in the Shoah and its lessons and implications, it encourages abstract reflection and responses to the concrete implications and lessons that the Shoah poses for the religious community. This difficulty is compounded by post-Shoah theologians and clergy who have not understood the implications or applied the lessons of the Shoah relative to the Germanic, Western influences that dominate the Christian theological enterprise. The tragedy takes shape in the perpetuation of oppressive teachings, the failure to confront the

Christian origins and justifications of genocide, and the failure to celebrate and to offer as role models Christian children, women, and men who rescued Jews from Nazis. Ultimately, the greatest defeat, regardless of which example of inhumanity we study, is the reticence to confront the failure of Christian institutions, leaders, and members to act in accordance with the teachings, example, and mandates of Jesus.

These charges are neither new nor unique. They are reflected in the anguish and outrage expressed by African-American theologians who charge the church for failing to confront the implications and learn the lessons of racism and slavery. They are known to feminist Christians who struggle to overcome male-dominated hierarchies and gender-biased teachings, and in Central American liberation theologies that challenge injustice, oppression, and in every theology that fails to take seriously, and attempt to overcome, the ascendant cultural and political power structures.

If the cycles of indifference and complicity are ever to be broken, and if Christianity is to be a positive force in preventing repetition of similar evils in the future, it must face these traumas and confrontations and address the second question, Considering what you have learned about what we suffered, who will you be? Only in this way shall there be probing self-examinations that lead to spiritual and intellectual, individual and institutional, transformations.

Those post-Shoah Christians who explore the second question must ask the next level of questions in response. At this level there are several areas the queries must probe—theological, institutional, and personal. The first may be daring theological questions about expectations of God that originated in and were perpetuated by doctrinal predominance in the Christian denominations. For instance, the post-Shoah faithful may be moved, as Rubenstein was moved, to ask if there is any longer a God or, minimally, to question the propriety of continuing to hold images and expectations of a God who is in control of the cosmos, whose power is unlimited, whose will is unchangeable, a God who knows in advance what will happen but who exercises no constraints. Clergy and theologians may feel compelled by the history of teachings about God to level their questions at God, but is not the real challenge of evil in the world and the suffering of persons directed at humankind and its structures and systems? Implicit at this level is the haunting question, Is it really sufficient to enter the dock and posit accusatory questions about God's place and role when a person suffers or when evil prevails over a people or in the world?

Relative to institutional self-examination, the Shoah demands that Christians dare to question and study the viability of the church: Can it be reformed in response to the Shoah, or is its place in history so polluted that it cannot survive? In this regard, post-Shoah Christians must come to terms with scandalous questions about the church and centuries of sophisticated theological inquiry that did not prepare the preponderance of confessing, practicing Christians throughout the European continent to turn aside the racial and religious hatred promulgated by the National Socialists, nor to protest or work to overthrow the Reich, or ultimately, to intervene on behalf of its victims. Indeed, we must ask, What are the implications of the certainty that so many Christians collaborated in the barbarities of the era and so few churches became communities of resistance and agents of compassion? What will post-Shoah churches learn from the experience of Nazi-era churches? Will they ignore the lessons and implications of history? How will they reform dangerous teachings and practices that could be used to turn believers against yet another group of human beings? What word will the church speak when modern-day haters grasp after the public will? What will be the role of the church in matters of global unrest, violations of human and civil rights, and acts of mass destruction?

As we examine the Nazi-era failings of an institution dedicated to grace, mercy, healing, justice, and love, and its dereliction in preparing its members to imitate those positive characteristics by acting compassionately and resisting evil, we must pursue a similar range of questioning and self-examination at the third or personal level. The Shoah lays bare the gaping chasm between Jesus' teachings about love and healing and the contrary actions of the majority of European Christians who either collaborated or were indifferent. Because so many professing Christians and churchgoing people were guilty of those charges, it is essential that individual Christians and the theological academies reexamine their experience of and confidence in *metanoia* (new thinking) and their reliance on *metamorphosis* (new life) in Christ. The mission of the theological community must be to assist individual Christians in their inquiry into what seems, in view of the Shoah, to be a romantic Christian reliance on teachings about the ultimate redeemability and wholeness of humankind, teachings that have only rarely had their genesis in the presence of burning children.

The final questions are more universal, belonging to those who survive suffering and evil, and to those who seek beneficial reformations and healing transformations after the Shoah. The questions are framed in the manner of the choice that Moses articulated on God's behalf when the Israelites were about to embark on the last leg of the journey to the Promised Land. The form of the question for survivors and witnesses is, What will you do with your experiences of suffering and indifference at the hands of Nazism? For the remainder of the human community, the question is, What will we do with our knowledge of the suffering of others, the complicity and indifference of the many, and the courageous compassion of the few? It is to these final two questions that I want to devote the majority of this chapter.

In the movie *Awakenings* there is a scene in which Leonard's mother, having made peace with the epidemic illness that left her son comatose and catatonic (*encephalitis lethargica*), reflectively commented to her son's visionary physician, Dr. Sayers, "When he was born healthy and fine I didn't ask why—I asked why when he became like this." This vignette is instructive as people of faith ponder the experiences that move them to question God's intention and role and to raise the familiar issues and explore the otherwise alien territory of theodicy. Most people accept the good that comes to them in life, accept it when pleasing things happen or life feels good and rich and blessed, without asking why or questioning its possible origins—and too often without even a grateful acknowledgment. Most frequently it is only when people reach or exceed the margins of their vulnerabilities, suffering, and pain that they invoke the protocols of theodicy.

Our natural selectivity in posing the questions in exclusively negative situations is one among many factors casting a dark shadow of suspicion on the theological enterprise of theodicy. It is instructive to think about the origins and place of theodicy in the same terms as the other doctrinally based teachings that have shaped believers' expectations of God and their understanding of God's intentions. Thornton Wilder's Brother Juniper, who sought an "Intention" in the twists and ways of life, in the novel *The Bridge of San Luis Rey*, expresses this struggle in simple terms after the bridge collapsed, sending five people to their deaths:

"Why did this happen to *those* five?" If there were any plan in the universe at all, if there were any pattern in a human life, surely it could be discovered mysteriously latent in those lives so suddenly cut off. Either we live by accident and die by accident, or we live by plan and die by plan.[3]

Because existence is replete with dangers, threats, and evil, we would do well to consider the sources and examine our attributions of responsibility, the better to assess the relevance of the historical approach of theodicy.

We know that there are disasters that result from the capricious acts of nature and that cause immense suffering for innocent persons. Earthquakes rend the faulted lands, hurricanes weave destructive paths, diseases and illnesses ravage vulnerable bodies, and people suffer and die. Accidents visit tragedy on all manner of people without regard to their stations in life.

Passenger planes crash, drunk drivers kill and maim, a rock gives way under foot or a rogue wave sweeps away, and always innocent people suffer. Evil acts by humans are legion in the world. The evening news briefly acknowledges the worst offenses, from the crimes against humanity in the Balkans to the violations of human rights in China, from a massacre of Muslim worshippers to a lethal terrorist raid on Israeli schoolchildren, from the willful mutilation of the natural ecology to sanctioned rapes and murders in Central America.

A more subtle, but no less destructive, expression of evil is silence in the face of another human being's oppression, suffering, and violation. Those who suffer in any tragedy want to know if others cared or responded; did everyone know what was done and by whom? A tragedy is compounded when victims learn that someone knew and did nothing, that government or institutions were silent bystanders. Wiesel's memoir *Night* was originally published under the title *And the World Kept Silent*. A significant part of Wiesel's struggle is with a world that knew and did nothing. In his novel *Town Beyond the Wall*, the protagonist, Michael, finally illegally returns to his hometown in search of something that continues to evade him. In the town's central plaza, he suddenly remembers the face in the window looking down over the Jews awaiting transport to the camps. It was the face of the "spectator." A person unmoved at any level and in any way by the plight of those he observed, Wiesel's spectator pretends not to be present and that the victims are also not there. The unresponsive world is personified by the indifferent, unfeeling, and inactive spectator.

SNAPSHOTS

The Shoah was a thief that stole life, robbed children of their youth, pillaged memory and tradition, pilfered the future, and deprived people of faith, joy, and hope. At the end of Ben Piazza's novel *The Exact and Very Strange Truth*, the child Alexander looked out from the train and thought:

Sometimes things change so sudden. Yes, like on a summer afternoon when a thunderstorm comes. The sky can be bright blue and all at once change to gray and then black. That is the way it is. Things change so sudden sometimes and that is the exact and very strange truth. Always and forever things change.[4]

For the first time since his father's death, Alexander cried, bending to the raw power of the exact and very strange truth: When someone dies, nothing is ever again the same. For victims, survivors, and witnesses after the Shoah, nothing was ever again the same. Everything had changed, forever.

I want to return to the two approaches taken by Pinchas Peli and Joseph Soloveitchik to the problem of suffering and evil in both our daily lives and systemically. In the first, a person who thinks about suffering and evil without finding meaning or understanding is rendered immobile and powerless. This person may be silent or indifferent in some future encounter. In the second, the suffering and evil are confronted, and whether or not meaning and understanding are found, the person makes very certain decisions about his or her values.

As I was preparing the chapters on theodicy and anthropology, a friend told me about a shattering experience in her life. It illustrates the dilemma and choice mentioned above. Rebecca Travis's college roommate Linda was kidnapped at random from the parking lot of her apartment complex. For three days, three men drugged her and drove her through the mountains on a rampage of rape and mayhem. One of the sadists turned state's evidence and told of Linda's last hours before they killed her. She begged her torturers to let her live; they responded by taunting, chasing, abusing, and finally murdering her. After actively participating in the regional search for her friend and enduring the graphic recounting of the terrors Linda suffered, Rebecca searched for meaning and understanding in the midst of the tragedy. Without finding peace or perspective, she asked, "I know that God did not will Linda's death. And I know that Linda's death is the result of very evil decisions made by very evil men. What I can never explain is why Linda had to feel such horror even to the very end. If God is not one who will intervene to prevent such things, why didn't God at least give her peace? What good is a God who allowed Linda's last thoughts to be ones of terror and despair, and not of hope and peace?" I will return to this traumatic story in a moment, after further reflecting on the second alternative in Soloveitchik's view.

TRANSFORMING SUFFERING AND DEATH INTO JUSTICE AND LOVE

How shall we find a way through and beyond the horrors of the Shoah, through and beyond traumas that exact their toll on our daily lives? What pathway will lead us to a framework of understanding and meaning that does not trivialize the suffering that others have endured and those calamities that directly touch our lives? What framework is sturdy enough to withstand the onslaught that follows catastrophe? A month before she was murdered at Auschwitz, Etty Hillesum, the Westerbork diarist, wrote to her friend Maria Tuinzing. Her words compose a warning to those who try to craft a personal understanding and meaning that will carry them through and beyond the study of the Shoah. It would be unconscionable to trivialize the experience of the survivors of the Shoah or of those who entrust to us the stories of their personal struggles, suffering, and pain. Her words point to a path that is not frail and will neither trivialize nor impair those who choose to be and to live differently because of the Shoah:

People sometimes say, "You must try to make the best of things." I find this such a feeble thing to say. Everywhere things are both very good and very bad at the same time. The two are in balance, everywhere and always. I never have the feeling that I have to make the best of things; everything *is* fine just as it is. Every situation, however miserable, is complete in itself and contains the good as well as the bad. All I really wanted to say is this: "making the best of things" is a nauseating expression, and so is "seeing the good in everything." I should like to explain why in greater detail, but if you only knew how tired I feel.[5]

What authentic constructs of understanding and meaning of post-Shoah life, values, theology, and behavior shall be offered to those who were robbed of their existence: to children who died with images of terror cavorting before their eyes, to parents who watched their children waste away or brutally die, to children who died with images of God eclipsing the terrors they were facing, to children who were slaughtered with frightful images and intimations of God warring for their final glimpse of life, and to the multitude of Rebeccas who shall never know what final images and thoughts that the countless Lindas carried away with them? We cannot excuse or justify the behavior of killers, but we can be different on behalf of their victims.

In a lecture at Stanford University on the life of the biblical patriarch Isaac, Wiesel reflected on suffering and evil, giving new meaning to Soloveitchik's second alternative in which suffering and evil are confronted and, whether or not meaning and understanding are found, a person makes very certain decisions about what values will direct the priorities of his or her life. Through the lecture, an unmistakable bond linked Isaac and the survivor of the Shoah. In that bond there exists a challenge to the manner of human being we will be when we witness, confront, resist, or endure suffering and evil.

Isaac will become the defender of his people. Why he? Because he suffered? But that is not a reason good enough! We believe that suffering confers no privileges;

it is what you do with your suffering that counts. And Isaac transformed his suffering into praise for [humankind] and praise of [humanity], rather than into hate and bitterness. . . . To be a Jew is to see what I have seen, remember what I have said and lived and endured and indicated, to do what I have done and go on doing it, or at least telling about it to some friends sometimes, and tell it all the time, not with tears, but with laughter.[6]

I have learned through the Shoah and its survivors, and from the lives and values of the rescuers, that meaning and understanding depend not on the reality of death or its many expressions but on who I am in the confrontation with death and its agents, and what I do in the midst of and after death has finished its work. I did not suffer the Shoah. In immersing myself in its aftermath, I suffered its consequences. I have attempted to be faithful to the voice and sufferings of its victims and to the witness and moral courage of those who rescued or otherwise resisted evil. I learned and appropriated from both groups the wisdom of Wiesel's autobiographical commentary on Isaac: "suffering confers no privileges; it is what you do with your suffering that counts." My task has been to perpetuate the truth of that lesson for the sake of the Shoah, and because elements in the world constantly threaten global peace and human security, I extend the lessons and implications in the hope of preventing repetitions or worse.

I have come to a new awareness of love and justice because I have confronted death and who I want to be in a world full of suffering and evil. Following the death of his thirteen-year-old son, Jerry Irish proposed a radical notion, a different way of perceiving one's self in the midst of loss, grief, and injustice. If a person is to be liberated from the grips of death or evil, suffering or oppression, that freedom comes when the person is able to perceive "Death as an occasion to love" and, I would add, and to do justice.[7]

In the cantata *Ani Maamin*, after the last of the three patriarchs has delivered his report, Wiesel's Narrator describes God's surprising response to the Shoah: God wept without constraint and "with—yes—love."[8] A survivor of suffering, evil, and death transformed the Shoah into the occasion for the Creator's love to be known. The flooding tears of God's love inspire hope in Abraham, Isaac, and Jacob. Wiesel gives them an additional expression of hope, their children, which is to say, hope for the future. Wiesel carefully maintains the tension between a hope for the future and the silence of the 1.5 million Jewish children exterminated in the Shoah. There cannot, dare not, be a simple or facile resolution of any manner of suffering, death, or evil.

The tragedy afforded the survivor/writer an additional occasion to find love and justice in the midst of murder and indifference. Though they cannot know it, the three patriarchs do not leave their audience and return to the Creation alone. They are accompanied by their God who loves, weeps, and smiles. Suffering, death, and evil become the occasion for God's presence amongst the survivors and in the world. The cantata ends with generation after generation of Jews singing the *Ani Maamin* chorus, in spite of and because of suffering and evil. The Reich did not ultimately eclipse the presence, silence the song, destroy the faith, or steal the hope.

What inspired this metamorphosis and why does it have such intuitive credibility as we seek to be different because of what we learn from the Shoah? In part, the answer may be found in a character study Wiesel wrote on the biblical prophet Jeremiah, the so-called Weeping Prophet. As with his conclusion about the lesson of Isaac's life, Wiesel's words about Jeremiah seem autobiographical and point to an essential post-Shoah route to life and blessing. Of Jeremiah he wrote:

[His] purpose is to teach his contemporaries and their descendants a lesson: there comes a time when one must look away from death and turn away from the dead; one must cling to life, which is made of minutes, not necessarily of years, and surely not centuries; one must fight so as not to be overwhelmed by history but to act on it concretely, simply, humanly.[9]

Always the evil and the hope, the need to secure justice and to live justly, must be held in tension. It is what a person does with his or her experiences of suffering, death, and evil that defines who he or she is and illuminates his or her values and faith.

DEATH, HOPE, AND RESISTANCE

Death subtracts and concludes, but love and justice multiply and create. Death divides, conquers, and plunders, but love and justice fulfill, complete, and reunite. Death isolates and then departs, often leaving in its wake stagnation and despair. Love and justice are generative, open and embracing, responsible but compassionate, crafting lives of integrity and investment. Death closes the future, threatening the faith and trust of survivors and succeeding generations. Considering the lessons and implications of the Shoah, love and justice offer a contrary vision of the present, for the sake of the future, and renew the commitment to active hope. Dietrich Bonhoeffer, from his cell in a Nazi death camp, struggled with living solely for the moment or dreaming of better times while abandoning the present.

In the midst of his suffering and with only limited hope of escaping execution, he rejected the alternatives and anticipated turning his fate into life and blessing and of robbing death of the last word in his life. He wrote:

We find both these courses equally impossible, and there remains for us only the very narrow way, often extremely difficult to find, of living every day as if it were our last, and yet living in faith and responsibility as though there were to be a great future. . . . There are people who regard it as frivolous, and some Christians think it impious for anyone to hope and prepare for a better earthly future. They think that the meaning of present events is chaos, disorder and catastrophe; and in resignation or pious escapism they surrender all responsibility for reconstruction and for future generations. It may be that the day of judgment will dawn tomorrow; and in that case, though not before, we shall gladly stop working for a better future.[10]

The lesson of the survivors, resisters, and rescuers is that we do not abandon hope or give.up on the future. We confront, struggle, and learn the history and stories of the Shoah, thereby diminishing the possibility of complicity in or indifference to evil and increasing the likelihood of altruistic interventions.

SNAPSHOT

With her permission, Rebecca Travis's husband Karl, a Presbyterian minister, shared with a grief support group for widows the story of Linda's tragic kidnap, rape, and murder and Rebecca's haunting question. One of the widows who more than once had contemplated and resisted allowing herself to die in the midst of a recurring illness, told of an unexplainable sense of hope that drove her to live on in spite of the grief and loneliness that she felt. Linking her experience and hope with Linda's will to live, she said, "It seems to me that the amazing thing about this woman's death is precisely that she didn't give up, that despite the atrocities committed against her for those three days she refused to give up her dignity. She wanted to live despite the degradation. She begged to live up to the very end. If the will to live in such situations is not God, I don't know what it is."

Only Linda knew what she was thinking while in the hands of her murderers and at the end of her life. Those who survive her or hear her story may choose to see in her courage and valiant struggle to be free and live, the passion and sustaining presence of God. The earlier discussion of theodicy compels me to believe that God faced and was a victim with her in every act of depravity inflicted upon her. God was also the source of her strength and dignity. Our tradition would have us take comfort in the fact that Linda was never abandoned or alone. The only response to Rebecca's question is to ask another question, with a more universal address: Who will we be, how shall we love and do justice when others suffer evil and death that we were not able to stop?

To submit to despair or helplessness is to cooperate in the labors of evil and death. To submit to theological doubt and mistrust is to begin to give death the final word in life—it is to do death's work for it, and there will be two victims: the one who suffered and died and the one whose faith in God and life suffers and dies. To affirm and bless life, to transform the work of evil and death into love and justice, is to reclaim what death and evildoers have taken from us in life and faith. Whether they are three murderers in New Mexico or a legion of killers and collaborators in Europe, we are forbidden to do their work for them or to give them the final word in our lives.

Given the approach I posit to theodicy and an anthropology of responsibility, a troubling question remains: Are we, am I, is the church, willing to free God from responsibility for the Shoah, and assess full responsibility to those who chose to take part in evil (the National Socialist plotters and planners, the killers, bystanders, equivocators, and collaborationists)—those who betrayed biblical Christianity and Jesus Christ? They exercised their free will, those who masterminded gas chambers, led mobile killing units, appeased the Reich, looked away, conformed, and otherwise cast their lot with the forces of evil. In the same way, those who chose resistance, rescue, and otherwise acted with human dignity and integrity exercised their free will and choices. "Free will" is represented in Judaism and Christianity as the "ability to make and execute one's own decisions, thus incurring accountability for what one does. . . . But we are moral agents expressing our authentic selves in our conduct."[11] Humanity, by virtue of free will, is accountable to God. Why should God be accountable to humanity for what people do, for the choices they make?

Maimonides addresses this understanding from the perspective of Jewish law: "Free will is bestowed on every human being. If one desires to turn towards the good way and be righteous, he has the power to do so. If one wishes to turn towards the evil way and be wicked, he is at liberty to do so."[12] Employing the positive alternative suggested in the model of Peli and Soloveitchik, a person is moved by the trauma of others and opened to them in such a way as to want to end their experience of suffering or evil. Faith reaches its zenith, the pinnacle of meaning, in those who, facing their own experience of suffering or evil, or that of another, or who consider taking part in or looking away from evil and suffering, instead choose life and blessing rather than death and curse. They who faithfully and biblically exercise their free will choose to act in ways that affirm life and are just, compassionate, peaceful, humane, and ultimately pleasing to God. When God asks of contemporary believers, "Where are your brothers or sisters?" we must be prepared to answer that we are moving toward them at that very moment; and when God demands to know, "What have you done?" we will be able to answer, "I intervened!"

Let us return to the story told by the Baal Shem of the special place in the forest, the fire, the prayer, and the story. Our lives are touched and changed by many events that are beyond our control. Whether a person survived the Shoah, attempted to save a roommate's life, or tries to craft meaning and change because of the suffering of others, the task is never to forget and always to tell the story that in spite of the depravity of the many, one maintained dignity; that in spite of what others may feel was absence, one knew God's presence; and that in spite of fear and the reality of evil, one had faith in God and held hope for life. In telling these stories to others, people can be moved to greater faithfulness, to hope, and to acts of goodness. The stories can empower people to refuse to give in to resignation, despair, or cynicism. The retelling of the stories can challenge people not to avert their eyes or otherwise engage in complicitous acts or to ignore the cries of the human family. It is all a lesson about the power of narratives: A story told about courage, compassion, or dignity in a particular time and situation can offer unimagined lessons for a completely different time and place. Through these stories the past looks over our shoulders to see who we will be and how we will act in the present. The future also looks over our shoulders for a glimpse of the harvest it must anticipate.

GRIEF, MEANING, AND STORY

In the Hasidic tradition there are three ascending levels of mourning: with tears—that is the lowest; with silence—that is higher; and with a song—that is the highest. Evil and death always seek to still the melodies of life, to silence our songs. The killers are still at work; therefore, the choristers must not allow their song to be stilled; neither the *Ani Maamin* nor the Gregorian chant. We tell the stories of victims and survivors, of rescue and resistance, so that the role models of dignity and heroism are not lost. Through the hearing and sharing of many such stories, death is transformed from an act of disenfranchisement to the occasion for love and justice; and we are enabled to determine who we will be, what values will inform our actions, and what we will do in the face of suffering or evil or death. Our ballad celebrates the stories of simple experiences of grace, the presence of dignity, and acts of courage in which common people muster the fullness of their humanity to resist death and evil as long as they have being.

Chapter Five

"To Act Justly . . ."

The most important of illusions is that the collective life of [human-kind] can achieve perfect justice. It is a very valuable illusion for the moment; for justice cannot be approximated if the hope of its perfect realization does not generate a sublime madness in the soul. Nothing but such madness will do battle with malignant power and spiritual wickedness in high places.

Reinhold Niebuhr[1]

They are timeless questions that may be asked in numerous variations. In Genesis, after Cain murdered his brother, God asked, "Where is your brother Abel?" In turn, Cain responded with a question, "Am I my brother's keeper?" And finally God asked, "What have you done?" Generations later, in the Gospel of Luke, a teacher of the law asked Jesus about attaining eternal life. Jesus put the question back to the canon lawyer who included in his response the mandate to "love your neighbor as you love yourself." Jesus acknowledged his correct reply, but the lawyer injected a caveat in question form, "Who is my neighbor?"

The prophets were unconcerned with the didactic niceties of probing questions and insightful answers. Amos bluntly admonished the faithful, "Seek good, and not evil, that you may live; . . . Hate evil, and love good, and establish justice in the gate. . . . Let justice roll down like a river and righteousness like an ever-flowing stream" (5:14–15, 24). Micah offered a formula for a faithful and holistic life: "This is what the Lord God asks of you: only this, to act justly, love tenderly, and walk humbly with your God"

(6:8). Jesus, perhaps inspired by Hillel's vision of a moral dictum ("What is hateful to you, do not do to another. That summary of law is the law, the rest is commentary"), taught his followers: "Always treat others as you would like them to treat you; that is the meaning of the Law and the Prophets" (Matthew 7:12).

In the same gospel, Jesus told a parable in which the protagonist, presumably the messiah of God, explained the theological basis for a just and compassionate life: "I was hungry and you gave me food; I was thirsty and you gave me drink; I was a stranger and you welcomed me; naked and you clothed me, sick and you visited me, in prison and you came to me." The faithful were confused and initially demurred because they had never seen him in those conditions, but he said to them, "Whenever you did this to one of the least of mine, you did it to me" (25:35, 40).

Without a trace of recrimination or animosity, an elderly survivor of the Shoah once wistfully queried a group of high school students, "Do you think the world will ever be different because of what we endured in the camps?" Rescuer Herman Graebe, hospitalized and near death, asked me, "Do you think it really made any difference?" Knowing that Graebe was self-critical because he was unable to save more people than he did, I assumed he meant to ask if his rescues made any difference. He interrupted as I sought to assure him that his efforts made a difference to the people he saved and to their offspring who would not have been born. "No!" he shouted. "Does it matter to anyone that Jews were murdered or that we tried to save them? Does my life make any difference with all the hatred and violence in the world today?"

The unrelenting presence of evil, suffering, death, oppression, and injustice invoke the fundamental question of the survivor who is compelled to ask, Will what I endured prevent someone else from suffering a similar fate? In the same manner, the witness who became positively involved demands, Are my words buried in the graveyard of historical memory, or are they born once again in those who will act justly and compassionately? Whether a person is a bystander or a perpetrator of evil, or wrestles with the decision to intervene, the suffering of others challenges humanity with God's question to Cain, "Where is your brother [sister]?"

Throughout Europe during the Nazi era, to be a faithful practitioner of Christianity and obedient to the biblical mandates for justice and kindness involved closing the gap that prevented goodness from overcoming evil, compassion from eclipsing indifference, and resistance from conquering collaboration. Every such act mattered, regardless of how great or modest, dangerous or safe, public or private. What individuals and institutions did or failed to do defined them relative to their place and identity in the historical-political milieu of 1933–1945. Too few closed the gap or used the occasion of increasing political oppression, systemic evil, and the imposition of death to focus and intensify their expressions of love and justice. In this regard, we must also include silence and indifference as component parts of complicity in evil and death. For that reason, the identity of the majority was unfocused and distorted, ensuring that their place was on the side of the killers.

For a faithful remnant, identity was forged in simple acts of kindness to strangers whom the Reich defined as "enemies." The identities of justice and goodness were formed in audacious acts of rescue, bold involvement in resistance, political opposition to the Reich, and such spiritual and ecclesiastical contention and inspiration as resulted from the actions of the Confessional Synod of the German Evangelical Church meeting in Barmen.

For those who transformed the horrors of the Shoah into their occasion to actively reflect the love and justice of their Creator and faith, there came a defining moment where a place in history and an identity were claimed, a moment in which both individuals and institutions made a choice that would be with them and mark the remainder of their existence. Just as Ben Piazza's "exact and very strange truth" of death holds that nothing was ever again the same, when people acted with compassion and courage in the Nazi era, their lives were forever changed. They shall never forget, but what they chose to do determined what and how they remember. During her interview for the film *The Courage to Care*, Dutch rescuer Marion Pritchard tells of being transfixed, a bystander, as Nazis threw Jewish children from an orphanage onto a transport truck. A woman ran up and protested, and the Nazis threw her into the truck. In that centering moment, Pritchard was changed and entered into rescue. While involved in rescue she was forced to choose between the Jews she was protecting and a Dutch police collaborationist. Because he would have killed the family of Jews she was hiding, she chose to take the policeman's life. She concluded her interview with a critical observation: "We all have memories of times when we should have done something and we didn't. And it gets in your way during the rest of your life."[2] The memory of evil and the sights and sounds of the terrors may never release their hold, but a greater knowledge prevails. Identity and being are affirmed and a measure of centering peace roots itself in those who acted in a manner that validated their faith and highest values. Even in the moral complexity of a situation in which a life was taken in order to spare the lives of the victims, there is the realization that evil was confronted and death was resisted.

I have attempted to honor the particularity of the Shoah, and at the same time I have sought to integrate its universal lessons and implications into my life and ministry. In this process, I have intentionally striven to avoid making the Shoah utilitarian, that is to say, to make it fulfill my own or some other purposes. At the same time that it was shattering my intellectual, professional, and spiritual paradigms, the Shoah was also forging new structures and models. These new paradigms provided me a new and different angle of vision, guided my perceptions, informed my interpretations, and directed my responses.

The lessons of the Nazi era have significance in the latter days of the twentieth century. And yet restraint and caution must be exercised in appealing to those lessons. If they are invoked casually, frequently, or as comparisons to modern events, the risk is that the lessons will be trivialized by careless generalization and overuse. While comparisons may be drawn between the events of separate historical eras or situations, it is more appropriate to avoid making comparisons in favor of referring to the lessons, enjoining the implications, and challenging people to action. Evil, suffering, oppression, and injustice cannot be compared; on the contrary, they must be resisted and terminated, and their lessons must be learned and transmitted. The lessons of evil from one epoch or experience are cumulative and speak to the next outbreak on the spiral of hatred and violence.

It is divisive and destructive to compare one person's suffering to that of another. When certain leaders of the Nation of Islam began comparing the unconscionable travesty of Africans forced into slavery to the experience of Jews in the Shoah, they tragically slipped, as do most who rely on this device, from comparison to quantification. Robbing the Shoah of it popularized name for their own use, their spokesperson proclaimed that "the holocaust of the African slaves was thousands of times worse than the Jewish Holocaust." Comparisons almost always give way to valuations and quantifications, which in turn diminish the experience and humanity of another, and huge chasms are gouged into the human landscape. I have never heard survivors of the Shoah compare their tragedy to that of African slaves, to the genocide of the Armenians, or to any other outbursts of evil. Few survivors make comparisons, most speak out against the forces that cause others to suffer, and they devote themselves to honoring the memory of their experience by tirelessly working to redress injustices suffered by others and to end modern genocidal activities.

Post-Shoah generations search for meaning in their own times, even as genocidal actions continue to flourish, oppression and injustice rage on, and while violations of human and civil rights abound. The paradigms that evolve from an authentic encounter with the Shoah have the power and authority to transform meaning, values, and identity and to quicken the conscience for justice. The task at hand is to learn the lessons and adopt the new paradigms, all the while honoring the memory of the Shoah as its voices speak to another generation.

IMPLICATIONS OF THE MESSAGES FROM BARMEN

> Listen not to the voices which speak the language of hatred, revenge, retaliation. Follow not leaders who train you in ways of inflicting death. Love life, respect life in yourself and in others.
>
>   John Paul II[3]

For clergy and theologians, one of the clarion lessons of the Shoah is to be vigilant for the works of injustice, hatred, and division. Vigilance leads to a paradigm of commitment to and involvement in activities that seek to end spirals of violence, threats to peace and stability, and that resist the political, social, economic, cultural, and religious forces that originate or are complicit in evil. One of the formative paradigms from the Shoah is the model of resistance formulated by the Lutheran, Reformed, and United Churches that, on May 31, 1934, approved the Theological Declaration of Barmen.

The Barmen Declaration was clearly a period piece, reflecting the divisions and struggles for identity and existence between the federation of German Confessional Churches in the German Evangelical Church and the National Socialist's Reich Bishop and the ultranationalist German Protestant Church (German Christians), the last two, respectively, appointed and founded by Adolf Hitler. Clearly, as the Reich commandeered control of both civil and ecclesiastical governments and sought to dictate the conditions of Christian faith, the Confessing Churches determined their place and identity in Germany.

The Barmen document divided its Protestant supporters from the "German Christians" by affirming central teachings of the Reformed tradition and rejecting Nazism's pagan ideologies. Many creeds and confessions are written and implemented in response to a perceived threat or a challenge to the faith or the church; Barmen was no exception. Employing a classic confessional format that included scriptural foundations, affirmations, and specific rejections of political impositions, the drafters of the Barmen Declaration addressed seven points related to "false doctrine, the use of force and insincere practices" threatening the unity of the German Evangelical Church.

The framers accurately perceived four basic threats to the church, specifically, and by extension, to the nation: first, that Hitler sought to assume from Jesus Christ the authority and allegiance of the churches and the loyalty of individual Christians; second, that the churches and their members were to be identified with a nationalist-ethnic agenda; third, that the calling and mission of the churches were to be united with and legitimated only in service to National Socialism; and finally, that churches and Christians were directed to conform their faith to a particular political ideology. With resolute bravery and a simple truth, the German Evangelical Church distinguished itself from other key leaders and institutions of the time with these words: "[We] may not keep silent, since we believe that we have been given a common message to utter in a time of common need and temptation."[4]

To be certain, early warnings were sounded in various quarters, but while the vast majority of Germans celebrated the revival of an economy ravaged by World War I, the rebirth of what was interpreted to be national pride and common purpose, and an emerging military-industrial alliance, the churches perceived an ominous threat on the horizon and publicly spoke in opposition. Thus, a segment of the church, a faithful remnant, began to break free of Reich ideology, declaring their obedience and loyalty to Jesus Christ rather than to *Der Führer*. As the German Evangelical Church courageously sought to distance itself from the political and spiritual controls of the Reich, it tragically failed to address the greater issues facing the German people, the society, and, ultimately, the world.

The Barmen Declaration was composed for the sake of the churches; it was the attempt by the churches to protect their own interests. On June 6, 1936, the German Evangelical Church submitted a Memorandum to Hitler. It was also a self-serving document and clearly sent the message that the interests of this church body were nearly exclusively parochial, that it was not a church for others! The Memorandum contains a single sentence weakly questioning anti-Semitism, in a modest paragraph devoted to a tempered rejection of Aryanization. A subsection of the Memorandum entitled "Morality and Justice" refers to the continuing existence of "concentration camps in Germany" but does so relative to the forced penal labor imposed on dissidents in the German Evangelical Church rather than in relationship to the fate of Jews bound for Dachau and the fulfillment of Hitler's promise to rid the world of Jews.[5]

In both Barmen and the Memorandum, the church failed to see beyond itself and in so doing failed to perceive the existent and emerging dangers posed by the Reich. It did not speak out on behalf of Jews who were the victims of brutal riots led by the SA (*Sturmabteilung*, German Storm Troopers), nor did it note the public burning of books written by Jews and other dissidents, and it did not explicitly acknowledge and decry the racist enactments of the Nuremberg Laws. During the period immediately preceding the drafting of Barmen and through the release of the Memorandum,

Jews were legally vilified and slandered and politically and socially isolated in preparation for liquidation. The core documents of church resistance failed to notice or protest those conditions! Furthermore, with its narrow perspective, the German Evangelical Church did not respond to the global political threats in spite of Germany's withdrawal from the League of Nations, mandatory conscription, the invasion of the Rhineland, and the divisive expository and written rhetoric of Chancellor Hitler.

It is understandable that the gathering at Barmen chose to be diplomatic in asserting that it did not mean to "oppose the unity of the German nation!"[6] This is the diplomacy of the so-called loyal opposition that cautiously conserves its favored position by attending to the subtleties of its public address. It was tragic, but the German Evangelical Church leaders, in spite of the evidence on every side, including that cited in their Memorandum, naively failed to understand that the Reich had no tolerance for opposition, loyal or otherwise. By the writing of the Memorandum, diplomacy gave way to a trivialization by politeness as the writers introduced their concerns:

The German Evangelical Church is closely associated with the Führer and his advisors through the intercession that it makes publicly and in private for the people, the State, and the Government. The provisional administration and the council of the German Evangelical Church consider, therefore, that they may undertake to give expression in the present document to the anxieties and fears by many Christians, in the communities, by the Councils of Brethren, and by the church leaders in regard to the future of the Evangelical faith and of the Evangelical Church in Germany, and on which they have meditated long and earnestly.[7]

Barmen and the Memorandum failed to address the fate of Jews and homosexuals publicly targeted by the Nazis. It is little wonder that Jews did not enjoy the widespread support of the church, even as biblically defined "strangers and sojourners." Jews were almost exclusively known in Christian theological circles for their role as alleged executioners of the Deity and their unwillingness to convert to Christianity. In a 1967 correspondence to Bonhoeffer's biographer, Eberhard Bethge, theologian Karl Barth noted his own failure, and by extension that of the churches, in the fate of the Jews:

It was new to me above all that Bonhoeffer, first and almost alone, viewed and attached the "Jewish Problem" so centrally and energetically from 1933 on. I have long since felt a sense of guilt that I did not also during the Church Struggle (*Kirchenkampf*), at least not publicly, emphasize its decisive character—e.g. in the two Barmen Declarations of 1934 produced by me.[8]

Homosexuals were simply outcasts, pariahs to the institutional church. They had virtually no protection at any level in German society. The fate of Jews and homosexuals was known to the church leaders, who chose not to intervene or speak out on behalf of these two primary target groups because the church was both anti-Semitic and homophobic. There was no witness for the fate of the homosexual community, but a warning about anti-Semitism from Karl Barth may sound for both. Barth struggled with the fact that had he understood the implication of the "Jewish Problem" as clearly as Bonhoeffer had, he would have defied the "Aryan paragraph." On later reflection, he concluded in his letter to Bethge: "A text including a petition against the Aryan paragraph would not have gained acceptance in 1934 by the general trend of thinking as well as by the so-called confessors."9

Barmen and the Memorandum failed to take clear, proactive stands against the Reich, the Reich Bishop, and the "German Christians." They did not give any direction to clergy and laity who might have chosen in conscience not to serve in the German army, nor did they offer support for those who might found or join resistance groups or take part in rescue efforts, and they did not turn their student programs into alternative, spiritual communities of resistance to the Hitler Youth. Neither of these important documents hints at a call for help to the League of Nations or offers a warning to other ecclesiastical judicatories to be vigilant relative to Nazis and National Socialism. The fifth paragraph of the introduction to the Memorandum quotes a line from Jesus to challenge the arrogance of the Reich. The quote may indict those who invoked it: "For what is a man profited, if he shall gain the whole world, and lose his own soul or what shall a man give in exchange for his soul?" The church was almost completely self-absorbed and may well have lost its own soul even as it sought to protect itself and its members from the very real dangers of Nazism. The Shoah is vitally important to the modern church that has not learned the lessons of Barmen, integrated the implications of Auschwitz, or transformed its theological foundation in response to Nazism.

In October 1945, as the death camps were emptied and sanitized, displaced persons camps were filled to overflowing, and the Allies were composing the War Crimes Tribunal, the Council of the Evangelical Church in Germany met in Stuttgart with representative of the World Council of Churches. In a welcoming statement the signatories offered a confession and expressed a hope:

We are all the more thankful for this visit, as we with our people know ourselves to be not only in a community of suffering, but also in a solidarity of guilt. With great anguish we state: Through us, inestimable suffering was inflicted on many peoples and lands. What we have often witnessed before our congregations we now declare in the name of the whole church: Indeed we have fought for long years in the name of Jesus Christ against the spirit that found horrible expression in the violent National Socialist regime, but we charge ourselves for not having confessed more courageously, prayed more conscientiously, believed more joyously, and loved more ardently. . . .

We hope to God that, through the common service of the church, the spirit of might and retribution which wants to become powerful anew, will be avoided throughout the world, and [that] the spirit of freedom and love, through which alone tortured humanity can find solace, comes to rule.[10]

The banality of the confession deadens the perceived historical significance of the declaration. The hollowness of this piece is underscored by the reference to suffering before guilt; the lack of any confessional recognition of the absence of institutional acts of systemic resistance, rescue, and conscience; the absolute disregard for the millions of Jewish dead being buried in literally thousands of mass graves in every Nazi occupied land; and the indirect triumphalist reference in the closing clause of the paragraph on hope.

LESSONS FOR THE POST-BARMEN CHURCH

In the language of the Bible, freedom is not something man
has for himself but something he has for others. . . .
Being free means "being free for the other," because the other has
bound me to him. Only in relationship with the other am I free.
                                        Dietrich Bonhoeffer[11]

How shall post-Shoah Christians and churches order their beliefs and actions so that they will never need to charge themselves after the manner of the gathering in Stuttgart? What positive lessons shall post-Shaoh Christians and their churches learn from the efforts of the Barmen drafters (hereafter I shall use *Barmen* to refer collectively to the Theological Declaration of Barmen and the Memorandum)? What is the model set before us by those who were compelled by the words of these documents to resist, to spend their very lives in the cause of stopping Hitler and terminating the Reich?

Without question, the pastors and laity of the German Evangelical Church were thoroughly endangered for speaking out on behalf of the churches and in resistance to the impositions of National Socialism. Many church leaders, both clergy and laity, were interned in concentration camps, tortured, or gave their lives in martyrdom. But, it must be said, the Nazis succeeded in diverting and narrowing the focus of the German Evangelical Church. As the churches, through Barmen, sought to preserve their institutional integrity and protect themselves from the influences of the "German Christians," they lost sight of the systemic evils of the National Socialists. They did not see the extreme dangers that the Nazis posed for Jews and homosexuals; worse, those who did see allowed their own prejudices to silence the impulse to humanitarian solidarity with all victims of the Reich. As an institution, the German Evangelical Church did not become a church for others.

The Reich took extraordinary steps to infiltrate and subvert and then to co-opt the churches. Clearly, the Reich was fearful of the potential moral influence wielded by the churches, particularly the German Evangelical Church. It was also aware of the long history of denominational anti-Semitism. As Hitler began confiscating Jewish businesses and property, he borrowed from the darkest recesses of Reformation history, mimicking Martin Luther's violent anti-Jewish rhetoric and proposals (as he did with his use of Luther's 1525 polemic on the Swabian Peasant Revolt, "Against the Robbing and Murdering Hordes of Peasants"). Hitler made special note of the time two brave bishops sought an audience with him to protest the Reich's anti-Jewish laws. Hitler informed them that he was only putting into effect what Christianity had preached and practiced for 2,000 years.[12] Reich officials were also aware of and capitalized on the divisions in the churches. The churches, having largely assimilated to the prevailing culture and political ideology, did not recognize or exploit the fear that the Reich clearly exhibited in its dealings with them, fear that was evident enough to be noted in the Memorandum as behaviors that tested the nettle of the churches.

The church leaders of Germany had the power to unify communities of believers and divergent denominations through moral discourse aimed at minimally preserving the common good and perhaps even the peace of the nation. The Reich would have encountered immeasurable difficulties if clergy, laity, and federations had presented a unified front, a common appeal to the highest altruistic values of Scripture, and a strong denial of behaviors that divided people from one another and, ultimately, murdered those who opposed the government. Because the churches misread or failed to read the signs of Reich apprehension, they chose to appear as the loyal opposition and later as obsequious bidders for Reich privileges. Absent systemic, explicit, unflinching, and public repudiation of the Reich, all manner of people, including the church leaders, where left at the mercy of a system that knew absolutely no mercy.

Various scholars of the era contend that one of the strengths of the Barmen Declaration and the Memorandum was their attempt to exhibit a measure of unity among the church opponents of the Reich. Some would have us

believe that this solidarity extended to the victims of the Reich. There was
certainly unity among those in the German Evangelical Church. For those
believers courageous enough to oppose Nazism, the solidarity of the
churches was critically important, but it is a mistake to think that the
solidarity extended to Jews, homosexuals, Gypsies, or all classes of resisters. Because it was blinded by its prejudices, in the case of homosexual
victims of Nazism, and its hatred, in the case of Jewish victims, the church
did not see these people as fellow sufferers but rather as deserving subjects
of vilification and appropriate objects of Nazi destruction.

By the time the Nazis came to power and began to magnify centuries
of anti-Semitic teachings, pogroms, and hatred, it was too late for a
systemic act of solidarity. Solidarity with victims must begin long before
there are public actions leading to victimization. Solidarity with victims
is a timeless, evolutionary, expansive, and consistent lifestyle. Without
an intentional, constant, empathic, egalitarian ethic, there can be all
manner of confessional verbiage, but there will also be tremendous
behavioral contradictions between the lofty words and the essential
concrete actions that must follow from the words.

It is the great disparity between the words and the resulting deeds that
temper the post-Shoah utility and importance of Barmen. That said, it
must also be noted that in spite of and because of the words, the deeds,
and the all too-human disparity between them, post-Barmen Christianity
must recognize and affirm the best efforts of the framers to be faithful
in their attempts to stand against evil, the inspiration they offered to
some, and the lessons they implore us to learn. In an essay on freedom,
Dietrich Bonhoeffer focused what would be both the struggle over and
the judgment on all three of the documents from the German Evangelical
Church:

The man of responsibility stands between obligation and freedom; yet he finds his
justification neither in his obligation nor in his freedom but solely in Him who has
put him in this (humanly impossible) situation and who requires this deed of him.
The responsible man delivers up himself and his deed to God.[13]

Following the admonition of Bonhoeffer that the church must be the
church for others and that Christians must be people for others, the churches
in every time and place must stand in solidarity with those who are hated,
objectified, oppressed, denied fundamental human and civil rights, victimized by alienating stereotypes, or otherwise isolated and treated unjustly by
any institution of society or government. The church of Jesus Christ is a
church for others. Our freedom, dignity, rights, and life exist in relationship

to the freedom, dignity, rights, and life of others. When churches participate in those behaviors that victimize, dehumanize, and isolate, as they did in the Nazi era with Jews and homosexuals, they abdicate their moral authority and witness, deny the justice mandates of Scripture, and disown the faith they confess. In short, they can no longer be the church.

The lesson of Barmen is that the example of the churches and the centuries of theological anti-Semitism were used by the Nazis to create scapegoats and division and then death camps. Until the churches and theologians reject and change these teachings of contempt, division, and triumphalism, we shall be useful to those who hate, oppress, and kill. The same principle holds for any aspect of church life that diminishes or isolates one human being from another, including racism, homophobia, and gender-ism. The role of the church is to instill the spirit of Galatians 3:28 and reflect the perspective and inclusiveness suggested therein, "There is no distinction between Jews or Gentiles, slave or free, male or female; you are all one in Christ Jesus." It is entirely a matter of perception, of how Christians see and relate to others. The calling is to see others as God sees humanity: beloved, whole, united, and esteemed.

Times of political, social, or economic crisis have traditionally led people to see their neighbors as the cause of whatever the problem and to treat them with suspicion and subject them to hostile, isolating behaviors. Scapegoating is a serious human failing that took root in post-World War I Germany as the economy staggered and the sense of a common national purpose evaporated. Jews became the foil in Hitler's ascent to power. To certain audiences, he portrayed Jews as dangerous, power-hungry, greedy merchants plotting to control the nation. To other listeners, he characterized Jews as vermin and parasites plaguing the body of the German nation. In either portrayal Hitler's solution was the same—eliminate them. This political variation on theological anti-Semitism alerts us to the dangers of unchecked teachings that dehumanize and alienate certain peoples and that are borrowed from the church by powers and principalities that have sufficient force of arms to take away freedom and life itself.

The role of the church is to be a moral voice when stereotyping and scapegoating infect the political establishment. The voices that instill fear and division must be met by the spiritual voices that value diversity and honor the unity of the human community. As I write these lines, around the globe nations are struggling for economic stability; citizens are generally suffering the attendant insecurities and responding by selecting scapegoats to blame for their social, economic, and political afflictions. There is presently in America a surging fear of so-called illegal or undocumented immigrants. The fear is fueled by unsubstantiated charges that people from south of the U.S. border have sapped the vitality of the national and regional economies. At the same time, African-American Muslims are preaching a message of hatred and destruction against Jews. With the disintegration of the Soviet Union and the resultant instabilities, virulent ultranationalists have inspired a resurgence of anti-Semitism. In one nation after another in Europe, there have been murderous outbreaks against "foreigners" and refugees. In the midst of all this, the religious communities are trying to find their moral voice in order to oppose the forces of separation and fear. It is a decisive moment as the religious communities choose where they shall stand, what they shall say and do. Silence is not a faithful alternative now, just as it was not for the Barmen Synod.

In light of Barmen and the shadows of the Shoah, the churches are challenged to embody their faith and values. The intimate bond between obedience, conformity, and popularity is the source of a significant ecclesiastical dilemma relative to the practice of justice. The German Evangelical Church interpreted itself as obligated by Scripture to be obedient to the state and consistently sought to favorably position itself with the government and its leadership. The confessional assertion that God ordains government gave tacit approval to the Reich. Barmen opposed what it considered to be unjust but duly sanctioned intrusions in the affairs of the churches by a government that Barmen had legitimated in its narrow conformity to Scripture. In seeking to maintain its power and privilege, Barmen did not question how the National Socialists came to govern over Germany; nor did it question the form of governance relative to the lofty, if limited, biblical definition of the role of government. It did not then challenge intrusions or the unjust and inhumane policies and actions by what should have been declared an unlawful government, unlawful at least by scriptural standards, beginning with those of the biblical prophets.

In retrospect, Barmen would have been a stronger statement to the Reich if it had publicly challenged the legitimacy of the government as well as confronted its authority and the legality of the sanctions and impositions on the churches. The only three differences might have been a swifter and deadlier elimination of church opposition than the Nazis initially planned; second, a more decisive and potentially more polarizing witness to the German people and the world; and third, having taken the risk of speaking its harsh truth publicly and moved to the very precipice dividing life and death, Christians would have fully known the liberation of Easter wherein death is rendered ultimately powerless.

The issues for post-Barmen Christianity are most likely to involve contention with legally established governments that are engaged in policies and actions that are not in the interests of humanity or the stability and peace of the world. The lesson we carry from Barmen is that church leaders must be more diligent in monitoring events in the world, more astute in their interpretation of events that threaten life and human rights, more forthright in commenting on those events and developing a public concern about them, and completely willing to risk imagined positions of power and privilege in order to act on behalf of the victims of history. The churches and synagogues of the United States, individually and collectively, remain one of the few and most potent voices in the struggle to prevent nuclear war, genocidal actions, and violations of human and civil rights and to promote the value of human diversity.

As with the parish clergy whose moving letters were collected and published in Helmut Gollwitzer's book *Dying We Live*, and in the witness of those who resisted or rescued in the Nazi era, contemporary congregational ministers, priests, and rabbis can create strategies to inform, mobilize, and lead their people to act on behalf of those "others" who are vulnerable, threatened, isolated, or scapegoated. Some of the most compelling testimony of the Shoah comes from the records of those clergy who chose not to conform, curry power and privilege, or turn against or away from "others" and the agonies of the world. Many of those pastors from the Shoah, as well as their contemporary counterparts, took the risk to act in spite of the fact that they were confronting harmful, immoral actions of duly established governmental and ecclesiastical authorities, in spite of the fact that their values and actions made them a distinct, nonconforming minority.

Situations are rarely clearly defined as good or evil, right or wrong, at their genesis. Evil can be evolutionary, initially appearing to be good and only later showing its true intention. That may explain how esteemed clergy mistakenly supported the initial rise of the National Socialist Party. Some in German churches saw the evolution of evil sooner than others. Some ignored the evolution because it played to their prejudices. It is, therefore, incumbent upon the clergy to be knowledgeable, thoughtful, set apart (in the Hebrew sense of "holiness," *kadosh*), and suspicious of popular movements in society and government. A warning, cynicism often masquerades as suspicion. To be suspicious is to maintain a healthy distance, to raise incisive, penetrating questions; and it is to generally avoid a hasty and uncritical position. Suspicion is constructive. Cynicism begins in mistrust and moves too quickly past questions to assertions. Cynicism is self-confident and often self-righteous as it takes a stand without bringing others through a process. For clergy, there must be the freedom of the informed conscience, of constructive suspicion, that allows them to critically and beneficially raise questions and in a timely fashion develop strategies and engage the powers and principalities when they are ill-willed and destructive. Václav Havel, writing as the president of the Czech and Slovak Federal Republic, suggested the intellectual, spiritual, and strategic framework for religious engagement at every level:

The law and other democratic institutions ensure little if they are not backed up by the willingness and courage of decent people to guard against their abuse. . . . It will do us no harm to occasionally remind ourselves of the meaning of the state, which is, and must remain, truly human—which means it must be intellectual, spiritual and moral. . . . What is needed is lively and responsible consideration of every political step, every decision; a constant stress on moral deliberation and moral judgment; continued self-examination and self-analysis; an endless rethinking of our priorities. . . . It is a way of going about things, and it demands the courage to breathe moral and spiritual motivation into everything, to seek the human dimension in all things. Science, technology, expertise, and so-called professionalism are not enough. Something more is necessary. For the sake of simplicity, it might be called spirit. Or feeling. Or conscience.[14]

The lessons of Barmen and Stuttgart must be addressed in the context of genocide. For decades, the world has feared the cosmic genocide of nuclear war. It is a geometric progression from the application of knowledge and technology that transformed euthanasia programs into an efficient genocide to the use of knowledge and technology to devise and deploy a nuclear or biological arsenal with the capacity to destroy all life forms. It required learned persons with advanced degrees in nearly every academic discipline, from medicine to engineering, to construct a policy of genocide, then to build the prototypes, and from social theory to theology to implement the program. Learned people abdicated the moral responsibility of learning by placing their knowledge in the service of evil and death. Today, with the closing of the chasm between Hitler's death camps and the instantaneous mass destruction of Hiroshima, and the proliferation of ever more sophisticated and potent weapons, Barmen confronts the moral uses of knowledge and technology, and, ultimately, the right of any nation to possess, let alone use, these weapons.

Today, cosmic genocide seems an increasingly distant possibility, while the more familiar forms of genocide known in the Shoah expand almost without restraints. The ongoing genocidal behaviors in Rwanda, the liquidations in Burundi, and the euphemistic "ethnic cleansing" in the Balkans remind the world that reason, civility, and tolerance are still fragile, vulnerable qualities even fifty years after Auschwitz, Hiroshima, and Nagasaki. As politicians consider the options to answer modern acts of genocide, weighing such things as "national interest," strategic capability, and multinational responses, the religious communities create an essential tension by their focus on "human interest," moral responsibility, the sanctity of life, and the ethical demands of faith. There is no way to avoid the questions that emerge from the consideration of political options, but there is always great partisan energy spent to avoid the parallel and equally important issues of human interest. The religious community dares not fail in its half of the shared responsibility to create the tension, voice the alterative issues and perspectives, stand with the victims of history, and prod the political systems to timely interventions. Outbursts of genocide need not be debated by the generations after Auschwitz and Hiroshima; they must be forcefully confronted and halted.

The human urgency is that, absent authentic, effective, systemic institutional transformations, one genocide prepares the way for the next. The genocidal slaughter of Armenians in 1915 was the precursor of German death camps and nuclear mass destruction in Japan, and those foreshadowed Cambodia, Rwanda, and Bosnia-Herzegovina. In order to avert the catastrophes that loom beyond the visible horizon of the history toward which we are moving, the religious communities must maintain the tension between the weighing of political options and the raising of moral questions. The calling of the religious communities is to tirelessly but joyously labor for the transformation of humanity and the priorities of its institutions and restore humankind's trust in and commitment to the common good, compassion, shared responsibilities, civility, diversity, and tolerance.

READING ABOUT JUSTICE AND ALTRUISM

> No one is useless in this world who lightens the burden of it for anyone else. And no one makes a greater mistake than those who do nothing because they can only do a little.
>
> William Sloane Coffin[15]

Deluged as we are by domestic threats and global horrors, most people need steady measures of hope, reassurances of the existence of a fundamental human goodness. We need the confirmation that common people, like ourselves, going about their daily routines can live and act with compassion and concern, rather than submit to cynicism, indifference, intolerance, or worse, inhumanity. We must ask ourselves as we struggle with the dichotomous and very human failings of the Nazi era and celebrate the enormous courage of the German Evangelical Church, What must we, and what can we, now affirm? And as we read the stories or view the films of resistance and rescue, we are compelled to ask ourselves, Have we a renewed commitment to justice and concern for the victims of history? We must know of ourselves and demand of our institutions, Has the repulsion we feel for Hitler's genocide sensitized us to the cries that emanate from contemporary crimes against humanity? Will they move us to speak out and act? Minimally, do we find from these encounters the strength to be helpful, compassionate, and just in our daily lives? If we find ourselves in need, will there be a Graebe, a Bonhoeffer, or a Schindler there for us? More important than that, when others are in need, will we have fostered the skills, courage, and compassion to be Graebe-, Bonhoeffer-, or Schindler-like in our responses?

AFFIRMATIONS

> It is as though after the shocks of recent history . . . people had lost all faith in the future, in the possibility of setting public affairs right, in the meaning of a struggle for truth and justice. They shrug off anything that goes beyond their everyday, routine concern for their own livelihood; they seek ways of escape, they succumb to apathy, to indifference toward suprapersonal values and their fellow men, to spiritual passivity and depression. . . . Paradoxically, though, this indifference has become a very active social force.
>
> Václav Havel[16]

Havel's assessment of life in Communist Czechoslovakia in 1975 is descriptive of a more general and contemporary malaise that may well have its roots in the Nazi era. In order that the vision of Amos, that "[j]ustice may roll down like a mighty river," and so that people might experience the truth of Micah's spiritual discipline to "[a]ct justly, love tenderly, and walk humbly with God," the post-Barmen, post-Shoah religious communities make affirmations that they must enflesh as they meet the dictates of the world's agenda.

We affirm that we are people of faith because of and in spite of the tragedies that humanity has visited upon itself, the injustices it has perpetuated, and the faithless complicity in evil that has scarred our traditions. In the shadow of the Shoah, we affirm our identity as people of faith, mindful that the confusion, tyranny, and spirit that prevailed in Nazism is latent in all of humanity and its institutions. After the manner of Moses, we choose life and blessing and reject the sacrifice of our faith traditions on the altar of a thousand-year Reich that failed and ended but whose foreboding spirit lives on, virulently infectious and global.

In the manner of Nazi-era religious resisters, martyrs, and rescuers, we declare ourselves to be people of faith and institutions for others. We affirm our identification and place beside and in solidarity with those who suffer evil, poverty, and oppression and endure violations of human and civil rights.

We affirm our commitment to the diversity of God's entire human family and our resolve to ensure that tolerance, understanding, and inclusion will replace hatred, rejection, and alienation.

As stewards of God's trust, we affirm our commitment to the sanctity of human life and our resolve to speak of and to work for justice and the peace that flows from it. As stewards we are partners with God in dispelling the forces of evil that seek to oppress and destroy. After the examples of prophets and teachers, and Jesus of Nazareth, we affirm our resolve to resist complicity in evil, indifference to injustice, and conformity to ill-willed or harmful social, economic, political, and ecclesiastical structures.

In the resplendent tradition of faithful, compassionate, and courageous women and men in the Nazi era, from Barmen to Stuttgart and from Flossenbürg to Dachau, we affirm our hope and trust in the just, gracious, and liberating commonwealth of God's reign and not in the transitory rule of ultimately fallible human institutions.

My ministry with youth and university students, and in my parish, demands that I create a tension between the generalization of Havel's experience under communism and a hope that is able to inspire and sustain me. Albert Camus offers a model of the tension and the challenge to people of faith:

Great ideas, it has been said, come into the world as gently as doves. Perhaps then, if we listen attentively, we shall hear amid the uproar of empires and nations, a faint flutter of wings, the gentle stirrings of life and hope. Some will say that this hope lies in a nation; others, in a [person]. I believe rather that it is awakened, revived, nourished by millions of solitary individuals whose deeds and works every day negate frontiers and the crudest implications of history.[17]

Perhaps for Christianity, if not for all religious communities, one of the most vital implications of the Nazi era is that we need not be—indeed, must not be—"solitary individuals." Evil divides, separates, and overcomes. Let people of faith pray and study according to their respective traditions, but let them together fulfill their highest values and callings by uniting to serve all of humanity. The examples of Nazi-era rescuers will point the way.

Chapter Six

Courage, Compassion, and Caring

"[T]here are pestilences and there are victims; no more than that. . . .

I grant we should add a third category: that of the true healers. But it's a fact one doesn't come across many of them, and anyhow it must be a hard vocation. That's why I decided to take in every predicament, the victims' side. . . ."

After a short silence the doctor raised himself a little in his chair and asked if Tarrou had an idea of the path to follow for attaining peace.

"Yes," he replied. "The path of sympathy."

Albert Camus[1]

As most students of the Shoah, I tried to fathom Nazi motives, reasoning, culture, religion, politics, economics, and worldview. As most who probe its depths and try to communicate its lessons, I struggled to understand what forces compelled so many cultured people to abandon the manifold positive elements of their society to join in the pathologies of Nazi leaders, frontline command officers, and their co-conspirators. I attempted to comprehend how Hitler, Eichmann, and Himmler could persuasively articulate to their SS subordinates that in building the death camps they were engaged in an enterprise that the world would eventually gratefully acknowledge. I sought to understand the forces that engendered the racial hatreds that fueled Nazi ideology regarding Jews. How did racial prejudices turn to hatred and then to destruction? I kept returning to the entry in Joseph Goebbels's diary, amazed at how words can indeed create worlds: "I, however, want to be able to hate. . . . Oh, I can hate, and I don't want to forget how. Oh, how wonderful it is to be able to hate."[2]

It has been in vain that I sought to understand the intricacies of mass murder. When I am overwhelmed by the complexity of the pathologies and the divergent interpretive voices, I think that Hannah Arendt's description of Eichmann on the stand in Jerusalem is a universal assessment of the Reich: "the banality of evil." After meeting the taxi driver in Kraków and listening to the story of his sister's brave compassion, and then at first superficially exploring the names that are memorialized and the selfless stories of goodness that are celebrated on *Yad Vashem*'s Avenue of the Just, I devoted myself to a firsthand study of the moral and spiritual development of the Righteous Gentiles (as they are known in Israel). My hypothesis was that these people shared certain characteristics, traits, and skills and that if the commonalties could be discovered, they might teach us how to prepare children, youth, and adults to be caring and helpful in their daily lives and courageously altruistic if ever they found themselves in extreme situations.

Their numbers were not legion, but the courage and compassion of the rescuers of Jews had as great an impact on my understanding of the Shoah as the horror and brutality. That is not to say that they are by any standard able to balance the scales. They could not; there were simply too few of them. They were a faithful remnant, precious few scattered over too much geography to effectively impact the movements of the Reich or to save every Jew. This faithful remnant reminds us of the power of a solitary life and, at the other extreme, of the tremendous strength of communal values that result in cooperative humanitarian efforts. In the example of their lives, they empower and restore a measure of self-confidence to those who invest themselves in labors for a just and peaceful world. In the words of Rabbi Harold Schulweis:

We must, for the sake of our sanity, make use of history to restore a sense of balance, to provide some moral symmetry to humanity. For non-Jews particularly, knowledge of the conduct and behavior of their contemporaries who rescued is no less essential. Let no one turn a deaf ear to the sound of accusation, to the noise of villainy, or to the voices of heroism. Instead, let us be justifiably proud of such nobility of character.[3]

In speaking of a "faithful remnant" of courageous and compassionate people, I am referring to a relatively small number of people, primarily Christians, who helped desperately endangered strangers, mostly Jews, who were social, political, cultural, economic, and/or religious outcasts. They offered help without regard for their own interests and took extraordinary risks all the while moderating the dangers to themselves and those they assisted. Another level of altruism was exhibited by those persons whose neighborly deeds gave limited, circumspect measures of comfort to refugees but who, for whatever reason, could not risk greater involvement. In virtually every nation, town, village, and city where the Nazis committed their crimes, there were countless acts of simple consideration and kindness: a knock on the door to warn of impending dangers; a shared piece of bread, meat, vegetable, or information; the gift of a blanket; the transmission of a message; the protection of a relic; a kind or hopeful word; and more. These good deeds were for some the precursors of more dangerous interventions, but in and of themselves these actions did not save lives and do not commend the helpful person for consideration as a Righteous Gentile.

Who were the Righteous Gentiles of the Nazi era, and what did they have in common? What follows is a sampling of their stories of intervention, courage, and compassion and a summary of my research findings. The actions of the righteous distinguish them from the killers, but I have not met a single rescuer who considered himself or herself to be a hero. Herman Graebe spoke for them when he said, "I am not some kind of hero. I only did what everyone should have done, what anyone could have done."

In most instances, I shall use only the first name of the rescuers, but wherever possible, I use the full name so that they might be remembered and celebrated by name. Many, however, preferred anonymity, in part because they were modest, self-effacing people and partly because they feared harassment by unrepentant anti-Semites, Nazis, and neo-Nazis. Several of the rescuers had collections of hate mail that followed after their deeds were publicly acknowledged. Herman Graebe had a full shoe box of hate mail, much of it containing threats that were explicit and detailed.

Various important scientific studies have followed my early research. Most notable is that of Professors Pearl and Samuel Oliner.[4] While our findings are different in several regards, their extensive work (including a control group composed of former Nazis) is a most vital contribution to secular and religious pedagogy. It should be noted that another small group of writers have concluded that there can be no reliable research or findings that itemize commonalities. There are even one or two studies that attempt to deny or greatly diminish the role of religious faith in the actions of the rescuers. Most of the writers in the latter two categories did not benefit from systematic interviews with both rescuers and the Jews whom they rescued. As with so much research on aspects of the Shoah, many of the survivors and witnesses have died, making the gathering, preserving, and evaluating of data considerably more difficult and these rueful interpretations less dependable. There are a large library of studies and a great many books recounting the stories of rescue. They are detailed in the bibliography.

The snapshot sections of the chapter will include illustrative stories of rescue. Most of the stories were told to me by the rescuer and corroborated by one or more persons who were rescued. Virtually all were noted in the Israeli archives, and whenever possible, the rescuers were honored by that grateful nation. In several instances, a Jewish survivor related an account of rescue and it was not possible, for a variety of reasons (i.e., because the rescuers had died, or their locations were not known, or they were inaccessible due to other geopolitical considerations), to secure additional details from the rescuer. I invite readers to freely use the findings and share these stories in sermons, religious school classes, and Bible studies.

The final section of this book includes liturgical resources and several important suggestions for using these stories. The three most critical suggestions are, first, that the reader carefully place the story of rescue in the larger context of the conditions that made rescue necessary in the first place, namely, the intentional, systematic mass destruction of European Jews. Second, be quite cautious not to give the impression that compassion and courage were the order of the day for Christians. The rescuers were a faithful remnant, not a multitude! Finally, Nazi-era rescuers were not morally gifted people. They were common folk going about their daily routines when they became involved in an effort to save the life of another person. Tempting as it is, to elevate them to some special status virtually assures that people will discount the potential for altruism, courage, and compassion in their own lives and fail to see themselves in the model of the common people who practiced human decency. They were simply good people who resisted evil and sanctified life by protecting others from death, and then they returned to their daily lives. Please carefully study the liturgical and educational resources and applications.

BACKGROUND

The heart has its reasons which reason does not understand.

Blaise Pascal[5]

I am sharing this information and retelling the stories of rescue because I believe it is the responsibility of the church and synagogue to establish communal values and to put them into practice, and because I am convinced that while these findings may not prevent evil people from coming to power and using their positions to harm others, we are able to teach and preach in such a way as to ensure a dramatic increase in the likelihood that countless institutions and people will have the necessary skills to undertake altruistic interventions. Often people will come to me after a lecture or having read the biography of Herman Graebe and explain that my findings confirm something they have known intuitively or supported a value, action, or style that previously had merely seemed to them to be "the right way." Not unlike rescuers in the Nazi era, these people have had no intentional, systematic preparation for acting in caring and helpful ways. A compassionate lifestyle is a foreign language that must be learned and regularly practiced. That people have not had intentional and systematic preparation explicitly underscores the importance of values formation and skill building. Implicitly, what this alerts us to is the fact that when people are ambivalent, confused, or allow their compassionate skills to atrophy, they are unlikely to engage in activities that contain significant risks or elements of exposure. Here now is what I discovered and some suggestions of how to prepare people to put into practice the highest humanitarian values of the Christian faith.

It is important to take note of the risks faced by rescuers. Would-be rescuers learned of the penalties for intervention in various ways: by word-of-mouth accounts of Reich regional government regulations, by very visible public warning notices, or by witnessing public punishments. In many Nazi-occupied areas, large warning signs were posted in prominent locations and offered a substantial reward (in Poland, for example, the reward Zl500 [Zl = Zloty], enough to be helpful in a wartime economy) to those who either exposed Jews in hiding or betrayed those who gave aid or comfort to Jewish refugees. The signs also announced that summary execution was the penalty for assisting or harboring Jews. One Polish rescuer was terrified by this notice that she read every day but not fearful enough to keep her from acting. Another rescuer, Irene Opdyke, witnessed the public execution of an entire rescuer family and the Jews they had hidden. Instead of deterring her compassion, it solidified her decision to continue protecting the twelve Jews she hid in the basement of the villa occupied by the Reich regional commander, her employer!

In towns with a Jewish population, the sudden arrest, detention, and eventual expulsion of every Jewish citizen, and the expropriation of their belongings and property, sent a message about the threat and power of the Nazis and their allies that chilled all but the strongest impulse to compassion. Because the threats were not idle and the punishments were speedy and severe, would-be rescuers rarely told even members of their families about their activities. The threat of accidental exposure or intentional betrayal was thereby minimized, and the hope was that the killers would not punish family members who were uninvolved. This helps explain why a great many interventions were single, serial rescues. That is, one person would intervene, usually rescuing one Jew, but possibly two or a family unit; and when that rescue was finished, the rescuer might retreat for restoration but usually started over again in a relatively short period. When we consider the general lack of skills, resources, and preparation for intervention, the magnitude of the penalties, and the possible suffering of one's family, whether involved or not, it is a wonder that as many people participated in rescue as did.

Rescues were effected in a variety of ways. Many rescues involved hiding and caring for one person at a time, for a period from a single day to as much as a year or more. Other rescuers had the resources to hide family units and small groups of Jewish refugees, generally numbering from two to fifteen persons. Mrs. Opdyke hid twelve Jews in the house where she worked. A Polish family hid thirteen Jews at a time on their farm. So-called underground railroads effectively moved endangered persons to safe or neutral locations. While concealment in a network of homes or other locations was essential to success, the primary purpose was moving people out of danger and beyond the reach of the Reich. The Danish sea rescues and the network of Seventh Day Adventists established by John Weidner are examples of this style of intervention.

A third mode involved several rescuers who enjoyed positions of trust in war-related industries or occupied zones, which in turn enabled them to use their positions of privilege to protect Jewish workers. Herman Graebe, in his capacity as an engineering manager working for the Reich Railroad Administration, saved or extended the lives of 2,000 to 3,000 Jews, Gypsies, and dissidents. In this role, he recruited and supervised large labor columns. When he became aware of the fate of the Jews in the Ukraine, he began requisitioning Jewish workers and protecting them. Eventually, he fabricated work orders, increased the number of Jewish workers, and then moved them to nonexistent sites away from mobile killing units and military fronts. Oskar Schindler, a German industrialist, protected more than 1,000 Jews through his factories and work sites in Poland and Czechoslovakia. He, too, commandeered Jewish workers and eventually selflessly protected them from certain death at the hands of the SS or the mobile killing units or in death camps.

A fourth mode of intervention involved communal rescues. These rescues most often involved an intentionally established group of people bound together by commonly held religious beliefs and values that were expressed in mutually agreed upon actions. The communities were self-contained, and the members were known to one another. The rescues by the Huguenots in the French town of Le Chambon-sur-Ligon and those coordinated by the Italian Catholic priest Rufino Niccacci illustrate this mode. In virtually every instance of communal rescue, there was a single person who acted as the catalyst and unifying force behind both the life of the community and the interventions.

In my study, I did not consider rescues that came under the following categories: first, interventions that were conditional, that is, involving any exchange of material goods or cash or based on a quid pro quo agreement. One rescuer's condition was an early variant on the "lifeboat ethic" in which he insisted that those he rescued have advanced university degrees. His rationale was that educated persons would be needed for the rebuilding of Europe after the defeat of Germany. Therefore, he would only save the best educated and most likely to contribute to reconstruction. He was not included in the study. Second, I did not consider rescues that employed violent means to achieve otherwise altruistic ends. Virtually all rescues were accomplished by stealth, cleverness, cunning, wit, and creativity. I did make an exception in several instances and included rescues where there was a sudden demand for self-defense in order to preserve the life of the rescuer or refugee. Finally, there was a fair-sized class of what I called "subversive rescues," most often conducted by Partisans or the Underground. Saving the lives of Jews was always secondary to the primary goal of subverting, inconveniencing, or otherwise negatively impacting Nazi operations. An example was the raid by Partisans on a train carrying Jews to a death camp in eastern Poland. The train was blown up, the tracks were destroyed, and all of the German soldiers were killed. The liberated Jews were left defenseless and had to seek help in a decidedly hostile environment. It is not known how many survived, but a participant in the raid later told me, "It was more important to stop the Nazis than rescue the Jews." Rescues in this category were not included in the study.

Rescuers reported a constellation of competing motives and reasons for engaging in these activities. Some rescuers felt it was their human duty. Others said it was a matter of obedience to the dictates of their religion. For one non-Christian rescuer who was a member of a theocentric philosophical group, intervention was motivated by the moral principles espoused by the founder of her organization. A woman who was saved by a Dutch rescuer whose forebearers affiliated with the New Amsterdam College Movement, which was known for Judaizing Christianity, said of her benefactress, "Being a true Calvinist she considered it her duty to help the Jewish people during the war." Interestingly, while most rescuers attended church or otherwise identified themselves as Christians, many of them had difficulty articulating a connection between their actions during World War II and what should have been familiar, related biblical directives such as the parable of the "good Samaritan," the aphorism known as the "Golden Rule," and the prophetic mandate to care for the poor, outcasts, widows, orphans, and strangers.

I found that most rescuers had never considered the motives for their actions. It simply never occurred to them to ponder why they did it. While it is virtually impossible to measure, I sensed that the rescuers had fully integrated their values and faith into their day-to-day lives, thereby composing a way of life. That may explain why the rescuers who knew the biblical passages previously mentioned had not overtly linked them to their own actions in the Nazi era. While we expect people to make their faith a way of life, religious beliefs and values need a larger context and regular rejuvenation in order to be vital and useful. It is essential for values, faith, and worldview to be reinforced, shared with a community of like-minded people, and constantly affirmed and celebrated.

André Trocmé, the pastor of the Huguenot community in Le Chambon-sur-Ligon, France, illustrates the importance of an intentional, regular discipline of study, reflection, prayer, and service in the context of a faith community. Every home in the Huguenot parish, numbering some 300, served as a hiding place for refugees fleeing Nazis and the collaborationist Vichy officials. Trocmé had regular pastoral and teaching contacts with his people. His manner of leadership development and linking faith to daily life resulted in a formidable rescue network that neither the Vichy police nor the Nazis could penetrate. Philip Hallie, chronicler of the rescues in Le Chambon-sur-Ligon, writes of Trocmé:

> Every two weeks he met with thirteen people, and they all discussed a passage they had been thinking about for those two weeks. Trocmé did not lay down an interpretation and ask them to carry it away with them; he helped stimulate their own interpretations and let them flower. Those thirteen leaders then went to thirteen different parts of the parish, and each tried to do with the people of his area what Trocmé had tried to do with them. . . . The local discussion groups doubled in size. . . . Above all, the ideas that came from each of these groups were, to use Trocmé's words, "fervent, practical, and concrete." The thirteen local leaders were called the *responsibles*, and it was they who became the backbone of the parish as far as sheltering and hiding refugees was concerned.[6]

In this Huguenot church there was a unity of values and practice that held the community together, reaffirmed faith and values, revitalized communal existence, and encouraged shared leadership and the spreading of risks when rescue efforts commenced. In the midst of daily work, regular study, worship, and rescue, Trocmé described a study process that illustrates how a community defines itself, acts on its values, and experiences integration and a sense of internal consistency and harmony: "Nonviolence was not a theory superimposed upon reality; it was an itinerary we explored day after day in communal prayer and in obedience to the commands of the spirit."[7]

The impact and effectiveness of this approach were seen in both the rescues and in a very powerful moment when a Vichy police chief and a German officer came to the manse to arrest Trocmé. A contingent of police and militia remained at the outskirts of town while the officers walked to the manse. At that time, refugees were hidden upstairs and downstairs in the Trocmé home. It was late when the pastor finally returned from making parish visits, on foot, and his wife, Magda, insisted that her husband be permitted to eat dinner. She set additional places at the table and served dinner to the officials arresting her husband. During the course of the meal, parishioners entered the home to offer words of encouragement to their pastor and to give him packets of food and supplies to sustain him while imprisoned.

Hallie recounts the scene as the officials later led Trocmé down the snow-covered street to the local jail:

On both sides of the crooked street . . . villagers lined up. . . . Standing among the villagers were refugees from Central Europe, and students from the Levenol School. There were also Darbystes, rival Protestants who did not believe in the necessity of having ministers or churches. As the three men walked down the street . . . the bystanders began to sing the old Lutheran hymn, "A Mighty Fortress Is Our God."[8]

During Trocmé's imprisonment, rescue work continued unabated. The rescue plan and the elegant manner in which parishioners and the larger community responded to the arrest and the police reinforced the faith, values, and practices of the church community. The community's perception of reality was affirmed, and its resolve to act and exist contrary to the prevailing norms was immeasurably strengthened.

When compassionate behavior, deeds that are caring and helpful, and interventions that save lives are fully integrated into the educational, liturgical, service, and spiritual disciplines of life in the Christian community, they create a sense of wholeness based on consistency between faith and values, and the translation of values into practices. In his 1974 studies of obedience to authority, Yale University professor Stanley Milgram sounded a clear warning about the absence of such consistency and wholeness with his conclusion that

[o]rdinary people, simply doing their jobs, and without any particular hostility on their part, can become agents in a terrible destructive process. Moreover, even when the destructive effects of their work become patently clear, and they are asked to carry out actions incompatible with fundamental standards of morality, relatively few people have the resources needed to resist authority.[9]

It is the task of church and synagogue to instill in its people the sense of peace and wholeness that is derived from the integration of faith, values, prayer, and service and to help them develop the requisite individual and communal skills both to resist ill-willed authority and to successfully put their faith into practice.

Inspired by the support of Rabbi Harold Schulweis, Perry London was the first scholar to study Nazi-era rescuers. From a modest initial sample, he found the following three commonalties that predisposed rescuers to their altruistic endeavors: first, a spirit of adventurousness; second, an intense identification with a parental role model of moral conduct; and third, a sense of being socially marginal.[10] Professor London and his Jerusalem associate, Robert Kurtzman, graciously assisted in the development of my research model and provided me all of their interview materials. I was able to confirm London's findings—but with certain qualifications and expansions. In addition, I made other discoveries.

MORAL MODELS

Rescuers report that one parent—occasionally, though rarely, both parents—served as an articulately moral parental rode model. It was not enough to be a moral person and by extension a model. It was essential for parents to establish, articulate, and teach their values and to practice those values with or at least in the presence of the child who would later become a rescuer. Very few rescuers reported that both parents articulated or practiced the same set of values. The reason for this is that often one parent was at work and the other was the primary teaching model; sometimes only one parent taught family values; and in other instances, there was clear disagreement about values or perspectives, but one parent deferred to the other. It is significant to note that in a contemporary time when there are many single-parent families, it was enough if one parent was an articulate moral model. The few rescuers whose parents held, articulated, and practiced the same values reported feeling absolutely no ambiguity about engaging in rescue. There was a sense in them that their values, faith, and practices formed a cohesive unit.

SNAPSHOTS

The parents of rescuers had a decided moral vocabulary and a practical collection of virtuous stories that gave a useful folk-wisdom or common sense quality to life. A Dutch rescuer told how his impoverished family regularly fed strangers at the family table prior to 1933. After the "guest" departed, his father would tell him that one could always find something to share with people who had greater needs. Once, in a casual remark that the rescuer remembered years later as he undertook his first intervention, his father made the usual disclaimer but went on to connect the feeding of strangers on a farm outside of Amsterdam to the biblical mandate to welcome and care for sojourners. In an almost identical situation, a Polish rescuer recalled how each night his father, who had the equivalent of a fourth-grade education and who taught himself to read, would recite a passage from the Bible and discuss it with the family. "My papa could make the stories so vivid that I believed them." Once, during a particularly difficult economic slump, the boy asked his father why their family shared food with a distant neighbor when all of them barely had enough.

I remember as if it was yesterday. My father lovingly wrapped his arm around my shoulders and said, "Don't worry, there will always be enough for us. God will provide for us just as He is using us to help our neighbor." Papa smiled and reminded me that Jesus fed thousands of people with only a few fish and then he recited his favorite words from the Bible, "Do unto others what you would have them do unto you." I never forgot that lesson.

A Hungarian rescuer recalled that his mother, who had been unfairly treated by both family and friends, always insisted that her son make honest and fair decisions. In this manner, she assured him, he could be proud of himself and confident that he was doing God's will. A German rescuer explained how her parents' teachings and practice of Christian love and kindness led her to the study and practice of nursing. She noted that nursing enabled her to live out her values. She first became a rescuer of Jews when a former patient whom she barely remembered furtively waited for her outside the clinic where she was employed. When she came out, the man explained that because he remembered her kind and caring ways from the earlier encounter in the clinic, he hoped she might help him find medicine for his sick child who was hidden in an empty building. She moved the family into her small apartment, lied to the doctor to get the medicine she needed, and hid the family for more than a year.

Herman Graebe's mother, Louise Kinkel Graebe, was the articulately moral model for her family. She held consistent, rigid but humanitarian views on right and wrong. She spoke freely and often of her faith and the values that it inspired. She was biblically literate and routinely quoted and commented on Scripture. She regularly attended the Lutheran church until a certain incident in her parish violated her values and she became less active. She was not doctrinaire; indeed, she had ecumenical interests that she pursued in weekly conversations with a local Roman Catholic sister. Through word and deed, she taught her sons to be egalitarian, charitable, and open.

Mrs. Graebe taught Herman to care for those who were needy or victims of society. We can trace directly back to her instruction and modeling her son's seasoned hospitality, his intense commitment to justice, and his skillful resistance to ill-willed, inhumane authorities. Herman Graebe remembered that his mother had certain favorite biblical stories and passages including the parable of the "good Samaritan" and that she often repeated the Golden Rule, admonishing her boys to live by its words: "Do unto others as you would have them do unto you." She was also a strong believer in Jesus' wisdom teaching in Matthew 22:39, "Love your neighbor as yourself." Mrs. Graebe would weave these passages into homey, unpretentious homilies in order to illustrate for her sons a particular value or to explain some kindness that she had performed.

Louise Graebe raised her son to be an independent and critical thinker. He described his mother as "the strong moral figure for me—she knew right and wrong." Her egalitarian approach set the stage for Herman's life and values: "She accepted people for their own worth, not because someone else told her about or spoke against them." In teaching her son to be a critical thinker, Mrs. Graebe would always ask him, "Fritz, what would you do?" in situations of ethical choice or complex interpersonal relations. This practice not only taught him how to think but, as you will read shortly, developed an anticipatory practice that virtually ensured that his altruistic efforts would succeed. I will continue this illustration later in the chapter.

ADVENTUROUSNESS

Prior to the war and before ever considering taking part in intervention or resistance activities, the rescuers showed a marked proclivity for adventure. They did not, however, engage in impulsive, reckless derring-do adventures. More accurately, they were risk takers who carefully calculated dangers in order to mitigate them. They routinely reported that they followed careful, extensive, and elaborate planning procedures that guaranteed they would experience the challenges and joys of whatever the adventurous activity while minimizing or eliminating injurious threats. Later, this practice was simply carried over in their rescue endeavors, which were, by any definition, adventuresome. Their rescues succeeded and they survived because they were able to plan their course and weigh the dangers in advance.

SNAPSHOT

John Weidner was an accomplished, award-winning downhill skier. He attended a Seventh Day Adventist college and lived in a dormitory where Jews, seeking safe haven from the collaborationist policies of the Vichy government, were hidden. It became obvious to Weidner and his fellow conspirators that they had to establish something like an underground railroad and move the Jews before they were discovered and the school raided. Contacts were established with other Adventists in towns and villages beyond a small range of mountains in the Alps. During the winter months, John Weidner and others escorted Jews across the snow-covered passes and trails, delivering their charges to Adventists who would then move them out along the line.

Each night before the morning when he took Jews on a particular route, Weidner would ski his intended course. In and of itself, skiing is an adventurous and usually risky sport. To ski at night without any illumination seems almost insane. When I asked Mr. Weidner why he took the nighttime ski, he looked incredulous, as if to demand, Isn't it obvious? He explained, "Each night I'd ski the route I planned to follow the next day. I did this because I had to be certain that Vichy or German snow troops had not moved into the area. If they had, then I would either cancel the trip, change the time, or take an alternate route." After a thoughtful pause, he continued, "Regardless, what right did I have to further endanger people who were already desperately endangered?"

Weidner was proactive and planful. He was a good skier, so he used the skills at hand, but in order to reduce or eliminate the dangers in this adventure, he had to handle the security issues in the middle of the night. It was clear that Weidner enjoyed the adventurousness of skiing and that the added challenge of outwitting the authorities added to the satisfaction he enjoyed. He did his security sweeps because he also knew that he had to act responsibly on behalf of the people who entrusted their lives to him. His compassion, the relocation of the victims, and securing their safety fulfilled his sense of religious calling. Weidner and the network saved not only Jews but also downed Allied aviators and others threatened by the Reich. Weidner was arrested and escaped several times, including from a cell moments before he was to be executed. He never betrayed his encyclopedic knowledge of the Dutch-Paris Underground, and for all of his heroic and compassionate activities, he was awarded the U.S. Medal of Freedom with Gold Palms and numerous honors from several European nations. The success of Weidner's ministry—because he spoke of his efforts as a calling, it is proper to refer to his activities as "ministry"—proves that effective altruism demands careful, preemptive, extensive, and elaborate planning.

RELIGIOUSLY INSPIRED NONCONFORMITY

Social marginality refers to a person's sense that he or she is not part of the mainstream of society or does not accommodate a popular norm or practice. It refers to those who listen to a voice that is different than the dominant voice, follow a conscience that is not informed by the preponderant ethic, or who for reasons beyond their immediate control exist outside the majority. Social marginality may be an intentional choice when the alternative violates a person's sensibilities, or it may result from isolating behaviors perpetuated by a larger or more powerful group of people. Whatever its genesis, social marginality serves to help people differentiate themselves, affirms their perspective, empowers them to persevere with their position, and most important, heightens their sensitivity to the plight of others whom they determine to also be socially marginal.

A significant corollary to what Perry London referred to as "social marginality" is what I have termed *religiously inspired nonconformity*. The story of the Dutch woman in the snapshot section explains the essential unity of social marginality and religiously inspired nonconformity if a person is to engage in high-risk rescue interventions. Over the course of my interviews, I discovered that rescuers nearly always defined themselves as nonconformists and almost uniformly engaged in at least an initial role exchange whereby their active imaginations placed them in the role of persecuted Jews. Social marginality, or more correctly, religiously inspired nonconformity, has the effect of isolating a person from an objectionable mainstream behavior, and at the same time that it is differentiating a person, it also enables them to exchange roles, which in turn increases the likelihood of an empathic response. More on empathy in the next section of this chapter.

SNAPSHOTS

One could not be more socially marginal than a Baptist in Poland; after all, Poland is a strongly and predominantly Roman Catholic nation. The Huguenots historically were a persecuted minority and certainly a socially marginal population in twentieth-century France. A Dutch-Calvinist-turned-Seventh-Day-Adventist would have been socially marginal, as would be the Roman Catholic nun who established rescue networks in predominantly Protestant regions of southern Holland (she would also be considered marginal on the basis of her gender, the vows she took when entering the order, and because of the way of life she followed as a nun) or the Protestant minister who did the same thing in a largely Roman Catholic region of Holland. The fourteen-year-old Polish Baptist girl who rescued and supported a father and daughter, Jewish refugees from a mobile killing unit, was marginal by virtue of her age, religion, and gender.

I interviewed a Dutch woman after *Yad Vashem* awarded her the highest honors of the Israeli government. The interview was long, and after four or five hours we took a coffee break. My questionnaire and checklist contained a variety of inquiries to elicit information about motivation. This woman did not answer any of them. She was silent, changed the subject, or answered a different, unvoiced question, but she would not talk about her motives. Over coffee and cake I explained that I did not understand her motives for saving forty or so Jews. She had saved one person at a time and once hid a family of three. She hid them in her closet, under her bed, or in a small crawl space in her attic. She shared her food and clothing. But why did she do these things?

She was pensive and quiet for a long time, toying with the handle of her coffee cup, before saying, "I honestly never thought about the question until you asked it. I'm uncomfortable with your question because it is quite unnatural." Again there was a period of silence before she said, "I did it because of what St. Paul said in Romans 12:2." In that specific passage of the correspondence to the church in Rome, Paul wrote, "Be not conformed to the standards of this world, but be transformed by the complete remaking of your mind. This is the only way to know the will of God—what is good, pleasing, and perfect to God."

Tears began to roll down her cheeks as she said to me, "If I had ignored the knock at my door, if I had refused to help, if I had betrayed the Jews, I would have been conforming to the standards of an evil world. But to share my home, to give them a little food and clothing, was to have a whole new mind. I believe I was doing God's will protecting these strangers in my own home."

We concluded our work for the day and agreed to meet the next morning. I want to share an additional story about this woman that is not directly related to religiously inspired nonconformity and social marginality but that is a very telling piece of information about the post-Shoah lives of many rescuers. The second day, again after several hours, I noticed that the Dutch woman was discreetly checking her watch. This continued for a time, and I finally asked her if I was imposing and if we should end the session. She assured me I was not and that we could spend as much time as I wanted. Soon, she was again looking at her watch. Feeling perplexed by her behavior, I mentioned that she was checking the clock and I felt uncomfortable continuing.

This woman was going to be in Israel for ten more days. She was to be feted by representatives of the World Jewish Congress in Tel Aviv, then she would visit a kibbutz where survivors whom she helped had settled after the war, and she was to be reunited with other survivors and their children and grandchildren (who would not exist without her interventions forty years earlier). She apologized and explained that she was preoccupied thinking about her Kirk in Amsterdam. At that very hour, members of the Refugee Resettlement Committee of her church were at the international airport waiting to welcome two families of refugees from off the South China Sea. She would have preferred to be on the tarmac to embrace these strangers and to welcome them to their new homes; however, she had no choice but to leave that to a committee she normally chaired! Forty years after the war, this woman was still providing safe haven for people fleeing murderous oppression—victims of evil and the world's indifference.

There was in very many of the rescuers I interviewed a consistent, lifelong concern for the poor and oppressed of the world. Once they had responded to the plight of Jewish refugees, they did not want to stop their interventions. At the end of the interview, I asked her a standard question, "Looking back, is there anything you would do differently?" She responded immediately that she would never again do such a thing alone.

It was terribly frightening every time I brought someone in—I didn't know what my neighbors would do if they found out; I had no way of knowing if there were spies watching. Because I was so fearful I waited a long time before helping the second person. I never told anyone until months after the war. I see now that was a mistake. You can see how I am doing it today! My entire church is involved, and if anything like the Nazis happened again, I would have everyone in my church hiding Jews—or whoever.

She was a living testament to the admonition "Be not conformed to the standards of this world."

THE EMPATHIC IMAGINATION AND THEATER ARTS

One of my hypotheses was that in their formative years, but not related to World War II, rescuers had developed sophisticated imaginations that enabled them to actually picture themselves in different circumstances, to comprehend the long-term consequences of the situations, and to preview various scenarios and roles that they and others might play in trying to resolve the situation. Rescuers who had nurtured an empathic imagination had the capacity to project themselves onto the particular stage and into the place and role of the victims. Approximately three-fourths of the rescuers had some degree of empathic imagination that served them in rescue. I also explored the relationship of empathic imagination and theatrical skills. Slightly less than half of the rescuers had any stage experience (school plays, public theater, amateur acting), and somewhat more than half regularly attended theatrical performances. Several of those with acting experience used the language of the stage to describe their interventions and, more important, employed their dramatic talents to effect rescue.

Sociologist Peter Berger has made an important linkage of social marginality and his notion of "ecstasy," or what I refer to as the *empathic imagination*. Berger defines *ecstasy* as "quite literally the act of standing or stepping outside the taken-for-granted routines of society. . . . While this begins as a state of consciousness, it should be evident that sooner or later there are bound to be significant consequences in terms of action."[11] It is Berger's contention that ecstasy is more likely to take place among socially marginal people than among those whose position is established or secure. The old aphorism "Put yourself in her shoes" is an invitation to ecstasy or role exchange, and it leads to a heightened empathy or awareness of what another person is experiencing and the long-term consequences of that experience. Persons who understand or define themselves as socially marginal can be expected to have a great sensitivity to those who are also marginalized.

During the war years, rescuers with empathic imaginations identified with the victims of the Nazis and literally pictured themselves in the situation of the endangered Jews. Exchanging roles by means of empathic imagining produced a strong commitment to intervene and set their minds to creating alternative means by which they could have a positive effect on the lives of victims. Those with acting skills used these talents to present themselves as the particular scenes demanded, in order to take command of a critical encounter or a dangerous situation. They mentally, and whenever possible, physically rehearsed the roles they would play, attending to such details as presentation, posture, breath control, wardrobe, placement, dialogue, and preferred outcome. There are several variations on the themes of empathic imagination and theatrical skills that will be presented following the next section.

SNAPSHOTS

The effect of empathic imagination, role exchange, and social marginality is illustrated in the story of an uneducated, impoverished farmer in

Holland. He saved an escapee who told him about the execution of Jews
and the mass graves in the forests. The rescuer said of the situation and the
victim, "He fell into my hands from the SD [the SS Security Service]. I
could hardly believe what he was telling me. Then I said to myself, 'This
thing [the executions] could happen to me or my family.' From then I had
no choice but to help these poor people." In this story, poverty and lack of
education are determinants of marginality, and the act of imagining himself
and his family becoming victims of an execution in the forest was an
example of role exchange.

Herman Graebe had by far the most well-developed empathic imagination of the rescuers I interviewed. He remembered always having had an
active imagination and intentionally fostering it over the years. His mother
helped forge it into an empathic imagination; recall how she would regularly
and in varied situations ask her son the question, "And Herman, what will
you do?" Graebe said of his mother's instructional device, "This was never
a rhetorical question; she always expected an answer. If we did not have an
answer or if the one we tried was not to her liking, she coached us to an
answer that agreed with her values." Graebe's visualizing skills turned to
artistic works and later to a successful profession as an engineer and
designer.

The extent to which Graebe's empathic imagination developed and
matured is shown in the profoundly moving scene enacted beside the mass
grave at Graebe's work site adjacent to the airport at Dubno in the Ukraine.
The first public account of this episode was when Mr. Graebe's sworn
testimony was read by Chief British Prosecutor Sir Hartley Shawcross as,
according to historian William Shirer, a "hush of horror" fell over the
courtroom of the Nuremberg Tribunal.[12] Mr. Graebe's testimony is recorded
in more than one hundred books in at least fourteen languages, but the
recounting I offer includes the personalized background and experience of
the rescuer, emotionally shared in his eighty-third year from his home in
San Francisco, California.[13]

A Jewish carpenter insisted to Graebe, the manager of the Reich Railroad
Administration work site, that a special unit of the German army (*Einsatzcommando*) was in the process of detaining and massacring the 5,000
Jewish civilians, including, he feared, his wife and child, in the neighboring
village of Dubno. He begged Graebe for permission to go and return with
his family. Graebe was skeptical, refused his petition, but immediately drove
to the airport to see for himself. When he arrived he found one of his German
staff in hysterics. Graebe walked around to the back of the hangar where he
found a huge mound of dirt and German soldiers and local militia men

standing guard over a long line of Jewish children, women, and men, all of whom had been forced to undress and stack their clothing in neat piles. Beyond the line, several military transport trucks were unloading more Jews who continued the ritual.

Graebe walked to the other side of the dirt mound and there watched German soldiers of the mobile killing unit order Jews in groups of ten to step down and move to the end of a dirt ledge dug into the side of the mass grave. On the far edge sat a German who smoked, nervously cracked jokes, and shot the Jews. Through cascading tears Graebe told me, "I watched as my own countrymen ordered Jewish women to hold their small children and infants in front of them so an SS man could kill two people with one bullet. In truth, the child died instantly, but rarely did the mother die immediately— it was a mortal wound and an agonizing death as one body fell on top of the others."

Graebe turned his attention back to the line of people waiting to be taken around the mound and murdered. In front of him stood a family with eight or ten members. They were talking quietly among themselves. An older, gray-haired woman cradled an infant in her arms and caressed its cheeks.

I saw an old man standing naked with his twelve-year-old son. The boy was also naked and crying. His father stroked his head and for a moment drew him close. Then the old man leaned over and whispered something in the boy's ear; I could not hear them. He pointed to the heavens and the two looked up; the boy smiled and then I heard the German officer scream out, "Next ten! Next ten! Quickly! Quickly!" The family began to move toward their destiny. A young woman with black hair sent me a terrible shock: In a controlled voice, as she passed her hands in front of her bare breasts and belly, she said, "Herr engineer, twenty-three, only twenty-three." I don't know how she knew who I was, but she called to me by my formal title. In seconds they were all dead.

Graebe's tears had turned to wracking sobs, and his nurse asked him to stop and rest. She gave Graebe a nitroglycerin pill, and we went to the kitchen for coffee and cake. As much as it hurt to remember, Graebe ignored the food and continued the account through his tears. I asked him how he knew that the man was old. He said, "He was my age; he just looked old because he was sick and malnourished." And the boy, how did you know he was twelve? "I didn't know, but he looked to be the age of my son who was visiting with my wife and staying in Sdolbonov" (Sdolbonov was a town approximately twelve miles distance from the execution site). His tone lightened as Graebe said, "I know precisely what I would say to my son in that moment. I would point to heaven, comfort him, and say, 'Do not be afraid because where we are going, there are no SS or mass graves.' "

Graebe became very quiet and finally said, "In that moment, when I was in such a state of shock and could do nothing, I heard my mother's voice say to me, 'Fritz, what will you do?' It was then that I knew I had no choice—I had to save the Jewish workers."

In Herman Graebe's empathic imagination, he and his son exchanged places with their Jewish contemporaries at the edge of the pit. He rehearsed the lines he would speak to his son in the final seconds. Though she had been dead for ten years, the voice of his articulately moral mother came from off stage and asked him the question that would set in motion an unprecedented rescue effort.

I measured Herman Graebe's sense of being socially marginal by comments he made about his short stature and the stuttering that afflicted his late adolescent years into his early twenties. Graebe indicated on several occasions that he was not comfortable with himself, a fact that limited his social contacts and for a time threatened his professional choices. Those factors and his experiences with peers who teased or took advantage of him likely heightened his sensitivity to the persecuted Jews he would later meet. There is more: Graebe also took a part in a school drama, before the accident that triggered the stuttering. Graebe used the techniques in an acting handbook to correct his stuttering. And every season he had tickets to all of the works performed by the Soligen Light Opera Company.

As the war years commanded his life, he transferred the acting skills of his youth, and he became a consummate actor, speaking of various significant confrontations with the Reich Regional Command as if he had been on stage. He carefully prepared for every performance—reviewing and rehearsing, considering his words and tone, practicing how he would present himself, and preparing for the inevitable improvisational twists that happen in unscripted encounters. Graebe used his dramatic skills to ingratiate himself to petty bureaucrats, in a gun barrel-to-gun barrel confrontation with a Nazi major preparing to send seven of Graebe's workers to their deaths, and in a brilliantly scripted scene in which Graebe entered SS headquarters in Warsaw after learning that they were maintaining secret files in preparation for arresting the engineer.

PREVIEWING FOR A PROSOCIAL, PROACTIVE LIFE

In order for compassionate acts to become a consistent and successful lifestyle, a person must be proactive and prosocial. Relative to Nazi-era rescues, proactive (the antithesis is to be reactive) and prosocial (the opposite is to be antisocial) behavior is characterized by (1) a careful, intentional plan to respond to oppression and threats against others in a responsible and cooperative manner; (2) anticipating the situations in which you will have a positive and beneficial impact on the lives of the victims; and (3) actively working for the security and well-being of the victims and one's self. When people develop the skills that help them feel self-confident and relatively secure about the levels of risk they can manage, they are more likely to engage in those activities or interventions. The following steps help protect altruists from impulsive, usually unsuccessful, and almost always needlessly hazardous interventions: first, intentionally previewing a course and an outcome; second, assessing personal and external tools to complete the undertaking; third, reviewing alternative courses and contingency plans; fourth, conservatively measuring risks against abilities; and finally, continuously rehearsing strategies.

In Robert Gardner's superlative educational video version of the book *The Courage to Care* (edited by Sister Carol Rittner and Sondra Myers; together the book and video are the most useful tools produced to date to introduce audiences to rescuers and the rescued), Magda Trocmé, who with her husband, Pastor André Trocmé, established and guided the church-wide rescue in Le Chambon-sur-Ligon, says,

> You don't sit down and say I am going to do this or that. You have no time to think. When a problem came, you have to solve it immediately. Sometimes people like you ask me "How did you take a decision?" There was no decision to take! Are you thinking that we are all brothers or not? Are you thinking it is unjust to be against the Jews, or not? Then let us try to help. Remember, in your life you will be across lots of circumstances that will need a kind of courage, a kind of decision of your own—not about other people, but about yourself.[14]

Unfortunately and quite unintentionally, Mrs. Trocmé encouraged the idea that most rescuers were not planful and proactive. To be certain, the Trocmés and many other rescuers did not wait until the critical moment when a rescuer stood at their doors to make their decision. They were, however, planful and proactive and therefore prepared to act rather than analyze, to respond when the knock at the door came.

In a variety of ways, rescuers prepared themselves for what they had to do. Pastor Trocmé's daughter noted that he regularly preached sermons about "peace and brotherhood." In his classes, he prepared church leaders to take the initial steps toward intervention. It was a logical and anticipated movement from talking about a compassionate and just lifestyle to actually living one. Other rescuers engaged in "self-talk," because they dared not discuss their plans with others. They witnessed things that happened in their communities, identified with the victims, and imagined, in brainstorming fashion, different things they might do in response to what they had seen. Some rescuers were exceptionally intentional about their planning, and more of them tended to be thoughtful about it, even if they lacked the specific skills to be methodical and planful. Having said that, I must also note that every rescuer in my research had thought in advance about the situation faced by the Jews and at least had a sense of what they needed to do.

THE FAITH AND SPIRITUALITY OF RESCUERS

The only reliable generalization about the faith and spirituality of rescuers is that ninety-eight percent defined themselves as people of faith, engaged in spiritual practices (prayer, study, and service), or were involved in a church. For many, church attendance was a matter of personal choice; for most, it was either a matter of habituation or a response to family, clerical, or social expectations. Institutional Christianity was, in those times, an ingrained part of the social fabric. While I made no attempt to determine the depth of faith, it was quite clear from the reports of the rescuers that they understood themselves to be people of faith.

The churches of Nazi-era Germany endured a tremendous internal challenge, and believers experienced confusion or distancing from the institution. On the one hand, there were those who linked Christianity, patriotism, and nationalistic fervor but who utterly failed to understand that at the heart of Nazism was a pure paganism poised to substitute itself for institutional Christianity when Nazism prevailed. On the other hand were the churches and religious leaders, such as those who supported the Theological Declaration of Barmen and otherwise resisted the National Socialist movement. Tossed into this mix was a Reich bishop carrying out the Nazi mandate to assume absolute control over the churches. The following vignettes highlight the dilemmas faced by various Christian rescuers and churches suffering a crisis of identity and future existence.

SNAPSHOTS

The sister of the taxi driver in Kraków was a devout Roman Catholic. Her brother told me that she was crushed and experienced a crisis of faith when the family priest (who was also a family friend) refused to support her efforts to save Jewish children by providing her with signed Baptism certificates. The crisis of faith grew out of the tension created by the inconsistency between what she and her family were taught by the priest in church and the failure of the priest to support the rescue effort that the family understood to be a faithful response to the teachings of the church. She died while rescuing the children and apparently without resolving the violation of trust and confidence.

Herman Graebe failed to gain the support of a particular Lutheran pastor he turned to for help. The experience embittered him against the Lutheran Church and its clergy. He remained a self-defined "spiritual man," which meant that he regularly prayed and read Scripture, but he did not often attend church unless his wife requested it. Unlike her husband, Elisabeth Graebe took great comfort in the church and the sacraments. While actively supporting her husband's rescue efforts in the Ukraine, she attended services and volunteered at her church.

For the Huguenot Christians of Le Chambon-sur-Ligon, the church and their faith were central aspects of personal and communal identity. The same was true for the Roman Catholic priests and church community of Assisi, Italy. Interventions that involved cooperative efforts between church members and clergy created a phenomenal sense of cohesion as church, faith, and rescue were integrated. There was no evidence of a crisis of faith or confidence in these settings.

The nonconformist Dutch rescuer learned after the end of the war that her minister honored her courage and compassion and regretted that he did not know what she was doing. They worked together in the relocation movement after the war—an activity with unqualified clergy support that she attributes to enabling the congregation to later support global refugee resettlement programs.

In an earlier chapter, I expressed my disdain for triumphalist tendencies in theology and ecclesiology. The idea that Judaism was inferior to Christianity or that God's covenant with Christianity superseded God's covenantal promises to Judaism, and the notion that Jews had to convert to Christianity in order to be redeemed or saved, played out curiously in several rescues. Triumphalist tendencies carried over into a number of rescues. The scene is set in one of Wiesel's novels in which a priest recalls his thoughts about rescuing a Jew who had escaped from a death train: "Here's a chance to save his soul, to bring him to the light, I said to myself. Kindness is a weapon and I decided to use it."[15] Unlike the cynical motives of the priest, rescuers who presented the claims of Christianity to Jewish refugees did not make it a condition for rescue. A Jew who was one of perhaps a dozen hidden on a farm graciously discounted the evangelical fervor of his rescuer and appreciatively remarked, "I knew she cared about all aspects of my life. She was very kind in every way. I told her I could not turn my back on my faith in the midst of this trial. She never brought it up again and we are friends to this day." Because there was an innocence in this and because the victims saw it as part of the general concern and kindness of the rescuer, I noted it as eschatological altruism—the deep and sincere concern for the spiritual salvation of a non-Christian. Still, I cannot justify the practice and abhor its modern expressions.

PERSONAL EXPERIENCES WITH SUFFERING AND DEATH

Nearly every rescuer had a pre-World War II experience with suffering or death that in some measure helped to inform their decisions to intervene. These experiences expanded their empathic imaginations and added a note of reality to their planning and decisions to undertake rescue. In formative years, those who became rescuers had not been spared personal encounters with the traumas of death, injury, or separation. Trauma and death tended to be experienced in the setting of a home or small clinic rather than in a distant hospital where the victim was isolated in a sterile cubical. This made the experiences more intense and personal. The parents of about half the rescuers spoke openly of their feelings and attempted to provide their perspective on the familial experience of death. Familiarity with suffering and death sensitized these people to the plight of sufferers; and because of parental involvement, it did not cause them to be fearful, repulsed, or morbidly attracted to suffering and death.

SNAPSHOTS

Herman Graebe's youthful encounters with death and suffering strengthened his resolve to combat them. He came to see the imposition of suffering and death in war as unnecessary and inappropriate. Graebe's brother suffered a crippling form of multiple sclerosis that led to his mistreatment by playmates and to an early death. Louise Graebe chose to create empathic imaginations in the youth who harassed her son by interrupting their behavior and calmly asking them how they thought her son felt when he was being teased. She continued, asking the children to put themselves in his place. Rarely, after this manner of intervention, did she need to scold or chastise. Graebe watched his mother, and it is little wonder that he had an enhanced sense of caring and an inclination to intervene on behalf of vulnerable people. Mrs. Graebe had a remarkable ability to forge and nurture the empathic imagination.

Graebe vividly remembered feelings from his late adolescence, at the end of World War I, when wounded soldiers returned home from the front. One young man from Gräfrath was badly wounded, much of his face had been obliterated by a bullet, and Graebe thought to himself that this youth and others like him had been wasted by such unnecessary suffering.

Others offered similar reports: A friend returning from World War I and suffering incredibly before dying caused one rescuer to become a pacifist, and the combination of the two fully sensitized him to Nazi brutalities in his city. A woman became a nurse because of the way her mother cared for a sick and dying grandparent in the family home. Her work in a hospital sharpened her awareness of suffering and victimization and directly influenced her decision to save Jews.

PREJUDICE MANAGEMENT

Historian Yehuda Bauer poses an essential question: "Under what conditions do anti-Semitic stereotypes become determinants of social and political action, and where do they recede before other considerations, such as considerations of ordinary human decency?"[16] In his early research, Perry London concluded that a significant number of rescuers were anti-Semites. Somehow these people were able to overcome political and cultural conventions that led to dehumanizing attitudes and ultimately to oppression and murder. All the rescuers in my study developed and held a more egalitarian worldview that enabled them to interpret the persecution of Jews and others as morally repugnant. Rescues took place where people had learned to recognize, confront, and change a bias or prejudice. Rescuers learned to value other human beings and not be afraid of racial and cultural differences or of pluralism generally.

A 1979 study of attitudes toward racial and religious minorities and women conducted by the Louis Harris Associates found: "The most salient idea to emerge from the study is the fact that familiarity does not breed contempt. To the contrary, familiarity breeds acceptance and respect."[17] Nazi-era rescuers who worked with or had Jewish friends or had knowledge of or experiences with Judaism substantiate this finding. The post-Shoah agenda is perfectly clear: If we are to forestall the crises in human behavior, we must instigate experiences of and instill respect for persons and cultures, traditions, and lifestyles that are not a regular part of a person's life experiences. The church, as a self-defined beneficiary of the universalization of God's grace and love, must develop as part of its central mission broad egalitarian and humanitarian beliefs and challenge ingrained, divisive judgments, stereotypes, and behaviors wherever they threaten the sanctity of life and the peace of the community.

SNAPSHOTS

The family of one rescuer had business associations with Jews for many years. The son who became a rescuer completed an apprenticeship with a Jewish merchant and later said, "They were not ruthless or corrupt in business like Hitler and the SA tried to make us believe."

Recall the story of the woman who held the unexamined belief that Jews suffered at the hands of history because they had abandoned the Ten Commandments, crucified Jesus, and failed to convert to Christianity. Her anti-Jewish sentiments and beliefs were contained by a greater commitment to human beings that she expressed in the following terms, "They were human beings and I could not let them suffer and die." She did not see how the Reich and its supporters held the same views and devised an extermination system on the basis of those beliefs. Fortunately, she maintained a value that was dominant to her theology, but the Nazis did not.

HOSPITALITY

Fundamentally, Christianity is a religion of welcome and hospitality. Roman Catholic theologian Henri Nouwen described the essential theological qualities of welcome and hospitality:

In a world full of strangers, estranged from their own past, culture, and country, from their neighbors, friends, and family, from their deepest self and their God, we witness a painful search for a hospitable place where life can be lived without fear. . . . That is our vocation, to convert the *hostis* into a *hospes*, the enemy into a guest and to create the free and fearless space where brotherhood and sisterhood can be formed and fully expressed.[18]

The practical expressions of hospitality include the welcoming and safeguarding of strangers or sojourners, feeding the hungry and providing drink for the thirsty, releasing the captives, ending oppression, embodying righteousness and justice, care for the sick and injured, attention to the needs of widows and orphans, giving clothes to the naked, and the provision of comfort for weary or besieged travelers. At the heart of their endeavors, but without engaging in reductionism, the rescuers were hospitable people who responded to scriptural mandates by providing food, drink, warmth, and other creature comforts, and respite and protection from dangers.

Rescuers often recalled that hospitality was a part of their childhood home life. Parents or grandparents welcomed complete strangers into the house and shared food and respite before sending the person on the way. The two biblical passages most frequently quoted or paraphrased by rescuers were the parable of the "good Samaritan," in which the least likely passerby responds to a man (who is also an enemy to the interventionist by virtue of divergent interpretations of their religion) who is the victim of a robbery and ends with Jesus' admonition, "Go and do likewise." The second passage was the parable in Matthew 25 in which Jesus is identified as having been treated with welcome and hospitality while imprisoned, without clothing, sick, hungry, thirsty, and a stranger. The parable ends with a call to the faithful to be welcoming and hospitable: "Whenever you did these things to one of the least of these . . . you did it to me."

SNAPSHOT

A Polish family living on a farm southeast of Białystok included thirteen people: father, mother, children, a set of resident grandparents, and several relatives who relocated to the farm because of the war. In the nearby town where they attended the Roman Catholic Church, the Nazis had posted a large sign warning the locals against giving aid or comfort to Jews and promising summary execution for that crime and also offering a cash reward for anyone who betrayed a Jew in hiding or anyone providing them any help.

The farm family knew about the threats and dangers, but they also knew about the refugees who tried to evade the Nazis and had heard the stories they told of the horrors befalling the Jews of Poland. With growing dismay about this situation, the entire family spent a dinner discussing the situation and their ethical obligations and decided that they had no choice but to hide as many refugees as they could. Over the intervening weeks, before undertaking their rescue mission, the family devised a plan and decided to take thirteen people. The mother's reasoning was commonsensical and simple, "We would save thirteen because we had thirteen places to hide people and because if anyone became suspicious, all they would find is thirteen dirty dishes, the usual dirty clothes, and unmade beds. No one would know." As fall approached, Jews were hidden in the attic, in a hollowed area under an abandoned rabbit hutch, in the barn, and in a small enclosure inside a hay mound. The family shared what food they had and expected in return only that the refugees would not come out of hiding during the daylight hours.

In the winter, very late at night after everyone was in bed, and with thirteen Jews hidden in various locations (except under the rabbit cage), the mother heard knocking at the front door. An old Jewish man wearing tattered clothes, a weather-beaten hat, and covered with snow, stood at the door. He had to have been at the end of his options and ready to accept whatever his fate. If these farmers were evil spirited he would die, but if they were compassionate, he might have a chance. The woman came to the door, carefully looked at him as she listened to his request, and then she welcomed him into the house. She went into another room, awakened her husband and their eldest son, and had them restack the firewood behind the wood cooking/heating stove while she prepared some food and a warm drink.

The old man spent the night sleeping in a space behind the wood stove, hidden by the rearranged cords. I asked the woman why she had her husband and son rebuild the wood pile and hide the man there rather than under a bed or in a closet. She responded, "When he first came in I saw at once that his hands and fingers were gnarled with arthritis and I saw pain in his face. I knew that he would be more comfortable with the warm penetrating heat of the stove."

It would have been enough to simply hide the man and go back to bed. This woman was not merely compassionate, welcoming, and hospitable; she had learned to carefully monitor her environment. It was as if she had built and installed an internal radar system that tracked the physical and emotional well-being of all those around her. For this woman, it would not have been enough to simply hide the old man. She saw another need, every bit as demanding as his fear, isolation, and poverty. While I lacked a formal means to measure the skill or characteristic of hospitality, I gradually realized that most of the rescuers were very observant, attuned to what was happening around them. Combine that quality with proactivity, previewing, and empathic imagination, and you have a very skilled and powerful person.

Rescues on the farm continued through the winter months. Several Jews had remained in hiding long term. In the late spring a neighbor apparently saw what she believed to be an illegal, undocumented refugee moving around on the property. She went to the nearby headquarters of the Reich regional government and demanded that the switchboard operator/receptionist, a local woman who had been pressed into service by the Nazis, take her to the commandant and give her the Zl500 reward because she knew where Jews were being hidden. The receptionist told the woman that the German officer was unavailable and offered to take the report and give her the reward. What the collaborator did not know was that the woman behind the desk was with the Underground.

After the woman left with her blood money, the receptionist got her son and sent him to warn the farm family of an impending raid. After several hours, she had to give the report to the Nazi. He in turn assembled his men and some militia and went directly to the farm. In the meantime, the thirteen hidden Jews were dispatched to the dense forest at the northern edge of the farm fields. The soldiers arrived, conducted a thorough, messy search, and found no Jews—only thirteen dirty dishes, stacks of clothes, and unmade beds, just as the woman planned it. But the German officer, either certain that the information was valid or because he wanted to make a point that would deter others, ordered the family of thirteen to line up single file in front of the house. The soldiers squared off in front of the family, the officer stepped between the two ranks, turned his back on the family, ordered the father and eldest son to step forward, pulled a pistol from its holster, spun, and shot them to death. Waving the gun at the family, he threatened, "Let that be a lesson to you!"

The next morning, before she had buried her husband and eldest son, the woman had hidden thirteen more Jews on the family farm. Finally, I had to ask her, "How could you have done that—so soon?" "You see," she responded, "they were certain that they had taught me a lesson. The lesson they taught me was that they would not come back because they were certain they taught me a lesson!" Though she never kept a count, by the end of the war she thought that they had saved another forty or fifty Jewish refugees.

Months later, as the tide of the war turned against the Reich, a major counteroffensive sent the German forces into retreat. Young soldiers were separated from their units and became the prey of Partisans, Underground, and angry locals who tortured and killed them. Early in the morning, at first light, one such young man cautiously moved toward the farmhouse. Having reached the end of his options, he decided that if these were revenge-spirited people, he would die, and if they were compassionate, he might have a chance. He knocked at the door and the woman answered. She understood that this man-boy was not one of those who executed Jews or murdered her husband and son. She gave him some food, and he departed wearing the clothing of the woman's husband and eldest son. She burned his uniform.

Jesus urged his followers to a high calling. He told them that they were to "Love your enemies." This woman, her husband and eldest son, and their family loved the Jews who were the enemies of their enemies, the Nazis—loved them unconditionally and unselfishly. But the love expressed to the young German foot soldier by the widowed mother sets the standard for fulfilling Jesus' mandate to "Love your enemies." Sustained by her strong faith and active participation in her parish church, this woman did not become bitter or resentful. When asked what she might do differently, she said, "Nothing really, except start sooner—perhaps save more people."

ALTRUISTIC COMMUNITIES OF FAITH

As noted earlier, most rescues were single, serial interventions and this was due in part to the fact that people were unable to surmount the fears and risks necessary to build cooperative groups of rescuers. The predominant reason, though, was that there were few communities of faith and networks organized to intervene. The majority of the rescues, being isolated, secret actions, almost universally involved a nearly disabling fear that could take weeks and months to overcome. If there was a longing in the hearts of rescuers, it was to share the responsibilities they had willingly taken on, to be in a mutually supportive relationship. To their eternal credit, rescuers overcame their fears and these longings, if not their isolation.

It is a severe judgment on the church that communities of faith were not enabled to become communities of compassion, led in such a way as to use the established relationships to build rescue networks based on the ethical mandates of Scripture. What does it say about the church— that there was not a common, unifying ethic fostering resistance and enabling intervention? What can the modern church learn from the most acclaimed religiously based communal rescues that emerged from long-standing congregations that shared a harmonizing and altruistic value system? The conclusion of my study was that a community that existed prior to the war and was not organized around a single, time-bound task could easily and successfully expand its agenda to embrace a religiously based enterprise such as rescuing Jews and other endangered people, provided that the religious community was not anti-Semitic. That is a description of those churches that shared common, humanitarian values, a uniformly embraced sense of moral responsibility, welcomed a diversity of skills, and became a supportive community of conspirators.

SNAPSHOT

To better understand the nature, importance, and success of such communal rescues, I encourage you to read two books that detail these interventions. The first, by Philip Hallie, *Lest Innocent Blood Be Shed*, tells the story of the Trocmés and the Huguenot Christians in Le Chambon-sur-Ligon. The second book is Alexander Ramati's account of communal rescues in Italy, *The Assisi Underground: The Priests Who Rescued Jews*.[19]

DID YOU KNOW?

There has been an on again/off again argument in the international legislative communities regarding the enactment of laws mandating altruistic interventions to save lives. Most laws are designed to keep people from harming others, and some laws have been enacted to protect those who engaged in so-called good Samaritan acts. It should be noted that during World War II the French Vichy government passed laws requiring citizens to prevent crimes and to rescue endangered persons. Pre-war Germany had similar codes, requiring rescue, that were expanded during World War II! Because Jews in Germany were not considered to be citizens, they were not protected by these culturally and racially biased laws.

Legislating morality, specifically rescue interventions, does little good if a society has lost its moral basis. In such circumstances, the laws that mandate moral behavior have no relationship to the will of society and the skills of the people.

TRANSITIONS

Life can only be understood backwards; but it must be lived forwards.
Søren Kierkegaard

The alarming, but not surprising, conclusion of my study is that victims in the Nazi era and today were and are left at the mercy of random and unpredictable interventions. Without radical efforts at preparing people to be proactive and prosocial, and providing the skills, values, and worldview that enable persons to act in caring and helpful ways, people who feel the impulse to compassion will be unable to translate values into actions. The good news is that most of what I have presented relates to skills that can be taught, rehearsed, and learned. As people learn and practice them, those who are in danger are more likely to be the recipients of direct, meaningful, and successful intervention. These skill-based proclivities do not develop out of nothingness, nor do they have a known genetic source. They must be practiced, affirmed, shared, and celebrated in ways that guarantee their continual refining and practice.

In the last public address before he was assassinated, the late civil rights leader Martin Luther King, Jr., offered a critical perspective based on the parable of the good Samaritan. It should be noted that this parable can be interpreted as a hostile criticism of Jerusalem's religious leadership at the time of Jesus. The key to the parable is that an unlikely person (there was a long history of serious enmity between Jews and Samaritans) stopped to offer help when two religious leaders could not do so, presumably because of ritual codes.

The first question that the Levite asked was, "If I stop to help this man, what will happen to me?" But then the good Samaritan came by. And he reversed the question: "If I do not stop to help this man, what will happen to him?" That is the question before you.[20]

That was precisely the question before each and every person who was asked to intervene, assist, rescue, hide, comfort, or protect Jews. Nazi-era rescuers asked the second form of the question and answered it with their faithful compassion.

Chapter Seven

The Stones Will Cry Out

In our own age we have been forced into the realization, that in terms of human relations, there will either be one world or no world.

Abraham Heschel

It was another of those confrontations between Jesus and the Jerusalem religious leadership, the Pharisees. It is an account that has historically lent itself to unfortunate and inaccurate comment, seeming to create yet another spiritual rift between Jesus and the Pharisees. It was the time of preparation for the Passover; Jerusalem was an occupied Roman military garrison with an imposed Roman regional government; pilgrims were massing in the holy city for sacred observances; and many of those present strenuously objected to the Roman occupation, and among those were some who fomented revolution and violent dissent.

The followers of Jesus shouted, "God bless the king who comes in the name of the Lord! Peace in heaven and glory to God." For Jesus, the timing was perfect, and his strategy was to present his message in the most dramatic way to the largest possible audience, distancing himself from the anti-Roman revolutionaries with his peaceful message. For the Pharisees, the timing was terrible. They did not want a surging, noisy, multiagenda crowd with a catchy but confrontational slogan to draw the attention and repression of the Roman authorities at the outset of a major religious holiday. The dissident claims of kingship would likely spark an intense and far-reaching response from Pilate unless the Pharisees could convince Jesus to calm his followers. They approached Jesus and asked,

"Teacher, have your disciples be quiet!" Under the circumstances this was a reasonable, if misunderstood, request.

True to his calling and identity, Jesus responded, "I tell you that if they keep silent, the stones will cry out!" The context and confrontation notwithstanding, for Christians, these words are the essence of Palm Sunday, the Passion week culmination of Jesus' ministry, and the only suitable introit to Easter. On another level, the proclamation that "the stones will cry out" speaks to people of faith about the nonverbal expressions of God's presence, majesty, and place in human life that cannot be silenced. Indeed, in the postprophetic period, for Jews and Christians, and for Christians in the postmessianic era, it is the wordless wonders that speak eloquently, at times with awesome simplicity, of God and Christ. Yes, the stones will cry out. I have always listened in the silence for the messages of God, sought reminders of the Creator in the grandeur of Creation, and attended to the song of the stones in matters of justice, love, and grace—in all that which dwells in silence and yet is so communicative and evocative.

> The only hope we have . . . lies in the building of a genuine spiritual union strong enough to withstand the dark attraction to chaos which has so often kept humanity in the shadow of its own violence.
>
> Theodore Hesburgh

It is estimated that 700,000 Jews died in Treblinka, the Nazi labor camp turned death camp in northeastern Poland. The entrance to Treblinka was intentionally deceptive, a plan of its commandant Franz Stangl. In 1942 he built a false railroad station with train schedules to spas and major European cities; installed a clock, ticket windows, signs to lavatories; carefully placed flowering pots around the platform; wove pine boughs through the barbwire fencing to make it invisible; and stationed a strategically situated Red Cross truck. Trainloads of Jews arriving to be executed were initially deceived and pacified as they were led into the kingdom of death.

At first, Stangl's death machine had to rely on carbon monoxide gas generated by engines from trucks and a submarine. Death was slow, torturous, and gruesome. Eventually, Stangl consulted physicians who employed their medical knowledge to help him find ways to hasten death and increase his body count reports to Berlin. Still later, they pointed him toward a quick and deadly insecticide to replace the carbon monoxide, Zyklon-B.

Today, there is nothing left of the former death camp. In its place a massive granite monument rises about the encircling pine forest, its crown a mass of faces chiseled under burial rocks and two outstretched hands barely reaching beyond the highest point. There was a mystical tranquillity that enveloped these haunting surroundings at the end of my first day visiting the former camp. An abundance of birds flitted and sang from the distant branches. Butterflies, propelled by a cooling breeze, moved effortlessly among the rustling spring leaves on the Aspen trees.

There is another element of the memorial, more stunning and captivating than the granite monument. Stones have been upturned and cemented in place. They reach far and wide, many bearing the engraved names of cities, villages, and towns from which the victims came.

As I sat among these stones, listening to the soft stillness as the Bible calls it, Jesus' words came back to me: "I tell you that if they keep silent, the stones will cry out!" The voices of hundreds of thousands of murdered Jews, crucified on the crossbars of spiritual hatred and political expediency, were silent, but on this day, the stones cried out for them. *"How shall we sing the Lord's song in an alien land?"* In the quiet moments, it became for me a symphony of remembered agony, but in order to deprive the killers of the final word, it was simultaneously a soaring chorus of the wordless truth that life and blessing must always prevail against death and curse. From their upturned position, the stones neither pointed accusingly nor beseeched weakly. On the contrary. They were at once rooted in the earth and cradled in the embrace of the Creator; they were the bridge between earth and heaven.

Somewhere, on a cobblestone path in this heart of the kingdom of death, I had picked up a stone and carried it around all day. Later, its point pushed painfully against my thigh—while holding the stone I realized I was holding holy ground. As every stone shouted out around me, I composed a prayer on a scrap of paper, enfolded the rock with it, and tucked it away in my pack. At every camp and memorial, I found another piece of "crying out" holy ground, enfolded each of these stones in a prayer on a scrap of paper, and carried them all to the Holy City.

In Jerusalem I first learned of a tradition in which prayers composed on scraps of paper are pushed into the crevices of the mighty stones that remain from the Western Wall of the ancient temple. I decided that the stones, imbued with holiness from the travails of evil, and the only prayers I could find within me, must meld into the holy rocks of Jerusalem. Each Sabbath, Friday and Sunday, I went to the Wall, recited one of the prayers, rolled it back with its stone, and entrusted it to the healing treasury of pilgrims' longings.

Two stones, one great and one small, struck, and a spark ignited the prayers, my soul, and thus the path to liberation was illumined.

On the final Sabbath when at last I held no more stones crying out, I lingered at the Wall long into the night. First one and then a skyful, stars rose above the dark, humid night air, glimpses of light for the vast darkness. A final prayer emerged, and with no more burdened stones in hand, I slipped over to the great stones of the Wall. Awash in predawn's dew—or were they tears? Whose?—the Wall received my prayer and set me on the path. The only prayer I preserved was the last one:

I followed Bethlehem's Star
'til it was clouded
by
Jews
from
Majdanek Birkenau Treblinka
Buchenwald Auschwitz
and a
thousand like places.
If I still follow the Star
it is because I realize anew
that
David's Star
and
Bethlehem's Star
are needed still.
I need them both
in spite of
because of
a thousand like places.
No more!
Never again!
The stones cry out!
Birth and Death
are linked
by
those who will not choose
between them.
The death of every child diminishing
let them be birthed to live
to see their star
unclouded.

II

LITURGICAL RESOURCES

Chapter Eight

Liturgy and History

The materials and resources that follow will assist in planning seasonal observances designed to meet four purposes: first, to honor the memory and the experiences of victims and survivors of the Shoah; second, to unite the lessons of the Shoah with the central act of worship in faith communities; third, to gratefully remember the faith, compassion, and moral courage of women, youth, and men who rescued Jews, peasants, dissidents, and others threatened with death at the hands of Nazis and their collaborators; and finally, to honor the memory and service of those in the military who liberated the death camps. Because 1995 is the fiftieth anniversary of the liberation of the death camps, the execution of Dietrich Bonhoeffer, and the end of World War II, a special community *Yom haShoah* service is included, as well as a study program and commemorative service honoring Protestant theologian, Resistance leader, and martyr Dietrich Bonhoeffer.

Also included are a brief section establishing the basic historical context of the Shoah, sermon (homily) notes and resources, quotations that may be used in sermons and classes, and an outline with resources for a church or interfaith study group. Most denominational calendars announce *Yom haShoah* observances, the national and international Day of Remembrance of the Shoah, which occur in the spring (the dates are listed at the end of Chapter Nine). Services and sermons are certainly appropriate in those days, but they should not be restricted to a single day or week in the year. Indeed, the themes suggested herein lend themselves to worship services in all of the liturgical seasons: Advent, Lent, Easter, and Pentecost; and at times when political, military, or societal circumstances dictate. For that reason, seasonal variations on services, prayers, and sermons are included. Please feel free to use or adapt any or all of this material to meet the needs of the particular worshipping community.

A BRIEF HISTORICAL CONTEXT FOR
COURAGE, COMPASSION, AND RESCUE

Services, sermons, and public remembrances of the Shoah and of those courageous and compassionate persons who rescued Jews and other persons threatened by the Reich must take account of the historical context that made intervention an essential but uncommon practice. Because surveys in various cultures have established that people are generally uninformed about the Nazi period, the preacher may not assume that the majority of worshippers in any congregation have a working knowledge of the Shoah. It is important to explain that the term *Shoah* refers to the circumstances and behaviors that sealed the fate of more than 6 million Jews who died and thousands more who survived the premeditated National Socialist Party policy of genocide. Because the term *the Holocaust* has been compromised by inappropriate general usage, most scholars and students of that era now prefer to use the Hebrew term *Shoah*. It will be helpful if there is some explanation of the change in usage and a definition of terms (please refer to the Notes, Chapter One, note 1).

Rescue does not take place unless human life is endangered. The need for intervention began to surface in the early days of the Reich, as Nazi policies were enacted and enforced in Germany and later in Nazi-occupied lands. Dissent and resistance were silenced, often with brutal force. The churches quickly came to know the price of dissent. Pastor Martin Niemöller spent seven years in a concentration camp for his efforts between 1933 and 1937, in Berlin, establishing the Pastors' Emergency League and circulating petitions supporting the primacy of Scripture over Nazi policy and rejecting Aryanization laws. In 1934, the Confessional Synod of the German Evangelical Church met in Barmen and approved the Theological Declaration of Barmen, which provided a firm and courageous foundation for ecclesiastical resistance to the antichurch, anti-Christian philosophy and practices of the National Socialist Party. Many of the clergy who signed it or spoke against the Reich were imprisoned and executed for their expressions of conscience.

The dangers expanded exponentially as the public provocations became painfully obvious. In 1938 party policies mandated the "Aryanization" of Jewish businesses—that is to say, the forced and uncompensated expropriation of all Jewish-owned commercial interests by the Reich, which in turn sold the business or inventory to the highest "Aryan" (non-Jewish) bidder. In October 1938, Jews from a number of German cities were detained and then transported to concentration camps in Poland. On November 7, 1938, a seventeen-year-old Jewish refugee living in France with his family received a letter from a relative taken to one such camp. Fearing for his own safety and that of his family, Herschel Grynszpan purchased a revolver, entered the German Embassy in Paris, and assassinated Ernst vom Rath, the third secretary of the legation.

Hitler seized on the killing as an opportunity to further foment anti-Jewish sentiments and to announce the discovery of a "Jewish plot against the highest officials of the Reich." Following vom Rath's death on November 9, the Nazis instigated the traumatic destruction of *Kristallnacht* (literally, "the night of broken glass") across Germany and Austria. Overnight, 191 synagogues were ravaged, thousands of Jewish businesses and homes were plundered, hundreds of Jews were assaulted, and hundreds of thousands were arrested.

After *Kristallnacht*, the unrelenting public beatings, humiliations, harassment, and social-racial stereotyping intensified. The tempo of hatred and division quickened as Jews in Nazi-occupied lands were brutally expelled from their homes and relocated in ghettos. Thousands were deported, placed in forced labor columns, or put to death in forests and mass graves by special German military mobile killing units (*Einsatzgruppen*). The Nazis quietly instituted an experimental killing program in which the mentally retarded, mentally ill, physically handicapped, and many dissidents were exterminated in a so-called euthanasia program. Jews were required to register and have their travel or identity documents officially marked to indicate that they were Jews. Soon, they were directed to wear either a yellow star, yellow patch, or yellow armband. Help did not come to the ghettos or labor or death camps in any organized fashion. Anti-Jewish laws were enacted in Romania and the Vichy government of France revoked the civil rights of Jews.

Ghettos were built and Jews were eventually forced to live in cramped, squalid quarters, sealed off from the community and from access to food and health care. The ghettos confined the Jewish citizens and expedited their movement to labor and death camps. Beginning in 1937, Jews were murdered in death camps scattered throughout Germany, and in central and eastern Europe. Less than a year after the German army invaded Poland, the most infamous labor death camp, Auschwitz, was ordered into existence by Heinrich Himmler. In little more than a year, Reinhard Heydrich appointed Hermann Göring to commence the "Final Solution," and six months later, the Wannsee Conference was convened to develop a strategy for the complete destruction of European Jewry. The primary death camps included Buchenwald, Auschwitz-Birkenau, Sobibor, Bełżec, Majdanek, and Treblinka.

Initially and for only a short time, the fate of European Jews was not widely known. That changed quickly as the Jews disappeared en masse from their communities, or were forced into the heavily guarded walled ghettos, and as all their rights and properties were taken away. The overwhelming majority of those who witnessed the fate of their neighbors did little or nothing to help; many participated or benefited from the catastrophe of the Jews. Further resistance to National Socialist Party policies was intimidated or crushed, and the Reich moved virtually uncontested to impose itself on all aspects of German national life and similarly in occupied lands. Tragically, the leaders of the Allied nations knew the fate of European Jewry but did not act on their behalf in spite of the incontrovertible evidence. In spite of official protestations regarding the provocative nature of such a mission and the dangers inherent in flying unescorted through enemy air space, and later, after years of denial, the United States Army Air Force admitted that it had indeed flown reconnaissance photo missions over Auschwitz-Birkenau. The nations of the "free world" knew and chose not to act. At the time the military took the photographs, the death camp was fully and efficiently operational. If the rail lines into the camp had been bombed or assaults mounted against it, it is likely that tens of thousands of Jews would have been saved from extermination.

It is against this backdrop that a faithful remnant of women, children, youth, and men, numbering between 10,000 and 12,000 (compared to the millions on the continent who could have responded, resisted, or intervened) began their bold and hazardous rescues. An additional, uncountable number of people acted in simple, caring ways: Some shared food or clothing, others gave warnings, a few looked away for a day or two while a stranger hid in a barn or an outbuilding, and many simply did not betray the Jews who passed briefly through their lives.

Many of the most courageous rescuers began their missions in simple, caring ways and graduated to more risky actions: hiding Jews in attics, under beds, and in barns. A few gave sanctuary in convents and monasteries. Some established underground railroads to move Jews away from danger. Several Germans (including Herman Graebe and Oskar Schindler) established "front businesses" and nonexistent work projects in order to requisition literally thousands of Jewish workers and then move them beyond the killing machine that the Reich had become.

The risks were tremendous, and the price of betrayed or discovered conscience and compassion was exacted summarily and publicly on makeshift gallows, before firing squads, or in death camps. Polish rescuers had every reason to trust the fate promised on signs posted throughout that nation: financial reward to those who informed on Jews and neighbors, and execution without trial for those who gave aid or comfort to Jews. And yet, thousands of rescuers and uncounted numbers of caring people who simply helped were undeterred. They overcame their fears, prejudices, and the combined forces of government, politics, religion, and society. They refused to conform to the murderous purposes of the Reich and its collaborators. Unlike the killers, the collaborators, and the indifferent bystanders, these people restore the hope of post-Shoah humanity, reminding us that in the biblical tradition it is always a faithful remnant that saves the faith and robs the executioners of the final word in history. They chose life and blessing over death and curse!

At the war's end, some of the rescuers testified against the perpetrators of evil. The testimony of German rescuer Herman Graebe opened the trials of those accused of Crimes Against Humanity. The rescuers have joined their voices as objective witnesses to the horrors of Nazism. They often labored tirelessly to bring the killers to justice. Now, by their witness, they unite their testimony with that of Jewish survivors to challenge ill-willed revisionists who claim the Shoah did not happen; denying the deniers who contend that it was contrived by world Jewry for some nefarious purpose.

The government of Israel regularly honors rescuers at *Yad Vashem*, the nation's Shoah Memorial and Research Center in Jerusalem. Those who receive the highest honors rekindle the eternal flame in the Hall of Remembrance, plant a tree on the Avenue of the Just, and are presented with a specially cast medal of honor. In New York City, the Jewish Foundation for Christian Rescuers (a trust of the Anti-Defamation League of B'nai B'rith) provides stipends for many former rescuers around the world, sponsors educational events to promote awareness of the rescuers and to encourage others to imitate their values and compassion, and is a resource center for those who want to know more about the rescuers.

There is another element of rescue, the Allied military liberation of the camps. In the months after Allied forces stormed the German lines on D-Day and as the Russian army began its push from the east, the extent of the murderous plan of the Nazis became widely known. As the tides of war shifted, the military liberators began entering the Nazi death camps. They faced the most horrific scenes and heard the most devastating appeals for assistance from the surviving victims of Hitler's genocide.

In 1979, the adaptation of Gerald Green's novel *The Holocaust*[1] aired as a television series nationwide. At the time, I was teaching an introduction to the literature of the Shoah to honors students at the University of Oregon. One of the students who lived in the community but resided in the dormitory told me this story: In the afternoon of the day that the series started, the young man's father called and asked him to come home—it was important. The father was waiting in the living room with a bulging file folder set on the table. The father told his son that there was a television program about to air, and he insisted that his son view it in its entirety.

It was an important program, he explained, because there were now people who publicly denied that the events depicted in the film really happened. At that point the father revealed painful memories that he had secretly harbored for thirty-four years. "All of what you will see is true. I was in the first unit of troops that entered Mauthausen [a death camp east of Munich with two satellite camps at Ebensee and Gunskirchen]. This is what we saw." The bulging file was opened, revealing photos of the camp and its victims. The long-buried shock of that experience finally found its release. He and the other American soldiers found a mass grave with 10,000 bodies. Famished skeletons reached out for comfort and liberation, friendship and food. It was a nightmare. More than 3,000 inmates died after the liberation because of the conditions they endured and their weakened state.

Mauthausen was a killing center for Jews, homosexuals, Gypsies, Jehovah's Witnesses, and prisoners of war. It was a place of profound physical brutality. Nothing in his war experience had prepared this father for what he witnessed and recorded on his camera. So great was his terror that he did not speak of Mauthausen until the television program came on. He wanted his son to know the reality of Nazism and the end result of fanaticism. He wanted his son to know the burden he had carried those many years. His experience was not unlike that of military liberators throughout the occupied lands of Europe. In 1985 a grateful nation acknowledged the labors and compassion of the liberators when the United States Holocaust Memorial Council convened a conference to honor them and to gather their accounts of liberation. No service of remembrance is complete without the witness of those who sacrificed so much to bring the war to an end and in so doing stopped the Shoah, freeing and ministering to the children, women, and men who survived.

Chapter Nine

Elements of a Worship Service Celebrating the Compassion of Christians Who Rescued Jews

AN ORDER OF WORSHIP WITH SEASONAL VARIANTS

Elements of this service may be adapted for Protestant, Roman Catholic, ecumenical, or interfaith services of worship. For interfaith or community services the prayers should be made inclusive in terms of denomination or tradition, and non-Christological so that all worshippers may participate fully. It is quite important that the language of worship be completely gender inclusive. If this service is adapted for a community-wide observance, it would be advisable to include among the participants Shoah survivors, Nazi-era rescuers, military liberators, laity, youth, civic dignitaries, rabbis, ministers, and priests.

INVOCATION

> God of Abraham and Sarah, Isaac, Deborah, and Jeremiah, You call us, through Your faithful servant Moses, to choose life and blessing. We remember a time when powers and principalities chose death and curse; a time when the evils of Nazism claimed the lives of children and parents, old and young, families and friends, liberators, rescuers, and those who resisted. For the sake of a better future, we remember, with gratitude, acts of faithful courage and compassion and pray that coming generations will be spared because we have not forgotten; because we have labored to sanctify life. Amen.

CALL TO WORSHIP [Lent or *Yom haShoah*]

Leader: Out of the depths I cry to you, O Lord!

UNISON: LORD, HEAR MY VOICE, GIVE EAR TO MY SUPPLICA-
TIONS!

Leader: Attune Your ears to the travesties permitted by silence;

UNISON: THE OFFENSE OF EYES AVERTED AND HELPING HANDS
WITHHELD;

Leader: The sin of closed borders and doors locked to those in need.

UNISON: OUT OF THE DEPTHS I CRY TO YOU, O LORD!

Leader: Lord, hear my voice.

PRAYER OF ADORATION AND CONFESSION

UNISON: CREATOR AND LORD OF THE WORLD, THROUGH
YOUR ENDLESS LOVE WE HAVE BEEN GRANTED LIVES
FULL OF FREEDOM AND HOPE. IN CHRIST YOU HAVE
SHOWN US THE WAY TO LIVE AND OFFERED US THE
FULLNESS OF JOY. BY CHRIST'S EXAMPLE WE KNOW
WHAT IT MEANS TO LOVE OUR NEIGHBOR. WE CONFESS
THAT TOO OFTEN WE ARE CONTENT TO LEAVE THINGS
AS THEY ARE, EVEN WHEN OTHERS SUFFER INJUSTICE.
THE SILENCE OF HISTORY AND OUR SILENCE IN HISTORY
CONDEMN THE INNOCENT. SAVE US FROM INDIFFER-
ENCE AND UNCARING. MAKE US INSTRUMENTS OF YOUR
JUSTICE AND PEACE AND KEEP US FROM COMPLICITY IN
EVIL. GRANT US THE WISDOM AND STRENGTH TO TAKE
RISKS, TO CROSS LINES OF ENMITY AND STRIFE, TO BLESS
AND SANCTIFY LIFE. IN CHRIST'S NAME WE PRAY. AMEN.

SCRIPTURE

Leviticus 19:2, 11–18	Matthew 7:12
Micah 6:6–8	John 1:1–5 [Advent]
Amos 5:14–15	Romans 12:1–12
Deuteronomy 30:15–20	I John 3:11–24
Joshua 2:1–24	Luke 10:25–37
Exodus 1:1–22	

SERMON (Homily)

[Advent or *Yom haShoah*]
"Glimpses of Light in the Darkness"

"The Final Word Belongs to Life!"

[Lent, Easter, Pentecost, or *Yom haShoah*]
"The Final Word Belongs to Life!"
"Be Not Conformed"
"Remembering for the Future"
"Celebrating Lives of Compassion and Courage"

AFFIRMATION OF FAITH (or may be used as a prayer after
the sermon)

UNISON: WE ARE A PEOPLE OF MEMORY. WE RECALL THE GOD
WHO PROMISED BLESSINGS AND DESCENDANTS TO OUR
FOREBEARERS SARAH AND ABRAHAM, AND WE RE-
CLAIM THAT PROMISE AFTER THE SHOAH. WE REMEM-
BER THE SACRIFICE OF ISAAC AND INVOKE HIS MEMORY
FOR THE PROTECTION OF ALL CHILDREN WHO ARE EN-
DANGERED. WE HAVE KNOWN THE WISDOM OF RIGHT-
EOUS JUDGES IN THE TRADITION OF DEBORAH AND,
WITH HER, CALL ON THE LORD TO TURN ASIDE THE
ENEMIES OF HUMANITY. THE PROPHET JEREMIAH IN-
STILLED IN US THE LOVE OF JUSTICE, AND WE LOOK TO
HIM TO FIND THE COURAGE TO RESIST THE FORCES OF
DEATH AND DESTRUCTION AT WORK TODAY. WE SHALL
NOT FORGET, NOR WILL WE CEASE FROM CHOOSING
LIFE AND BLESSING. OUR MEMORIES OVERFLOW WITH
GOODNESS AND SADNESS; THE MAGNITUDE OF PAST
EVILS DEFY OUR WORDS AND PRAYERS, BUT WE SHALL
NOT GIVE THEM THE FINAL WORD IN LIFE. WE REMEM-
BER AND ARE CHANGED.

HYMNS

"O God of Vision"
"Live into Hope of Captives Freed"   Jane Parker Huber
"When Israel Was in Egypt's Land"   African-American Spiritual
"Song of Hope"   Alvin Schutmaat
"What Does the Lord Require"   Erik Routley
"Here I Am, Lord"   Daniel L. Schutte
"By the Babylonian Rivers"   Ewald Bash
"Zion's Song"   Penny Penrose

BENEDICTION

Leader: We conclude our service, reciting the words discovered on the wall
   of a cellar in Cologne, Germany, where Jews sought refuge from Nazis
   and collaborators:

UNISON: I BELIEVE,
   I BELIEVE IN THE SUN,
   EVEN WHEN IT IS NOT SHINING.
   I BELIEVE IN LOVE,
   EVEN WHEN FEELING IT NOT.
   I BELIEVE IN GOD,
   EVEN WHEN GOD IS SILENT.

SEASONAL VARIATIONS

For Advent (The pre-Christmas season of lights)

CALL TO WORSHIP

Leader: Scripture promises that God's enduring light will forever penetrate
   the darkness of history and human life.

UNISON: WE LIGHT THIS ADVENT CANDLE AGAINST THE
   DARKNESS OF NAZI EVIL AND REMEMBER THE LIGHT
   CAST BY THE RIGHTEOUS CHRISTIANS WHOSE COMPAS-
   SION AND COURAGE KEPT ALIVE THE SPARK OF HUMAN
   DECENCY.

Leader: We gather to worship the One God whose light continues to lead
   us in ways of justice and peace.

PRAYER OF ADORATION AND CONFESSION

UNISON: YOUR STEADFAST LOVE ENDURES FOREVER, O GOD;
   THE LIGHT OF YOUR ETERNAL STAR HERALDS YOUR
   NAME IN EVERY TIME AND THROUGHOUT CREATION. YOU
   HAVE CALLED US TO DO JUSTICE, TO LOVE TENDERLY, AND
   TO WALK HUMBLY WITH YOU. YOU GIVE VISION BEYOND
   THE DARKNESS THAT DIVIDES PEOPLE FROM ONE AN-
   OTHER. YOU GRANT COURAGE TO ACT IN CARING WAYS
   AND INSPIRE COMPASSION TO OVERCOME HUMAN HURT.
   FORGIVE US WHEN WE SING OF PEACE ON EARTH RATHER
   THAN LABOR FOR IT; HAVE MERCY WHEN WE SAY, "DO
   UNTO OTHERS," BUT FAIL TO CARE FOR OTHERS AS WE

WOULD WANT THEM TO CARE FOR US; AND SAVE AND
REDEEM US WHEN EVIL DEEDS ECLIPSE THE ANGELIC
PROCLAMATION OF GOOD TIDINGS. LET OUR LIVES RE-
FLECT THE LIGHT OF THIS HOLY SEASON, NOW AND
EVERY DAY. IN CHRIST'S NAME. AMEN.

*For Lent (The season of reflection and repentance before Holy
Week and Easter)*

CALL TO WORSHIP

Leader: "The Lord is my shepherd; I shall not want.

UNISON: THOUGH I WALK THROUGH THE VALLEY OF THE
SHADOW OF DEATH, I SHALL FEAR NO EVIL, FOR YOU,
LORD, ARE WITH ME. . . .

Leader: You prepare a table in the presence of my enemies, anoint my head
with oil and my cup overflows.

UNISON: SURELY YOUR GOODNESS AND MERCY SHALL FOL-
LOW ME ALL THE DAYS OF MY LIFE."

Leader: Let us worship the God of life and light! (based on Psalm 23)

LITANY OF ADORATION AND CONFESSION

Leader: Shepherd God, You guide us in paths of righteousness.

UNISON: THE DARKNESS BECKONS AND WE OFTEN SUCCUMB
TO ITS SEDUCTIONS, FOLLOWING PATHS OF EVIL.

Leader: Let us walk as children of light, laboring on behalf of what is just
and good.

UNISON: SAVE US FROM COMPLICITY IN THE WORKS OF DARK-
NESS: FROM PARTNERSHIP WITH INJUSTICE, INDIFFER-
ENCE, AND SELF-INTEREST.

Leader: The choice Moses gave the Israelites is the choice awaiting every
person of faith: "I set before you life and death, blessing and curse;
therefore choose Life."

UNISON: MAY ALL THAT WE DO AND SAY BEAR WITNESS TO THE
GOD OF JUSTICE AND COMPASSION. MAY OUR LIVES BE
SPENT IN THE SERVICE OF THE ONE WHO BRINGS SALVA-
TION, WHO CALLS US TO PUT ASIDE THE DARKNESS AND
LIVE IN THE LIGHT.

For Easter (The celebration of the resurrection of Jesus Christ)

CALL TO WORSHIP

Leader: Death is defeated, new life rises from the grave, and hope is reborn. Christ is risen!

UNISON: CHRIST IS RISEN INDEED!

Leader: This is the day that the Lord has made.

UNISON: LET US REJOICE AND BE GLAD IN IT!

PRAYER OF ADORATION AND CONFESSION

UNISON: LORD GOD, YOU CAUSE NEW LIFE TO BURST FORTH; WE TASTE HOPE, WE FEEL THE CHAINS OF FEAR AND OPPRESSION FALLING AWAY; WE SEE LIGHT AND KNOW THE RENEWAL OF HEART AND MIND AS THE STONES ARE REMOVED FROM THE TOMBS OF OUR LIVES. THE EARTH IS FILLED WITH DEATH, LIVES ARE SHATTERED, FAITH IS STRAINED, AND YOUR FAMILY LOOKS FOR SIGNS OF PROMISE AND CONFIDENCE, HOPE AND TRUST. ON THIS MOST HOLY DAY, WE PAUSE TO REMEMBER AND GIVE THANKS FOR FAITHFUL WOMEN, CHILDREN AND MEN WHO RESISTED THE FORCES OF DEATH AT WORK IN OUR HISTORY. IN THEM WE FIND A FULL MEASURE OF HOPE, THE SUSTAINING VISION OF LIFE AND COMPASSION, AND THE STRENGTH TO LABOR AGAINST THE FORCES OF HOSTILITY AND INJUSTICE IN OUR TIMES. THE STONES OF OUR ENTOMBMENT ARE ROLLED AWAY, AND THE FUTURE OPENS TO LIGHT AND FRESHNESS AS FEAR AND DISTRUST ARE DISPELLED. THE RADIANT BEAMS OF NEW HOPE AND UNDERSTANDING SCATTER THE SHADOWS OF SELF-INTEREST, INSECURITY, AND ENMITY. CHRIST IS RISEN! LET US LIVE FOR GOD'S JUSTICE AND PEACE. AMEN.

Remembering the Liberators

It is appropriate to remember the military liberation forces on Memorial Day, on *Yom haShoah* and in sermons or services where their deeds are the focus of public gratitude and attention. Public or community services are enriched by the presence of and the opportunity to express gratitude for the courage and compassion of the liberators. Some community observances honor both liberators and rescuers in the same service.

If it is appropriate to use hymns in the service, the following should be considered for inclusion:

"O Beautiful for Spacious Skies"
"Lift Every Voice and Sing"
"Eternal Father, Strong to Save"

INVOCATION

God who leads us beside still waters, you will for all in your
Creation quiet contentment, wholeness, and peace. But there are
times when evil prevails and chaos interferes with your will. In
those times the cosmos resounds with the agonies of war,
struggle, death, and much sorrow as it mourns its losses. Nations
rise up against nations, weapons of war and strength of arm
replace justice and peace as our refuge and consolation. Even
when the cause is just and war is the only way to resist evil, we
must confess that we have failed—failed to find peaceful ways
to resolve our conflicts. From the tragedy of war, we seek to
learn new and peaceful ways for nations and peoples to work
out their differences. Today we gather in grateful remembrance
of those who risked all in the service of ending the evils of the
Nazi era and whose mission led them to liberate the poor and
oppressed, those who were starved and orphaned, the brutalized
and abandoned. Through the thankfulness of history may they
know your peace and see themselves as your servants. In
Christ's name we pray. Amen.

It is possible that a member of your church, synagogue, or community
was part of a military unit responsible for liberating one or more of the
camps, or that there are men and women who served in medical corps or
with the Red Cross and were assigned to the death camps to provide care
for the victims. Local veterans organizations and the United States Holocaust Memorial Council may be useful in identifying such persons. The
liberators may be publicly recognized, and the minister, priest, or rabbi may
briefly recount the nature of their work or experience. The liberators may
be asked to meet with adult and youth groups to speak more fully about the
meaning of their experiences.

PRAYER OF REMEMBRANCE AND THANKSGIVING

Righteous God, ruler of nations, we remember and give thanks
for faithful men and women who boldly and bravely set themselves in harm's way and who, by their kind and caring ways
with victims of evil, bore witness to your righteousness, justice,

and love. Their eyes have recorded horrors that other of your children have endured, horrors that no person should be subjected to or made to remember. And yet the visions do not easily relinquish their hold. We pray for them the healing of memories, for the certainty that their cause was just and their mission in keeping with your will. The witness of their lives is an example for the generations. Grant, O God, that we may take into our lives the legacy of their faithfulness and goodness. With reverence and affection we remember the victims and give thanks for the compassion of the liberators.

BIBLICAL LITANY OF REMEMBRANCE

Leader: Our help is in the name of the Lord, (Ps. 124:8)

UNISON: WHO MADE HEAVEN AND EARTH.

Leader: What does the Lord require of us? (Micah 6:8)

UNISON: TO DO JUSTICE,

    TO LOVE TENDERLY, AND

    TO WALK HUMBLY WITH GOD.

Leader: What is the true worship that we should offer? (Rom. 12:2)

UNISON: DO NOT CONFORM TO THE SCHEMES OF THE WORLD,

Leader: But be transformed by a complete renewal of your mind,

UNISON: SO THAT YOU WILL KNOW WHAT IS THE GOOD AND ACCEPTABLE AND COMPLETE WILL OF GOD.

Leader: Whatever you would have people do for you, do the same for them: This is the meaning of the Law and the Prophets. (Mt. 7:12)

CONGREGATION: THOSE WHO WAIT FOR THE LORD SHALL RENEW THEIR STRENGTH, THEY SHALL MOUNT UP WITH WINGS LIKE EAGLES, THEY SHALL RUN AND NOT BE WEARY, THEY SHALL WALK AND NOT FAINT. (Isa. 40:31)

UNISON: LET JUSTICE FLOW LIKE A STREAM, AND RIGHTEOUSNESS LIKE A MIGHTY RIVER. (Amos 5:24)

For Yom haShoah (The Day of Remembrance of the Holocaust)

The primary elements of the service can be used here provided that they are inclusive and thoroughly avoid Christological references.

INVOCATION

God of Abraham and Sarah, Isaac, Deborah, and Jeremiah, You call us, through Your faithful servant Moses, to choose life and blessing. We have gathered to remember a time when powers and principalities chose death and curse. We gather to reclaim and honor the memories of those lost to the evils of Nazism: children and parents, old and young, families and friends, liberators and rescuers. We remember for the sake of the future. We remember unspeakable horrors and pray that coming generations will be spared because we have not forgotten; because we have labored to sanctify life. Amen.

For Pentecost (The day when the Creator's life-giving spirit came upon Christ's followers)

CALL TO WORSHIP

Leader: The Spirit of the living God fills and renews us.

UNISON: I WILL SING TO GOD AS LONG AS I LIVE. I WILL SING PRAISES TO MY REDEEMER WHILE I HAVE BEING.

Leader: Let us lift our voices to the God who inspires us to live justly, love tenderly, and walk humbly; whose spirit makes us bold and faithful.

UNISON: LET US WORSHIP THE SPIRIT OF THE LIVING GOD!

LITANY OF ADORATION AND CONFESSION

Leader: Spirit of God, descend upon us and renew our lives with joy and hope, mercy and forgiveness.

UNISON: WHERE OUR LIVES OR THE LIFE OF THE HUMAN FAMILY HAVE BECOME A DRIED AND LIFELESS DESERT, LET OUR ACTS OF COMPASSION AND OUR WORK FOR JUSTICE BE AN OASIS OF HOPE. LET THERE BE A REBIRTH OF TRUST FOR THOSE WHO SUFFER AND ARE OPPRESSED. LET OUR FAITH BE A BEACON OF CONFIDENCE FOR THOSE WHO HAVE LOST CONFIDENCE IN YOU OR IN YOUR CHURCH.

Leader: Keep us from the wilderness of uncaring and indifference;

UNISON: EMPOWER US BY YOUR SPIRIT TO BRING LIFE AND BLESSING AND TO TURN ASIDE DEATH AND CURSE.

Leader: Let us cherish the gifts and fruits of freedom and where others are enslaved, grant us the vision and courage to seek the end of their bondage.

UNISON: HAVE MERCY ON US WHEN OUR LIVES SERVE A LESSER CALLING THAN YOUR JUSTICE, O GOD, CREATOR OF ALL HUMANKIND. AMEN.

DATES: ANNUAL DAY OF REMEMBRANCE

The government of Israel established the internationally accepted date for the annual "Holocaust Remembrance Day," on the Hebrew calendar, as the twenty-seventh of the month of Nissan. The following dates for the annual public commemoration are set aside jointly by the Israeli government and the United States Holocaust Memorial Council:

1995	Thursday, April 27
1996	Tuesday, April 16
1997	Sunday, May 4
1998	Thursday, April 23
1999	Tuesday, April 13
2000	Tuesday, May 2

OTHER SIGNIFICANT DATES FOR COMMEMORATION

May 31, 1934: The German Evangelical Church, meeting in the First Confessional Synod, unanimously adopted the Theological Declaration of Barmen.

June 4, 1936: The Council of the German Evangelical Church sent its "Memorandum Submitted to Chancellor Hitler."

February 4, 1906: Dietrich Bonhoeffer was born.

April 9, 1945: After being implicated in the unsuccessful *Abwehr* resistance and conspiracy, Dietrich Bonhoeffer was transferred from the Buchenwald death camp to Schöenberg, and then to the Flossenbürg concentration camp where he was executed on this date. Within ten days, Allied military forces liberated Flossenbürg.

Chapter Ten

Sermon (Homily) Notes and Resources Celebrating the Christians Who Rescued Jews During the Nazi Era

INTRODUCTION AND SERMON RESOURCES

The following notes and resource lists will assist you in preparing a sermon (homily) suitable for a Christian worship service in which the *Shoah* is remembered and the courage and compassion of Christians who rescued Jews are celebrated.

It is not possible for a single sermon to do justice to the scope of the history and implications of the Nazi destruction of European Jewry. If the liturgical calendar or lectionary permit it, consider developing a sermon series in which several homilies focus on the history, issues, implications, and lessons of the Shoah. The following suggestions illustrate a possible three- or six-part sermon series (the number of sermons depends on the preacher's desire to broaden the individual foci and expand on them according to his or her interests).

First Sunday: "A Living Faith in an Age of Atrocity." In this sermon the focus may be on the questions and issues of theodicy—How do people of faith confront evil and suffering given the teaching of their traditions and affirmations of faith? It may begin with a brief history of the Shoah, or the history can be woven into various parts of the sermon, as they relate to the primary theme of faith in the midst of human suffering. The themes related to theodicy could be expanded to several sermons and class sessions.

Second Sunday: "Responding in an Age of Atrocity: Complicity or Compassion." The dual focus of this sermon would be on the role of both the German Church and the contemporary struggle to act responsibly in times or situations of evil. The preacher could expand on three possible responses or roles in light of denominational teachings and individual responsibility: complicity in evil, indifference, and resistance. This sermon would not go into the issue of rescue.

Third Sunday: "The Challenge of Compassion." This sermon would focus on and celebrate the courage, compassion, and faithfulness of Christians who rescued Jews during the Shoah. The sermon outline and the actual sermon text that follow give the preacher a variety of alternatives for homilies on this theme.

An optional fourth sermon in the series would be a reflection on "Building a Moral Society." Developing from the foundation of the preceding three homilies, this sermon would challenge the community of faith to imitate in the daily lives of its members the values and compassion of the Nazi-era rescuers and the spiritual, moral, and political conscience of the Resistance. The sermon could confront the often debilitating realization that people of faith reside in a world where countless individuals lack a moral foundation or do not participate in communities that nurture prosocial values and moral accountability, and where governments do not have either an ethical perspective or a sense of global responsibility. From that confrontation develops a challenge to live faithfully and act morally and altruistically on behalf of the common or societal good.

When preaching about the Christians who rescued Jews, several points should be noted:

First, few if any, of the rescuers considered themselves to be heroes or heroines; on the contrary, they were common people going about their customary routines rather than professional altruists or politically motivated interventionists. We do them a disservice and discourage caring and helping behavior in others when we portray role models as being unlike the common person.

Second, every act of compassion took courage, but not all interventions were selfless or life endangering. Some were simple acts of human decency, while others were filled with risk—both forms should be acknowledged and celebrated.

Finally, the rescuers who risked their lives or undertook extraordinary interventions were a faithful remnant numbering in the range of 10,000 to 12,000 (based on the honors bestowed by the Israeli government at *Yad Vashem*), from among the millions of persons in central and eastern Europe who could have assisted but did not.

SERMON BACKGROUND RESOURCES

A sermon celebrating the Christians who rescued during the war is enriched by sharing the stories of their activities. In addition to the resources and illustrations provided in the next chapters, the following texts are readily available in libraries and bookstores and will provide ample narrative anecdotes and sermon illustrations:

Carol Rittner and Sondra Myers, eds., *The Courage to Care* (New York University Press). This book is based on the video of the same name and provides narratives, background information, and suitable quotes from a cross section of rescuers and those whom they rescued. Some of their remarks are quoted in the next chapter.

Philip Hallie, *Lest Innocent Blood Be Shed* (Harper and Row). This is a deeply moving account of the highly successful rescue network established by Pastor and Mrs. André Trocmé from the French Huguenot church in Le Chambon-sur-Lignon. Full-length and classroom versions of the video, *Weapons of the Spirit*, are available to rent or purchase. Eyewitnesses and participants tell the story of the Huguenots and those whom they rescued.

Nechama Tec, *When Light Pierced the Darkness* (Oxford). The author offers a collection of personal remembrances and interviews with Polish nationals who rescued Jews.

Alexander Ramati, *The Assisi Underground* (Stein and Day). Ramati tells the story of the priests in the parish of Assisi, led by Fr. Rufino Niccacci, who protected 300 Jews.

Douglas Huneke, *The Moses of Rovno* (Dodd, Mead). This is the story of a German Christian who saved or protected the lives of several thousand Jews and others targeted by the Nazis. The epilogue identifies a cluster of traits, skills, and characteristics common to the rescuers with applications for those who would be caring and helpful today (only available from 240 Tiburon Boulevard, Tiburon, California 94920).

Samuel and Pearl Oliner, *The Altruistic Personality* (Free Press). This book is the result of a thorough scholarly study of the sources of altruism, based on interviews with rescuers and a control group of former Nazis.

Elie Wiesel and Albert Friedlander, *The Six Days of Destruction: Meditations Towards Hope* (Paulist Press). The authors, Shoah survivor and London rabbi, prepared this collection of six readings and reflections on the Shoah and sample liturgies. They are primarily suitable for synagogue, community, or interfaith *Yom haShoah* observances, but the stories and lessons have universal appeal.

Franklin Littell and Hubert Locke, eds., *The German Church Struggle and the Holocaust* (Wayne State University Press). This book is an enduring and important series of essays, by key thinkers, on the role of the German churches during the Shoah.

HONORING A RESCUER

It is possible that a Christian rescuer lives in or near your community. If so, you may wish to honor that person by having him or her present in the worship service, for an adult class, a forum for older elementary through high school-age students (college groups also), and/or for an interfaith forum (bringing together a neighboring synagogue and the church). Many rescuers are invited to speak in public, private, and parochial schools where they bring a note of realism to the study of what may seem to the young to be a distant and slightly abstract history. The Jewish Foundation to Sustain Christian Rescuers can assist you in determining if a rescuer lives in your area and might be available to participate (c/o Anti-Defamation League, 823 United Nations Plaza, New York, New York 10017).

RESOURCES FOR A CHILDREN'S SERMON

Many pastors and rabbis include in their services a reflection time or object lesson for children and youth. The theme of celebrating goodness, courage, and caring is very appropriate for these age groups. The liturgist may use this portion of the service to introduce and honor a visiting rescuer or survivor.

A variety of biblical stories can be used to bridge Scripture, rescuers, and the day-to-day lives of young people. Those passages are noted in the next section of this chapter. One of the most effective ways to ensure the investment of children and youth in a reflection or object lesson is to ignite their empathic imaginations and get them talking about an experience they may have shared in common with those in the primary and biblical stories.

Our assumption must be that the vast majority of children and youth in church and synagogue settings are goodwilled human beings who want to act compassionately and that they generally lack developed, in-place skills to consistently and successfully respond altruistically. At the very least, a reflection that unites Scripture, a rescuer story, and the lives of the young people will provide them with an additional moral role model, a sense of what it means to act in altruistic ways, and encourage them to look for daily opportunities to be caring and helpful.

The children's sermon might begin with a brief, dramatic rendering of the story of "the good Samaritan." The core message of this story is that one (the Samaritan) who was the least likely person to help the badly injured man by the side of the road (the Jew) actually put aside his distrust and risked helping a stranger who was also an enemy. Jesus' admonition at the end of the story, "Go and do likewise," is the challenge to all believers. Take care not to make the story anti-Semitic by condemning the religious people who passed by without helping. Remember, if they touched a dead body, they were ritually unclean for an extended time. Rabbinic Judaism has partially resolved this dilemma, permitting actions that save a life, even if taken on the Sabbath.

It is now time to ask the children if anyone has acted in a caring way toward them or if any of them have ever been saved from danger. Shift the focus and ask them to think of a time when they were caring or helpful toward someone else, or if there was a time when they helped someone who was in trouble or endangered. Encourage a few of them to briefly share an experience.

Next, give a brief summary of the Nazi-era experience of the Jews. I avoid going into an explicit recitation of the horrors. Children often lock into the violence more than into the compassion and courage. Finish the lesson with the story, preferably, of a child or youth rescuer, or if necessary, of an adult rescuer. Ask the children how the rescuer fulfilled Jesus' directive to act like the "good" Samaritan. In their daily lives, most young people will be faced with a range of opportunities to be caring and helpful, but it is unlikely that any of them will face circumstances of the magnitude of the Shoah; however, some of them may find themselves in emergency situations. Two observations: First, people who act in caring and compassionate ways in their daily lives are more likely to recognize and respond altruistically to a more demanding situation. The objective is to help children ground their lives at home, in school, and in play groups in personal values and behaviors that are routinely oriented toward the well-being of others.

Second, given the modern perils that endanger children, it is worthwhile taking the time to brainstorm with them how they might act when someone is in danger or special need of help and a young person feels compelled to do something to respond. It is important for them to understand that the best thing they can do is seek the assistance of a parent or a known adult, or dial the free emergency phone number and summon help. Under no circumstances should a child place his or her life in direct and imminent danger or submit to such perils as abduction.

If the liturgist is retelling an account of rescue, whenever possible, the focus should be on youngsters who rescued during the war. The following books are available in libraries and bookstores:

Claire Huchet Bishop, *Twenty and Ten* (Puffin Books). This classic is a true account of twenty French children who hid and protected ten Jewish refugee children during the occupation. It is a very touching and courageous story.

Milton Meltzer, *Rescue: The Story of How Gentiles Saved Jews in the Holocaust* (Harper and Row). This collection of well-written accounts of rescue is suitable for older children and youth but easily adaptable.

Johanna Reiss, *The Upstairs Room* (Bantam Books). This is another classic, written this time from the perspective of a Jewish youth who was hidden and protected. It is also adaptable for a children's sermon.

SERMON NOTES

Biblical texts appropriate to the observance are listed, with optional sermon titles, in Chapter Nine. The following outline can be adapted for use with any of the texts, and the liturgical seasons can be observed to augment and enrich the meaning of both the sermon and the seasons.

Prologue

Rabbi Harold Schulweis has observed that most people know the names and deeds of Adolf Hitler, Adolf Eichmann, Klaus Barbie, and other Nazi killers. Very few, however, can identify John Weidner, André and Magda Trocmé, Irene Opdyke, Herman Graebe, or Raoul Wallenberg. Rabbi Schulweis and other scholars of the Shoah stress the importance of knowing the horrible offenses committed by the first group of people, the kind of government they backed, and the forces that guided their behavior. It is equally important to know about those who did not conform to the routines of the killers or become bystanders—who resisted daily acts of inhumanity by protecting and aiding those who were vulnerable to the Nazi machine. *To study only the killers is to leave people with a one-dimensional view of humankind; to celebrate only the goodness of the few is to trivialize the suffering of millions.*

Narrative

Of the times and of the rescuers, Nobel Laureate Elie Wiesel has written, "All the gates of compassion seemed to have closed on us. . . . Only a few had the courage to care. . . . In those times, one climbed to the summit of humanity by simply remaining human."[1] What does it mean to "simply remain human?"

Illustrations

For Pastor and Mrs. Trocmé and the Huguenots of Le Chambon, who had only heard about the fate of the Jews, it meant building a carefully coordinated, parish-wide effort to shelter, feed, and protect Jewish refugees from Nazi and French Vichy authorities. Their efforts were successful in spite of arrests and overwhelming odds. Their story is told in Philip Hallie's book *Lest Innocent Blood Be Shed* and in Pierre Sauvage's film *Weapons of the Spirit*.

For fourteen-year-old Stefka, a Polish farmgirl, it meant that on a cold winter day, when she met a young Jewish refugee and her very sick father, she had to trust a comment she overheard her parents make about helping Jews. When her mother and youngest brother sought refuge away from the troops, and after her father and brother were taken away by a Nazi labor recruitment unit, Stefka spent more than a year solely responsible for the two hidden refugees and her farm. She succeeded in her dangerous and complicated mission.

For Knud Dyby (pronounced Die-be), who had been a member of the Danish Royal Guard and an apprentice printer in Copenhagen, it meant joining the underground. In the fall of 1943 when German forces began arresting Danish Jews, Mr. Dyby organized a fleet of small fishing boats to carry Jews past Nazi patrols and on to safety in Sweden. Though Mr. Dyby was betrayed by collaborators and went into hiding, he continued his efforts. Like nearly all rescuers, he does not consider his work to have been heroic—only a part of his human duty.

A Dutch woman made the moral choice to save forty-two Jewish neighbors. She deftly avoided questions from those who sought to understand her motivations. Finally, she responded to one. With simplicity and clarity she said, "You know what St. Paul wrote in Romans 12:2. That is why." She quoted the passage, "Be not conformed to this world, but be transformed by a complete renewal of your mind." She then said, "To conform would have meant betraying or killing Jews. To be transformed meant saving them. That was my only choice."

Herman Graebe, a German engineer working on the railroads in the Ukraine, summarized what it meant to "simply remain human" when he said, "I only did what everyone should have done, what anyone could have done." Mr. Graebe knew, however, that not everyone had the skills, the commitment, the opportunities, or the values to save the lives of desperately endangered persons. As the Nazis retreated in near defeat, Graebe commandeered a forty-car train and took nearly 350 of his Jewish workers from the Ukraine to Warsaw, from Warsaw to Dusseldorf, and from there he led them to the Allied military forces and safety. He saw and responded to the many opportunities he observed to act altruistically. He was also in a position of power that enabled him to do things, such as take control of an entire train and direct it to carry endangered Jews into the land of the killers. Graebe carefully and intentionally planned his rescues in order to minimize danger and ensure success and safety for his Jewish workers. After the war, he routinely advised people to prepare themselves to act in ways that were caring and helpful.

Questions to Include or Address in a Sermon

1. What enabled the Christian rescuers to act as they did in the worst situations?

2. How can we reconcile the moral actions of the Lutheran pastor Martin Niemöller and the fatal equivocations of so many other religious leaders in most of the other nations?

3. Many Americans fought the Nazis, fully committed to "making the world safe for democracy." Even so, U.S. and Allied military and foreign policymakers, with full and incontrovertible evidence, ignored the fate of the Jews. Why? What are the implications of this fact for the positions taken by governments relative to global human rights violations and genocide treaties?

4. Why did the German Confessing Churches take a stand against National Socialism while so many other churches failed to speak out or act? And yet, why did their statement contain obvious vestiges of centuries-old anti-Semitism?

5. Why did more than two-thirds of Polish Jewry die, while nearly all Danish Jews survived the Shoah?

6. What can we learn from the rescuers that will help us to be compassionate and involved today? Please refer to the next section on implications and applications.

Implications and Applications

Nazi-era rescuers embodied the biblical vision of a humane society by refusing to conform to destructive, ill-willed authorities and by actively observing the biblical mandate not to stand idly by when others suffer, are oppressed, or victimized.

Rescuers bore witness to the teaching of Scripture that says, "Love must not be a matter of words or talk; it must be genuine and show itself in action" (I John 3:18). These Christians consciously linked their faith and their concern for others in such a way that they were empowered to save lives.

Although we do not live in a Nazi-like era or society, we are called to a daily living that, in smaller ways, reflects the caring, kindness, and service of the rescuers. By living with compassion day by day, we will be able to act with courage and compassion in the most difficult of times. Most rescuers began their efforts with very simple acts of kindness and decency that led them to ever bolder acts that protected lives.

In a time of rising incidents of anti-Semitism, racism, hate crimes, and violence, we are called to confront, reject, and resist the forces that lead to malevolence, division, and destructive behavior.

An important contemporary lesson from the Shoah and the rescuers is that we are not exempt from active concern about modern global forces of death, nor can we tolerate any remnants of the silence, indifference, unchecked stereotypes, and moral lassitude that fueled the Nazi era. Governmental policies that do not respond to incidents of mass murder, wholesale violations of human and civil rights, or genocide cannot be tolerated.

These various issues may focus contemporary applications and comments on such concerns as the increasing incidence of hate crimes and anti-Semitism nationally and internationally, the reassertion of the neo-Nazi and white Aryan movements, the effects of poverty and social marginalization, nuclear threats, dangers to the fragile global ecology, violence directed toward refugees and immigrants, and situations in which basic rights are violated. Examples that come to mind include, but are not limited to, the fate of peoples in the genocide occurring in the Balkan states; the election of a Russian nationalist who is dangerously xenophobic; anti-immigrant legislation and sentiments in the United States; attacks on refugees in England, Germany, and France; and the violations of fundamental human rights in China. Additional specific contemporary illustrations can be inserted and considered as appropriate.

Conclusion

We remember the Shoah, its victims, and its lessons; we celebrate and seek to imitate the compassion of the rescuers; and re-commit ourselves to a faith that calls on us to "turn aside evil, love good, and maintain justice at the gate" (Amos) and that commands us, "do not conform to the world, but show in the way you live, the new mind which Christ has given you" (St. Paul in Romans). How shall we together fulfill these biblical mandates and live faithfully in our times?

A MODEL SERMON CELEBRATING NAZI-ERA RESCUERS

Title: "Be Not Conformed"

Scripture: Micah 6:8, Amos 5:14–15, and Romans 12:1–12 (emphasis on 12:2)

Text: Refer to the historical context section of Chapter Eight and integrate elements of the history as you deem appropriate.

Rabbi Harold Schulweis, the spiritual leader of the Valley Beth Shalom Synagogue in Encino, California, was the first to recognize the importance of remembering and learning from the courage and compassion of the Christians, the non-Jews who saved Jews from the Nazis and their collaborators. Rabbi Schulweis observed that most people know the names and deeds of Adolf Eichmann, Hitler, Klaus Barbie,and the other masterminds of genocide. Very few, however, can identify John Weidner, André and Magda Trocmé, Raoul Wallenberg, Irene Opdyke, Herman Graebe, or Knud Dyby; and were it not for the movie by Steven Spielberg, few people would know or remember Oskar Schindler.

It is imperative that we know what horrible offenses the first group of people committed, the sort of government they backed, and the forces that guided their behavior. It is equally essential for us to know about those who did not conform to the routines of mass murder or become indifferent bystanders; who instead resisted the daily acts of inhumanity by protecting and aiding Jews, dissidents, Gypsies, homosexuals, and others targeted by the policies of the National Socialists in Nazi Germany.

Because of the sheer magnitude of their numbers and their profoundly evil deeds, we know more about the Nazi killers than we do about the compassion and courage of the rescuers. We would have hoped that tens of thousands of people in central and eastern Europe had acted with the altruism of a Wallenberg or Schindler, Trocmé or Dyby, but that was not to be the case. Because of this fact, we must remember, speak of, celebrate, and learn from the studied bravery and goodness of that remnant—numbering less than 20,000—who remained faithful and moral, who selflessly saved lives. To exclusively focus on the killers is to leave people with a one-dimensional view of humankind; to celebrate only the goodness of the few is to trivialize the suffering of millions. Today, we seek the balance so that we might have hope and at the same time take a vow on behalf of those who suffer at the hands of history.

Of the times and of the rescuers, Shoah survivor and Nobel Laureate Elie Wiesel has said, "All the gates of compassion seemed to have closed on us. . . . Only a few had the courage to care. . . . In those times, one climbed to the summit of humanity by simply remaining human."* What does it mean to "simply remain human"? For Pastor and Mrs. André Trocmé and the Huguenots of Le Chambon-sur-Lignon, France, who had only heard about the fate of Jews, it meant building a carefully coordinated, parish-wide effort to shelter, feed, and protect Jewish refugees from Nazi and French

---

* Elie Wiesel, quoted in *The Courage to Care*, edited by Carol Rittner and Sondra Myers (New York: New York University Press, 1986), p. XI.

Vichy authorities. Their efforts were a success in spite of arrests, killings, and overwhelming odds.

For the fourteen-year-old Polish Baptist farm girl Stefka, it meant that on a cold winter day, when she met a young Jewish refugee and her very sick father, she had to trust a comment she overheard her parents make about helping Jewish refugees. When her father and youngest brother were taken away by a Nazi labor recruitment unit, Stefka spent more than a year solely responsible for the two hidden refugees and the farm. She succeeded in her dangerous and complicated mission. Her family was reunited, and the two Jewish refugees, who tragically lost everyone else in their family, survived.

For Knud Dyby, who had been a member of the Danish Royal Guard and an apprentice printer in Copenhagen, it meant joining the underground. In September 1943, when German forces began arresting Danish Jews, Mr. Dyby organized a fleet of small fishing boats to carry Jews past Nazi patrol boats and on to safety in Sweden. Dyby was betrayed by collaborationists and went into hiding but continued his efforts in great secrecy. Like so many of the rescuers, Mr. Dyby does not consider his work to have been heroic, only a part of his human duty.

There are troubling, timely questions that must be asked: What enabled the righteous to act as they did in the worst of circumstances? Why did ninety percent of Danish Jewry survive the Nazi onslaught while ninety-five percent of the Jews in Poland, Latvia, and Luthuania perished? Why did the Orthodox leaders in Bulgaria protect Jews while the churches of Slovakia sanctioned the killing? Why did the Confessing Churches in Germany take a stand against National Socialism while so many other churches either failed to speak out and act or supported the Reich? How can we reconcile the moral actions of the German Lutheran pastor Martin Niemöller with the equivocations of Pope Pius XII or the conformity with evil of Reich Bishop Mueller? Many Americans went to war against Nazis fully committed to "making the world safe for democracy." Even so, U.S. and Allied military and foreign policymakers, with full and incontrovertible evidence, ignored the fate of the Jews. Of that travesty, Dr. Irving Greenberg wrote, "[A] war that was being fought to save democracy in general betrayed the most fundamental responsibilities of humanity and democracy."†

There are moments and experiences in the life of each person and nation, circumstances when a moral choice must be made. Such choices in the Nazi era spelled the difference between life and death. The king of Denmark made a moral choice that foiled the plan of the Reich to divide the peoples

---

† Irving Greenberg, quoted in *Auschwitz: Beginning of a New Era?* edited by Eva Fleischner (New York: KTAV Publishing House, 1974), p. 37.

of a nation. Unlike Jews in all other occupied lands, the Jews of Denmark did not wear yellow stars or patches. We must ask: How many Jewish lives would have been saved if the Allies had chosen to bomb the tracks leading into Auschwitz rather than photograph them or, less dangerously, sent envoys with visas and other papers, as Sweden sent Raoul Wallenberg into Hungary? Herman Graebe, a leading German engineer and project manager assigned to the Reich Railroad Administration, made a moral choice as he watched a mobile killing unit destroy the Jews of Rovno in the Ukraine. He became a prey of Gestapo informants as he successfully aided thousands of Jews throughout the Ukraine and Germany.

A Dutch woman made the moral choice to save forty-two Jewish neighbors. Years later, she deftly avoided questions about her motivations until in an interview I asked her simply, "Why did you save Jews?" She responded with equal simplicity and clarity, "You know what St. Paul wrote in Romans 12:2. That is why." She recited the quotation, which was in the morning lesson, "Be not conformed to this world, but be transformed by a new way of thinking." She then said, "To conform would mean betraying or killing Jews. To be transformed meant saving them. That was my only choice." There were, and there are, moments of encounter and confrontation, and moments of moral choice. Between 1933 and 1945, only the few chose for life and on behalf of humanity.

Today, we remember and honor the righteous Gentiles, as the nation of Israel refers to them; we honor them not with certificates, trees, and medals but in our hearts and by our commitment to remember their courage and to perpetuate their compassion in our lives. We shall honor them by searching our own hearts and preparing ourselves not only to make the moral choices but to live daily a caring and humane lifestyle. We honor them by covenanting with them to teach our young people to be just, moral, life affirming, humane, and compassionate.

Nazi-era rescuers embodied the biblical vision of society by refusing to conform to destructive, ill-willed authorities and by actively observing the scriptural mandate not to stand idly by when others suffer, are oppressed, or are victimized. By their lives, they bore witness to the Christian Scripture that teaches, "Love must not be a matter of words or talk; it must be genuine and show itself in action" (I John 3:18). Although there are global evils that mimic the Nazi era, we do not live in that time. In our personal lives, we are called to a daily living that, in modest ways, reflects the caring, kindness, and service of the rescuers. In our national life, we are called to reject and resist the forces that lead to hatred, division, and destructive behaviors and government policies.

As global citizens, we must learn a most critical lesson from the Shoah: that we are not exempt from active concern about or resistance to modern global forces of death. Neither can we tolerate any vestige of the silence, indifference, unchecked stereotypes, and moral lassitude that contributed to the Nazi era. Today, for us, it is the peoples of the Balkan states who cry out for peace, protection, and justice; it is the voice of the proposed victims of a xenophobic Russian nationalist that we hear from the East; and it is the violations of human rights in China that arrest our attention. The knock at our doors today may not be from European Jewish refugees but rather from Central Americans fleeing modern-day versions of Nazi mobile killing units. Regardless of their origins, we must learn from the Jews and the rescuers of Jews how we shall live and serve our Lord today, here.

We remember the Shoah, its victims, and its lessons; we remember, celebrate, and imitate the compassion and decency of the rescuers; and we recommit ourselves to a faith that calls on us to "turn aside evil, love good, and maintain justice at the gate" (Amos) and that commands us, "Do not conform to the world, but show in the way you live, the new mind which Christ has given you" (Paul in Romans).

FOLLOW-UP ON THE SERMON

An intergenerational education forum affords congregants the opportunity to enter into a dialogue with the sermon and to reflect on the implications of the Shoah and the actions of the rescuers. Very often it is possible for such programs to be either ecumenical or interfaith. In Chapter Twelve, there is an outline for a three-part study program that can be adapted for a variety of uses and settings.

Chapter Eleven

Quotations and Aphorisms Focusing on the Faith and Moral Courage of Nazi-Era Rescuers for Use in Sermons and Illustrations

The following materials can be used in sermons, study groups, and post-sermon dialogues to illustrate or reinforce various points about the Shoah and Nazi rescue.

HAROLD M. SCHULWEIS

Rabbi, Temple Valley Beth Shalom, Encino, California, and founder of the Jewish Foundation for Christian Rescuers

The tragedy of the Holocaust cannot be reversed. What remains to be done is to raise the sparks of human decency out of the impenetrable darkness. There is an obligation to recognize goodness, not just with rhetoric, but through deeds of loving kindness. (Conference on "Moral Courage," 1991)

ELIE WIESEL

Shoah survivor, author, and recipient of the Nobel Peace Prize in 1986

If someone suffers and he keeps silent, it can be a good silence. If someone suffers and I keep silent, then it is a destructive silence. If we envisage literature and human destiny as endeavors by man [humankind] to redeem himself [itself], then we must admit the obsession, the overall dominating theme of responsibility, that we are responsible for one another. I am responsible for his or her suffering, for his or her destiny. If not, we are condemned by our solitude forever and it has no meaning. (Quoted in *Harry James Cargas in Conversation with Elie Wiesel*)

There were so few [Christian rescuers] because indifference is a very comfortable position. You don't have to worry that the Gestapo or KGB will knock on your door. . . . [The night before our family was sent to Auschwitz] a member of the Hungarian police told my father that if he was to learn of our fate he would come to us. I remember that night there was a knock on the window. It didn't take much courage, a knock on the window. Because of that man I carried the image of the Righteous Gentile for years. (From a lecture at Lynchburg College, Lynchburg, Virginia)

PASTOR MARTIN NIEMÖLLER

Minister and early leader of the Resistance to National Socialism; arrested in 1937 and imprisoned for seven years for his public opposition to Adolf Hitler and Reich policies.

In Germany they came first for the Communists, and I didn't speak up because I wasn't a Communist. Then they came for the Jews, and I didn't speak up because I wasn't a Jew. Then they came for the trade unionists, and I did not speak out—because I was not a trade unionist. Then they came for the Catholics, and I did not speak out—because I was a Protestant. Then they came for me and by that time there was no one left to speak up. (Quoted in *Exile in the Fatherland: Letters from Moabit Prison*, edited by Hubert G. Locke)

PRIMO LEVI

Primo Levi was born in Turin, Italy, and trained as a chemist; arrested and sent to Auschwitz in 1944 for his efforts with antifascist resistance, he survived and became a prolific author.

Levi writes of Lorenzo, an Italian civilian worker who brought him a piece of bread and the remainder of his ration every day for six months:

I believe it was really due to Lorenzo that I am alive today; and not so much for his material aid, as for his having constantly reminded me by his presence, by his natural and plain manner of being good, that there still exists a just world outside our own, something and someone still pure and whole, not corrupt, not savage . . . something difficult to define, a remote possibility of good but for which it was worth surviving. . . . Thanks to Lorenzo I managed not to forget that I myself was a man. (Quoted in *Survival of Auschwitz*)

ANNE FRANK

It's really a wonder that I haven't dropped all my ideals, because they seem so absurd and impossible to carry out. Yet I keep them, because in spite of everything

I still believe that people are really good at heart. I simply can't build up my hopes on a foundation consisting of confusion, misery, and death. I see the world gradually being turned into a wilderness, I hear the ever approaching thunder, which will destroy us too, I can feel the suffering of millions and yet, if I look up into the heavens, I think that it will all come right, that this cruelty too will end, and that peace and tranquillity will return again. In the meantime, I must uphold my ideals, for perhaps the time will come when I shall be able to carry them out. (From *Anne Frank: The Diary of a Young Girl*)

DIETRICH BONHOEFFER

Protestant (Lutheran) theologian executed by the German government for resisting National Socialism and working with the underground

There remains for us only the very narrow way, often extremely difficult to find, of living every day as if it were our last, and yet living in faith and responsibility as though there were to be a great future. . . . Some Christians think it impious for anyone to hope and prepare for a better earthly future. They think the meaning of present events is chaos, disorder, and catastrophe, and in resignation or pious escapism they surrender all responsibility for reconstruction and future generations. It may be that the day of judgment will dawn tomorrow; and in that case, though not before, we shall gladly stop working for a better future. (*Letters and Papers from Prison*, edited by Eberhard Bethge)

HERMAN F. GRAEBE

A German Christian and engineer assigned to manage the development of Nazi railroad services through the Ukraine; Mr. Graebe was honored by the Israeli government as a Righteous Gentile for saving 348 Jews by taking them through Poland and Germany and delivering them to the safety of the United States Army; he also saved or aided thousands of Jews, peasants, dissidents, and Gypsies in occupied lands.

Most of the Jews I had saved in Rovno were dead. I found it very hard to accept the limitations imposed on me by fate. My cunning should have been more effective than all the rifles of the Reich. My only consolation—and it took me a long time before I could accept it—was the knowledge that I gave some people a reprieve, an opportunity, a moment of life in a sea of death. Sometimes, now years later, I think of more things I could have done to save more people. I am not sure that anything would have worked better. I only wish that the people I had rescued could have been saved to see life on the other side of the war. (Quoted in *The Moses of Rovno*, by Douglas K. Huneke)

A DUTCH RESCUER OF JEWS

She hid forty-two Jews in her apartment during the occupation, one at a time, each in a closet, attic, or under a bed; a devout Calvinist, she turned to Scripture to explain the source of her compassion and courage.

"Why did I hide Jews?" A long silence followed as she pondered a question that she later said she had never once considered. Finally, she responded, "You know what Saint Paul said in Romans 12:2. That is why I did it. He wrote, 'Be not conformed to this world but be transformed by the complete renewal of your mind, so as to know what is the acceptable, perfect, and good will of God.'" Another long silence ensued before she concluded, "If I had turned my back, ignored their [Jews'] knock at my door, or acted like the collaborators, I would have conformed to the evils of the world. But to hide Jews was to be transformed and freed so I could do the will of God." (Quoted in "Glimpses of Light in a Vast Darkness: A Study of Era Rescuers," by Douglas K. Huneke)

MAGDA TROCMÉ

With her husband André, the pastor of the Huguenot church in the French village of Le Chambon, Mrs. Trocmé was honored by Israel for turning their church into a community of rescue.

It is important, too, to know that we were a bunch of people together. This is not a handicap, but a help. If you have to fight it alone, it is more difficult. But we had the support of people we knew, of people who understood without knowing precisely all that they were doing or would be called to do. None of us thought that we were heroes. We were just people trying to do our best. . . . In the end, I would like to say to people, Remember that in your life there will be lots of circumstances that will need a kind of courage, a kind of decision of your own, not about other people, but about yourself. I would not say more. (Quoted in *The Courage to Care*, edited by Carol Rittner and Sondra Myers)

MARION PRITCHARD

Dr. Pritchard hid Jews in her family home in the Netherlands and was forced to kill a Dutch police officer who tried to betray a Jewish family to the Nazis.

It did not occur to me to do anything other than I did. . . . I think you have a responsibility to yourself to behave decently. We all have memories of times we should have done something and didn't. And it gets in the way for the rest of your life. . . . Being brought up in the Anglican Church . . . imbued me early on with a strong conviction that we are our brothers' keepers. When you truly believe that, you have to behave that way in order to be able to live with yourself. (Quoted in *The Courage to Care*, edited by Carol Rittner and Sondra Myers)

Chapter Twelve

Outline and Resources for a Church or Interfaith Study Group

Liturgical observances of the Shoah and events honoring Nazi-era rescuers are greatly enriched when people prepare in advance and when they have an opportunity to reflect together following such events. Observances and study groups have the most impact when they are interfaith and intergenerational. Wherever possible, a study group should include church members, congregants from a neighboring synagogue, and if appropriate, congregants from other churches or ecumenical associations; and special emphasis should be given to having participation from students from both traditions (middle school through high school age).

The following format has met with success in a variety of situations and may be adapted to meet the needs of an individual congregation or an interfaith program. Each session should last ninety minutes and include informal time at the beginning and end and a short break in the middle.

OUTLINE FOR CHURCH OR INTERFAITH STUDY GROUP

Session I. The Historical and Personal Context of the Shoah

A. The minister or rabbi, or a local teacher or professor, knowledgeable in the antecedents, history, and consequences of the Shoah should make a thirty- to forty-five-minute presentation on that topic. The Holocaust Classroom Posters series (available from Holocaust Resource Centers or the regional offices of the Anti-Defamation League) that portrays the period of the Nazi era may be effectively used to illustrate the context of the war years.

B. A survivor of the Shoah may be invited to speak on his or her personal experiences of the Shoah. Adequate opportunity should be given for the presentation and for the study group to interact with the survivor. This is always a moving encounter that is very useful in transitioning the group from abstract historical review to a personalized, firsthand report of the experience. Most local or regional Jewish Federations or Community Relations Councils will assist in arranging for a survivor to speak. Sometimes it is helpful if the survivor is able to attend each session and to participate with other members.

C. A former military person who participated in the liberation of the death camps may be invited to speak about his experiences.

D. Participants may view a video such as *Night and Fog* (twenty-eight minutes; a gripping, very graphic documentary with a distinct moral message) or *Genocide* (fifty-two minutes; explicit, chronological documentary). These films should be fully previewed because the visualizations may be difficult for some people to watch.

E. Preparation for the next session should include the reading of *Night* by Elie Wiesel, a history of the Shoah should be started, and at least one of the texts on the rescue of Jews should be read.

Session II. An Introduction to Rescue

If it is at all possible, arrangement should be made to invite a rescuer to speak to the class. Costs can be shared with local schools and civic organizations that may also feature presentations by the rescuer. In either the absence of a rescuer or after a rescuer has spoken, follow this session outline.

A. View the video *The Courage to Care* (twenty-eight minutes). The booklet with the video offers a limited study guide with discussion questions for viewers.

B. Participants divide into groups that are balanced by tradition and age. The groups should review and discuss the following:

1. Personal reactions to experiences related by survivors and rescuers on the video.

2. What enabled the rescuers to act as they did? What qualities, characteristics, and values did the rescuers share in common? (Note: In the epilogue of the book *The Moses of Rovno*, by Douglas Huneke, there is a listing and description of a cluster of common characteristics and skills shared by rescuers. The epilogue may be copied and distributed solely for use by this class. Similarly, Samuel and Pearl Oliner, in their book *The Altruistic Personality*, have compiled a careful and extensive listing of traits and characteristics. These two resources may be useful in giving the

discussions an additional focus. There is a range of research and thinking about the commonalities, with some scholars describing different characteristics.)

C. The participants return to the full group and share their reactions to the video and their observations about the rescuers.

D. View the classroom version of the video by Pierre Sauvage, *Weapons of the Spirit* (thirty minutes).

E. Once again the groups should be formed and the questions discussed relevant to the second video. Some people may wish to read and comment on Philip Hallie's book *Lest Innocent Blood Be Shed*, which chronicles the rescue efforts of Pastor and Mrs. Trocmé in Le Chambon.

F. Preparation for the last session should include the reading of an additional book about rescue, and the book on the history of the Shoah should be completed.

Session III. Conclusion

A. The minister and rabbi should be prepared to address the biblical and theological roots of anti-Semitism. This discussion should be concise and used to establish that *(1) the Shoah had its origins in centuries of theological and social anti-Judaism and (2) Nazi-era rescuers were able to overcome centuries of religious, political, and social prejudice in order to act altruistically.* In that sense, rescuers represented a remnant or minority perspective, and their actions were predicated on religiously inspired nonconformity. A well-regarded resource for preparation is Father Edward Flannery's book *The Anguish of the Jews: Twenty-three Centuries of Anti-Semitism*.

B. A Nazi-era rescuer may be invited to meet with the class and describe his or her experiences and rescue activities. If it is not possible to have a rescuer speak, a survivor of the Shoah who was rescued may be asked to speak of that experience. If neither a rescuer nor a rescued survivor is available, you may wish to show the video *Weapons of the Spirit* during this session rather than in Session II. You may prefer to show the longer video *The Avenue of the Just* (fifty-seven minutes) and conduct similar small-group discussions based on the viewer reaction to the film.

C. The facilitator(s) of the program should conclude with a presentation on the implications and lessons derived generally from the Shoah and specifically from the activities of the rescuers. The primary question to be addressed in concluding this session and the series is, How shall we be different because of what we have learned through this encounter with genocide and compassion?

Session IV. Concluding Observance

Integral to the study program is an observance that either begins or ends the study or comes after the second session. The larger community may be invited to participate in the observance.

Leaders of youth and college-age groups may follow the general format suggested above for programs directed at these grade levels.

Church libraries would do well to include a collection of the books and video resources noted in the outlines for the service and sermon and in the list of quotes. The presence of the texts will encourage further study and interaction in classes and may contribute to the formation of an interfaith dialogue group that continues after the observance and that might cover a wider range of topics.

ADDITIONAL RESOURCES

Video/Film Guide

A. Rescuers
   The Courage to Care
   The Avenue of the Just
   Weapons of the Spirit (full length)
   Weapons of the Spirit (classroom length)
B. History
   Night and Fog
   Genocide

Unless otherwise indicated, the audiovisual resources are available from the Braun Center for Holocaust Studies of the Anti-Defamation League (823 United Nations Plaza, New York, New York 10017) or from regional offices of the Anti-Defamation League.

Study Programs and Poster Series

Witness to the Holocaust. A video and seven-session study program with a guide ably written by Isaiah Kuperstein, Henry Hausdorff, and Doris Gow and distributed by CLAL—National Jewish Center for Learning and Leadership (421 Seventh Avenue, New York, New York 10001).

The Holocaust Classroom Poster Series can be ordered from the Anti-Defamation League.

Books Suitable for the Study Group

Milton Meltzer. *Rescue: The Story of How Gentiles Saved Jews in the Holocaust.*

Philip Hallie. *Lest Innocent Blood Be Shed: The Story of the Village of Le Chambon and How Goodness Happened There.*

Elie Wiesel. *Night.*

Samuel P. Oliner and Pearl M. Oliner. *The Altruistic Personality: Rescuers of Jews In Nazi Europe.*

Douglas K. Huneke. *The Moses of Rovno.*

Nechama Tec. *Dry Tears: The Story of a Lost Childhood* and *In the Lion's Den: The Life of Oswald Rufeisen.*

André Schwarz-Bart. *The Last of the Just.*

Chapter Thirteen

For the Life and Service of Dietrich Bonhoeffer: A Service of Remembrance and Gratitude

HISTORICAL-BIOGRAPHICAL CONTEXT

Dietrich Bonhoeffer was born the sixth of eight children, the youngest of four sons, in Breslau (Wrocław, Poland) on February 4, 1906, to Karl and Paula Bonhoeffer. His father was a professor of psychiatry and chief of the clinic in that community. Paula Bonhoeffer studied to be a teacher, raised her children, and initially taught them at home. Her origins were in the aristocracy, and her father was a professor of theology and, briefly, the pastor to Kaiser Wilhelm II. In the 1930s Paula Bonhoeffer assisted her son's pastoral and theological colleagues who needed connections, protection, or counsel. In 1912, Karl Bonhoeffer was appointed to the faculty of Berlin University, and the family resettled in that city.

In 1923 Dietrich Bonhoeffer began his theological studies at Tübingen. His studies eventually took him to Berlin, later to service as an assistant pastor in Barcelona, and in 1930 to studies at Union Theological Seminary in New York City. In the fall of 1933 Bonhoeffer joined Pastor Martin Niemöller in taking serious exception to the impact on the church of the Aryan Clause (*Arierparagraph*), which was introduced in April 1933 to exclude non-Aryans (read: Jews) from membership in all political, social, and cultural associations and to purge Jews from most positions in the public sector and from participation by converts in and ordination to ministry in the German church. The 1935 Nuremberg Laws codified these policies in general law. Bonhoeffer consulted with Niemöller in the establishment of the Pastor's Emergency League, which surprisingly found quick and reasonably good support for its resistance to the Aryan Clause.

In spite of the initial successes, the German church authorities prevailed, and in short order Bonhoeffer simultaneously felt seriously at odds with many of his colleagues and at the same time felt compelled to honor his fear of the personal hubris that might ultimately divide him from them. In October 1933, Bonhoeffer elected to go into a self-imposed exile from the church struggles and his homeland, an exile that he saw as a sojourn in the "wilderness." Before leaving to assume the pastoral post with two German Lutheran congregations in London, Bonhoeffer went on retreat with a number of his closest students. One of those present, Winfried Maechler, recorded Bonhoeffer's despairing words, spoken over a simple meal: "We must now endure in silence, and set the firebrand of truth to all four corners of the proud German Christian edifice so that one day the whole structure may collapse."[1]

During his London years, Bonhoeffer's commitment to a pacifist agenda took form after the example of Ghandi, whom he longed to visit and observe firsthand in India, a significant goal that he never realized. Pacifism, specifically a working practice of nonviolence, seemed to Bonhoeffer the only way to polarize resistance to the Reich and to foil the divisive policies of the National Socialists. During this period, Bonhoeffer sought to find a model for life in Christian community. The urgency he felt was driven by the factious end of the churches under Nazism and by the theologian's profound commitment to the future of the church. Bonhoeffer envisioned a church that had a global perspective and an ecumenical spirit, a church that existed for others, and both saw and responded to "the great events of world history from below, from the perspective of the outcast, the suspects, the maltreated, the powerless, the oppressed, the reviled—in short, from the perspective of those who suffer."[2]

In 1934 the Reich bishop ordered that the "Old Prussian preachers' seminaries" be closed and that proof of Aryan origins be required of candidates for ministry and newly ordained clergy. The German Evangelical Church decided that it had no choice but to resist the orders of the Reich bishop by establishing its own "preachers' seminaries" and invited Bonhoeffer to be the director in Berlin-Brandenburg. Filled with a renewed spirit and buoyed by the hope that emerged from his dream of such an endeavor, Bonhoeffer accepted and began his work in 1935. His biographer, Eberhard Bethge, described this transformation:

The approaching task acted as a catalyst for everything that had been preoccupying Bonhoeffer during the past few years: a theology of the Sermon on the Mount, a community in service and spiritual exercises, a witness to passive resistance and ecumenical openness.[3]

During that time and until the Reich closed the seminaries in 1937, Bonhoeffer maintained his ecumenical commitments and his schedule of meetings with church leaders on the continent. The intellectual and spiritual legacy of the preachers' seminaries is to be found in two of Bonhoeffer's books that explore Christian community and the Christian life—*Life Together* and *The Cost of Discipleship*, respectively. Following the arrest and imprisonment of Pastor Niemöller and the closing of the seminaries, great difficulties ensued for the seminarians, and once again, Bonhoeffer began to feel isolation and alienation from many of his colleagues in the ministry and from his homeland.

After *Kristallnacht* ("the night of broken glass"), November 9, 1938, Bonhoeffer's resolve for pacifism and nonviolence were severely tested. His response to the wanton destruction of synagogues and Jewish properties and the silence of his fellow pastors seemed prophetic:

His seminarians recalled his remark . . . that, "if the synagogues are set afire today, tomorrow the churches will burn." In the Bible he used for prayer and meditation, these words from Psalm 74:8 are marked with the date, November 9, 1938: "they say to themselves: Let us plunder them! *They burn all the houses of God in the land*" (these last words are underlined in his Bible).[4]

From 1937 to 1940, Bonhoeffer served beside and taught the pastors of congregations in Koeslin and Sigurdshof in a variation on the preachers' seminary model. In 1940, two days after completing this tenure, the Gestapo closed the seminary and churches. Later that year, Bonhoeffer was officially silenced by the Gestapo and required to regularly report to the local police. Less than a year later, the Nazis prohibited him from publishing his works. It was during the fall months of 1940 that Bonhoeffer was introduced, through his brother-in-law Hans von Dohnanyi, to the *Abwehr*, the Wehrmacht's intelligence corp. Admiral Wilhelm Canaris, the head of the *Abwehr*, and his associate, Colonel Hans Oster, recruited Bonhoeffer to join their resistance to Nazism by serving as a contact with European churches and as a courier.

Throughout these tumultuous years, Bonhoeffer wrestled with three core dilemmas. Bonhoeffer traveled to the United States to teach, but this evasion stirred deep conflicts in the man of conscience. In the first dilemma, he struggled with how it would be possible to participate in the reconstruction of the German nation after the war if one did not actively participate in ending the war. The security of teaching in a distant country and of building a support base in New York City was not as commanding an alternative as returning home to labor among the relatively few colleagues who were risking everything in the cause of resistance to Hitler and the National Socialists. After several weeks of soul searching while in residence at Union Theological Seminary, he returned to Germany.

The second Bonhoeffer dilemma challenged the theologian's intense commitment to pacifism and nonviolence. He pondered losing his own soul if he participated in a plot to assassinate Hitler in order to stop the ravaging war and the genocide against the Jews. His logic was that Hitler's actions were killing millions of innocent people, and it would be better for one person, Bonhoeffer, to risk all and bring the killing to an end than to allow it to continue unabated. Bonhoeffer's critical explorations of "cheap and costly grace" in his book *The Cost of Discipleship* presage his later struggles. The struggle is briefly reopened in *Letters and Papers from Prison*, with a strong assertion about the correctness of risking one's soul to end evil.

The third issue for Bonhoeffer focused on his spiritual life and how to maintain the essential balance between spiritual disciplines and the all-encompassing biblical mandates for peace and justice. Bonhoeffer's life and writings are compelling precisely because he was able to find and sustain that balance and to allow his spirituality to inform his decisions regarding exile in New York City and the matter of his pacifism. His prayers, poems, and reflections are an enduring beacon for contemporary people of faith who must confront grave ethical dilemmas all the while honoring the vital need for a strong inner life and spiritual practice. Clearly, Bonhoeffer's spirituality prevented him from succumbing to the pervasive violence of those times.

The lessons and example of the Bonhoeffer dilemmas are timeless: to stay or to leave, and to relinquish and violate a core, defining ethical standard in order to accomplish a presumed "greater good." A risk then was, and is today, great: to abandon a spiritual life in the face of incredible political troubles and human demands, and thereby risk destroying the potential for inner peace that would, on one hand, sustain the efforts and, on the other, would deter Bonhoeffer from cooperating with the varied forms of violence he was resisting. Bonhoeffer's writings bear witness to a wisdom born of a spiritual discipline that made his resistance fruitful and faithful.

Bonhoeffer made his peace with the central issues he faced and moved forward in resistance to the evils of the Reich. In 1941, with the construction of Auschwitz well under way, the Reich instigated the first deportation of Jews from Berlin. The *Abwehr* conspirators felt compelled to begin a rescue operation to save Jews in Berlin with whom they had worked. Code named "Operation 7," the initial plan was to save seven specific Jews destined for the camps. The plot relied on the pretext that the Jews were actually *Abwehr* agents on a mission for the Reich, and the seven were secreted out of Germany into Switzerland.

Word of the success raised tremendous suspicions among the Gestapo in Berlin who were already investigating the *Abwehr*. In April 1943 the Gestapo arrested several of the co-conspirators, including Bonhoeffer and Dohnanyi, all of whom were held and interrogated at Tegel Prison. Following Klaus von Stauffenberg's failed attempt to assassinate Hitler, the Gestapo and Reich security forces launched relentless, massive efforts to identify all factions of the Resistance. In the course of their thorough searches, they uncovered the secret files of Admiral Canaris. The discovery led to the arrest and imprisonment of Bonhoeffer's brother Klaus and Eberhard Bethge, among others. A nearly completed plot to help Dietrich escape was abruptly stopped at his direction so as not to place his brother's life at risk because of the retaliations that would certainly follow an escape attempt. Here, Bonhoeffer's concept of a Christian as a "man for others" found its most intensely personal expression in an action that sealed his fate.

Bonhoeffer was transferred to the Buchenwald death camp and then to Schoenberg. While this was occurring, the Reich security command was, at the direction of Adolf Hitler, preparing the disposition of the cases in the *Abwehr* conspiracy. Bonhoeffer was transported to Flossenbürg where, on April 9, 1945, he was hanged along with Admiral Canaris and Colonel Oster. On the same day, Bonhoeffer's brother-in-law was executed in the Sachsenhausen death camp. Through a fellow inmate, a British officer who was with him in the last hours at Flossenbürg, Bonhoeffer sent a message to his close friend Bishop Bell of Chichester. The message speaks of the faith that transcended the very human fear of suffering, death, and evil, and it looked beyond the gallows and the dying Reich to a greater vision: "This is the end—for me, the beginning of life. Tell him [Bell] . . . with him I believe in the principle of universal Christian brotherhood which rises above all national interest."[5]

LITURGICAL RESOURCES

The following prayers, litanies, hymns, and sermon outline are drawn from the life and writings of Pastor Bonhoeffer. The initials and numbers following direct quotations refer to a specific text and page number in books by or about Bonhoeffer (additional information is contained in the bibliography).[6] Because most people will not know much of the life of Dietrich Bonhoeffer and only a few will be familiar with his writings, I suggest that a sermon be woven together using the preceding historical context (detailed histories of Bonhoeffer's life and a listing of his books are included in the bibliography), the history of the Shoah in Chapter Eight, and reflections on salient quotations listed in the sermon outline. This format allows the primary focus to be directly on Bonhoeffer. The preacher is responsible for the reflection and contemporary applications. Because in Bonhoeffer's time there was not even a measure of the contemporary sensitivity to the implications of language that is gender exclusive, and in order to ensure that all worshippers are genuinely included in all aspects of the service, I have made the quotations gender inclusive.

HYMNS

"By Gracious Powers"   words by Dietrich Bonhoeffer
                            Tune: "Intercessor" by C. Hubert H. Parry

The text to this hymn is by Fred Pratt Green and is based on Bonhoeffer's poem entitled "New Year 1945" and is included in the Memoir by G. Leibholz (CoD, p. 20). Bonhoeffer composed the poem while incarcerated in a Nazi prison in Berlin as that city experienced a massive bombardment.

"Today We All Are Called to Be Disciples"   by H. Kenn Carmichael
                                             Tune: "Kingsfold" CMD
                                             by Ralph Vaughan Williams

"A Mighty Fortress Is Our God"   by Martin Luther
                                             Tune: "Ein' Feste Burg"
                                             (isometric)

"Be Thou My Vision"   Tune: "Slane"

INVOCATION

Creator of the Universe, we gather as a community of faith and invite your presence in the words of your faithful servant, Dietrich Bonhoeffer:

"I want to see the turning of the times,
When luminous signs stand in the night sky,
And over the peoples new bells
Ring and ring.
I am waiting for that midnight
In whose fearfully streaming brilliance

The evil perish for anguish
And the good overcome with Joy. . . .
See, O humankind,
Holy strength
Is at work, setting right."

(PFP, p. 21)

THE CALL TO WORSHIP

(L: Liturgist lines; C: Congregational lines; U: UNISON response)

L: "If I preach faith and grace alone, . . . then you ask:

C: "What about the Christian life?

L: "If I discuss the Sermon on the Mount, . . . then you ask:

C: "What about eternal life?

L: "If I interpret the very real and sinful life of some person in the Bible, then you ask:

C: "Where are the eternal verities?

L: "And all these questions really express only one concern:

U: "HOW CAN I LIVE A CHRISTIAN LIFE IN THE REAL WORLD, AND WHAT ARE THE FINAL AUTHORITIES FOR SUCH A LIFE, WHICH ALONE IS WORTH LIVING?"   (MTW, p. 43)

L: Let God speak to us through Word, prayer, and song. Through silence, sharing, and service Christ shall be the center of our lives.

U: LET US WORSHIP THE LIVING GOD!

LITANY OF CONFESSION AND THANKSGIVING

L: "It is not the purpose of the Bible to give information about the origin of evil but to witness to its character as guilt and as the infinite burden of humanity."

(CaF, p. 65)

C: "We have been silent witnesses of evil deeds; we have been drenched by many storms; we have learnt the arts of equivocation and pretense; experience has made us suspicious of others and kept us from being truthful and open; intolerable conflicts have worn us down and even made us cynical. Are we still of any use?"   (BEM, p. 113)

L: "We must take a definite step. What does this mean? It means that we can only take this step aright if we fix our eyes not on the work we do, but on the word with which Jesus calls us to do it."   (CoD, p. 72)

U: "THE CHURCH CONFESSES THAT SHE HAS WITNESSED THE LAW-
LESS APPLICATION OF BRUTAL FORCE, THE PHYSICAL AND
SPIRITUAL SUFFERING OF COUNTLESS INNOCENT PEOPLE, OP-
PRESSION, HATRED AND MURDER, AND THAT SHE HAS NOT
RAISED HER VOICE ON BEHALF OF THE VICTIMS AND HAS NOT
FOUND WAYS TO HASTEN TO THEIR AID."   (BEM, p. 119)

L: "I believe that God can and will bring good out of evil, even out of the greatest
evil. For that purpose God needs human beings who make the best use of
everything. I believe God will give us all the strength we need to help us to
resist in all times of distress. . . . I believe that even our mistakes and
shortcomings are turned to good account. . . . I believe that God is no timeless
fate, but that God waits for and answers sincere prayers and responsible
actions."   (LLP, p. 11)

U: "THERE IS A VERY REAL DANGER OF OUR DRIFTING INTO AN
ATTITUDE OF CONTEMPT FOR HUMANITY. . . . NOTHING THAT WE
DESPISE IN THE OTHER PERSON IS ENTIRELY ABSENT FROM
OURSELVES. · . . . THE ONLY PROFITABLE RELATIONSHIP TO OTH-
ERS. . . . IS ONE OF LOVE. . . . GOD DID NOT DESPISE HUMANITY,
BUT BECAME ONE OF US FOR OUR SAKE."   (LLP, p. 9)

L: The Lord have mercy.

C: Christ have mercy.

SILENT REFLECTIONS

L: "Our past is always kept before us by thankfulness and penitence." (LLP, p. 70)

C: "In ordinary life we hardly realize that we received a great deal more than we
give, and that it is only with gratitude that life becomes rich."   (LLP, p. 46)

U: "YOU MUST NEVER DOUBT THAT I AM TRAVELING WITH GRATI-
TUDE AND CHEERFULNESS ALONG THE ROAD WHERE I AM BE-
ING LED. MY PAST LIFE IS BRIM-FULL OF GOD'S GOODNESS, AND
MY SINS ARE COVERED BY THE FORGIVING LOVE OF CHRIST
CRUCIFIED. I AM MOST THANKFUL."   (LLP, p. 208)

ASSURANCE OF PARDON

L: "People go to God when they are sore bestead,
    Pray to God for succour, for God's peace, for bread,
    For mercy for them, sick, sinning, or dead;
    All people do so, Christian and unbelieving.

C: People go to God when God is sore bestead,
    Find God poor and scorned, without shelter or bread,
    Whelmed under weight of the wicked, the weak, the dead;
    Christians stand by God in God's hour of grieving.

U: GOD GOETH TO EVERY PERSON WHEN SORE BESTEAD, FEEDETH
BODY AND SPIRIT WITH GOD'S BREAD; FOR CHRISTIANS, PA-
GANS, ALIKE GOD HANGETH DEAD, AND BOTH ALIKE FORGIV-
ING." (LLP, p. 192)

SCRIPTURE

Psalm 119 (see MTW, p. 103)

Psalm 50:1–6 (see MTW, p. 73)

Romans 12

Matthew 5:1–12

HOMILY-SERMON NOTES

I propose a sermon-homily style that relies on the recitation of Bonhoeffer's words with the reflections and contemporary applications provided by
the preacher. Wherever possible, I have grouped the quotations by themes.
Bonhoeffer's writings abound with evocative, meaningful aphorisms; his
words spark insights and challenge us fifty and more years from their
composition. The listing of quotes is obviously not comprehensive. It has
been inspiring and instructive to reread the Bonhoeffer library in preparing
for this book. You are well advised to read again and select passages from
the books written by Bonhoeffer and to be guided by Eberhard Bethge's
invaluable biography.

On Grace: Cheap and Costly

Cheap grace is the deadly enemy of our Church. We are fighting today for costly
grace. (CoD, p. 45)

Cheap grace means grace sold on the market like cheapjacks' wares. The sacraments, the forgiveness of sin, and the consolations of religion are thrown away at
cut prices. Grace is represented as the Church's inexhaustible treasury, from which
she showers blessings with generous hands, without asking questions or fixing
limits. Grace without price; grace without cost! The essence of grace, we suppose,
is that the account has been paid in advance; and, because it has been paid,
everything can be had for nothing. (CoD, p. 45)

Cheap grace is the preaching of forgiveness without requiring repentance, baptism
without church discipline, Communion without confession, absolution without
personal confession. Cheap grace is grace without discipleship, grace without the
cross, grace without Jesus Christ, living and incarnate. (CoD, p. 47)

Costly grace is the gospel. . . . Such grace is *costly* because it calls us to follow, and
it is *grace* because it costs a person his/her life, and it is grace because it gives a

person the only true life. It is costly because it condemns sin, and costly because it justifies the sinner. Above all, it is *costly* because it cost God the life of God's Son . . . and what has cost God much cannot be cheap for us. (CoD, pp. 47–48)

An Advent Theme

Bonhoeffer carefully observed the seasons of the Christian year. In the 1943 season of Advent, Bonhoeffer wrote to his fiancée, Maria von Wedemeyer-Weller:

A prison cell, in which one waits, hopes . . . and is completely dependent on the fact that the door of freedom has to be opened from the outside, is not a bad picture of Advent. (LLP, p. 168)

A Baptism Theme

On May 21, 1944, Bonhoeffer wrote in the midst of an air raid, offering the counsel to direct the memory of such occasions into spiritual channels that solidify resolve and commitment:

If in the middle of an air raid God sends out the gospel call to God's kingdom in baptism. . . . [I]t is a kingdom stronger than war and danger, a kingdom of power and authority, signifying eternal terror and judgment to some, and eternal joy and righteousness to others, not a kingdom of the heart, but one as wide as the earth, not transitory but eternal, a kingdom that makes a way for itself and summons people to itself to prepare its way, a kingdom for which it is worth while to risk our lives. (LLP, pp. 151–152)

On Death and Resurrection

Easter? We are paying more attention to dying than to death. We are more concerned to get over the act of dying than to overcome death. Socrates mastered the art of dying, Christ overcame death as "the last enemy" (I Cor. 15:26). There is a real difference between the two things; the one is within the scope of human possibilities, the other means resurrection. It is not from *ars moriendi*, the art of dying, but from the resurrection of Christ, that a new and purifying wind can blow through our present world. . . . If a few people believed and acted on it in their daily lives, a great deal would be changed. To live in the light of the resurrection—that is what Easter means. Do you find, too, that most people do not know what they really live by? (LLP, p. 132)

On Church, State, and Justice

The state which endangers the Christian proclamation negates itself. (ToF, p. 139)

[T]here are three possible ways the church can act toward the state: in the first place . . . it can ask the state whether its actions are legitimate and in accordance with its character as state, i.e., it can throw the state back on its responsibilities. Second, it can aid the victims of state action. The state has an unconditional obligation to the victims of any ordering of society, even if they do not belong to the Christian community. . . . [T]he church may in no way withdraw itself from these two tasks. The third possibility is not just to bandage the victims under the wheel, but to jam a spoke in the wheel itself. Such action would be direct political action, and is only possible and desirable when the church sees the state fail in its function of creating law and order. (ToF, p. 139)

On a Place to Stand

In a message to his fellow conspirators at the end of 1942:

We have for once learned to see the great events of world history from below, from the perspective of the outcast, the suspects, the maltreated, the powerless, the oppressed, the reviled—in short, from the perspective of those who suffer. (ToF, pp. 38–39)

I should like to speak of God, not on the boundaries but at the center, not in weakness but in strength; and therefore not in death and guilt but in humanity's life and goodness. . . . God is beyond in the midst of our life. The church stands, not at the boundaries where human powers give out, but in the middle of the village. (ToF, pp. 42–43)

On Liturgy and the Fate of the Jews

Renate Wind reflects on Bonhoeffer's commitment, in the "preachers' seminaries," to a communal life that was, in Bonhoeffer's words, "not monastic segregation but innermost concentration for service outside." "It was," from Wind's perspective,

not . . . a flight from reality, as in other groups which came into being at this time and which attempted to get over the wretchedness of church politics by retreating into new liturgical forms, religious aesthetics, meditation, and song. To these Dietrich objected, "Only those who cry out for the Jews may sing Gregorian chant." (SiW, p. 116)

W. H. Auden met Dietrich Bonhoeffer in 1939 and after the war composed the poem, "Friday's Child," which he dedicated, "In memory of Dietrich Bonhoeffer, martyred at Flossenbürg, 9 April 1945." The poem should be considered as a suitable ending for a homily-sermon or as a printed cover for a special bulletin. The poem is included in PFP, pp. 90–91.

HOMILY–SERMON ALTERNATIVES

An engaging alternative to a standard sermon format would be to select four congregants who would meet in advance of the observance to learn about and reflect on Bonhoeffer's life and works. They would agree to read and discuss *Letters and Papers from Prison, The Cost of Discipleship,* and one other book or collection of their choosing. Each congregant would select one of the Bonhoeffer quotations and prepare a five-minute personal reflection or response to it for the sermon-homily. These should be personal responses that might include lingering questions and contemporary challenges. Care should be taken to include a high school or college student, and a balance of women and men. The preacher would initially set the historical context for Bonhoeffer's life and work, and then the congregants would offer their insights. The preacher would conclude the sermon in a manner agreed upon by all of the participants.

Another alternative would be a dramatic reading of Elizabeth Berryhill's compelling two-act play based on Bonhoeffer's life. The play, *The Cup of Trembling*, may be adapted for use in a regular Sabbath service or staged as a special event. A study guide prepared by Donald Stauffer is also available. If the play is adapted for a regular worship service, care should be taken to abbreviate other aspects of the service.

AFFIRMATIONS AND CONFESSIONS

The congregation may be asked to stand and recite one of the following:

"Who Am I?"   (LLP, pp. 188–189)

"Stations on the Way to Freedom"   (E, p.15)

"Stations" may be used in its entirety or by combining two of the subsections (Self-discipline and Action, Self-discipline and Death, or Action and Death).

BENEDICTION

L: "I fear that Christians who stand with only one leg upon the earth also stand with only one leg in heaven."   (letter to Maria)

C: "It may be that the day of judgment will dawn tomorrow; and in that case, though not before, we shall gladly stop working for a better future."   (LLP, p. 16)

U: WHAT DOES THE LORD GOD REQUIRE OF US, ONLY THIS, TO ACT JUSTLY, TO LOVE TENDERLY, AND TO WALK HUMBLY WITH GOD.

(Micah 6:8)

PREPARATORY OR FOLLOW-UP STUDY

It is important that congregations have an opportunity to engage in in-depth discussions and study of Bonhoeffer's life and writings. The bibliography contains a list of books by and about Dietrich Bonhoeffer and a compilation of study resources including video and leader's guides.

INTERFAITH STUDY

A remembrance of Dietrich Bonhoeffer affords a community the opportunity to gather from a variety of traditions and cultures. A series of interfaith responses, under the theme "Dietrich Bonhoeffer: A Legacy of Faith and Conviction," might be convened as a community forum series. The following topics and speakers suggest themselves from Bonhoeffer's writings:

- A local minister: "Pastoral Reflections on Bonhoeffer's Life and Ministry"
- A local rabbi: "Jewish Reflections on *Letters and Papers from Prison*"
- A Shoah survivor: "A Survivor's Perspective: The Bonhoeffer Legacy"
- An African-American minister: "An African-American Response to Bonhoeffer" (this may include a response to his work around South Africa)
- A panel of clergy and laity: "Acts of Resistance Then and Now"
- A woman minister/layperson: "A Feminist Reflection on *The Cost of Discipleship*"
- An Asian perspective: "Liberation and 'Third-Eye Theology' and Bonhoeffer"
- A public showing and panel discussion of the video *Dietrich Bonhoeffer: Memories and Perspectives*

Notes

CHAPTER ONE

1. From 1945 on, the word *Holocaust* referred exclusively to the genocidal destruction of European Jewry. More recently, politicians, peace activists, environmentalists, revisionists, and others have taken the name for their own uses, without sensitivity to the anguish their corruption of the language causes the survivors. In addition to problems created by the contemporary misuse of the word *Holocaust* there is a linguistic concern. *Holocaust,* as it is frequently used in Scripture, refers to a sacrificial offering that is totally consumed by fire on an alter. The usage implies a certain voluntary quality or a martyr's willing self-sacrifice, both in response to a particular value system or theology. Multitudes of the victims of the Shoah were consumed by fire, but they were not sacrificial in the ritual sense of the term. I prefer and will use the Hebrew ascription, Shoah, which refers to a sudden catastrophe that is destructive and devastating. Shoah is becoming the commonly used reference to the attempt by the Nazis to destroy European Jews and Judaism.

2. Elie Wiesel, *Night, Dawn, The Accident* (New York: Hill and Wang, 1972), p. 41.

3. William L. Shirer, *The Rise and Fall of the Third Reich: A History of Nazi Germany* (New York: Simon and Schuster, 1960), pp. 239–240.

4. Wiesel, *Night,* p. 38.

5. Richard Selzer, *Mortal Lessons: Notes on the Art of Surgery* (New York: Simon and Schuster, 1976), p. 27.

CHAPTER TWO

1. Frederick Buechner, *Listening to Your Life,* comp. George Connor (San Francisco: HarperCollins, 1992), p. 14.

2. John Roth, "Asking and Listening, Understanding and Doing: Some Conditions for Responding to the Shoah Religiously," in *Contemporary Christian Religious Responses to the Shoah*, vol. 6, ed. Steven L. Jacob (Lanham, Md.: University Press of America, 1993), p. 206.

3. Elie Wiesel, *The Gates of the Forest* (New York: Avon Books, 1966), pp. 36–37.

4. Ibid., p. 192.

5. Ibid., p. 193.

6. Ibid.

7. Irving Greenberg, "Cloud of Smoke, Pillar of Fire: Judaism, Christianity, and Modernity After the Holocaust," in *Auschwitz: Beginning of a New Era? Reflections on the Holocaust*, ed. Eva Fleischner (New York: Ktav Publishing House, 1977), p. 23.

8. Martin Niemöller, quoted in *The Christian Century*, March 21–28, 1984, p. 296.

9. Gitta Sereny, *Into That Darkness: An Examination of Conscience* (London: Picador edition, Pan Books Ltd., 1974).

10. Adolf Hitler, *Mein Kampf* (Boston: Houghton Mifflin, 1971), p. 640.

11. Paul van Buren, "The Status and Prospects for Theology" (address to the Theology Section of the American Academy of Religion, Chicago, Ill., November 1, 1975).

12. Jules Isaac, *Jesus and Israel*, ed. Claire Huchet-Bishop (New York: Holt, Rinehart and Winston, 1971), pp. 401–404.

13. Ellis Rivkin, *What Crucified Jesus?* (Nashville: Abingdon Press, 1984), p. 124.

14. Harry James Cargas, *Harry James Cargas in Conversation with Elie Wiesel* (New York: Paulist Press, 1976), pp. 47–48.

15. Walter Wink, *Transforming Bible Study: A Leader's Guide* (Nashville: Abingdon, 1980).

16. From a personal conversation witnessed by the author.

17. "Elie Wiesel n'est-il pas particuliérement le héraut de la mémoire de la Shoah," in *Le mal et l'exil: Dialogue avec Philippe de Saint-Cheron,* ed. Philippe de Saint-Cheron (Paris: Nouvelle-Cite-Rencontres, 1988), pp. 51–52, cited in Marcel Dubois, "The Memory of Self and the Memory of God in Elie Wiesel's Jewish Consciousness," in *Elie Wiesel: Between Memory and Hope*, ed. Carol Rittner, R.S.M. (New York: New York University Press, 1990), p. 67.

CHAPTER THREE

1. Nikos Kazantzakis, *Report to Greco* (New York: Bantam Books, 1966), p. 494.

2. Richard Rubenstein, "Some Perspectives on Religious Faith After Auschwitz," in *The German Church Struggle and the Holocaust*, ed. Franklin H. Littell and Hubert G. Locke (Detroit: Wayne State University Press, 1974), p. 262.

3. Elie Wiesel, "Talking and Writing and Keeping Silent," in Littell and Locke, *The German Church Struggle,* p. 274.

4. Ibid., pp. 271–272.

5. Elie Wiesel, *Night, Dawn, The Accident* (New York: Hill and Wang, 1972), pp. 71–72.

6. Elie Wiesel, *Ani Maamin: A Song Lost and Found Again* (New York: Random House, 1973), p. 75.

7. Ibid., p. 93.

8. Ibid., p. 97.

9. Ibid., p. 103.

10. Ibid., p. 105.

11. From a private conversation between Mr. Graebe and the author.

12. Denise Levertov, "Mass for the Day of St. Thomas Didymus," quoted in *Cries of the Spirit: A Celebration of Women's Spirituality*, ed. Marilyn Sewell (Boston: Beacon Press, 1991), p. 257.

13. Eberhard Bethge, *Bonhoeffer: Exile and Martyr* (New York: Seabury Press, 1975), p. 115.

CHAPTER FOUR

1. Elie Wiesel, *The Town Beyond the Wall* (New York: Holt, Rinehart and Winston, 1964), p. 118.

2. Elie Wiesel, *Ani Maamin: A Song Lost and Found Again* (New York: Random House, 1973), p. 75.

3. Thornton Wilder, *The Bridge of San Luis Rey* (New York: Washington Square Press, 1963), p. 5.

4. Ben Piazza, *The Exact and Very Strange Truth* (New York: Farrar, Straus, and Co., 1964), p. 329.

5. Etty Hillesum, *Letters from Westerbork* (New York: Pantheon Books, 1986), pp. 111–112.

6. Elie Wiesel, "The Binding of Isaac" (a lecture at Stanford University, May 6, 1974).

7. Jerry Irish, *A Boy Thirteen: Reflections on Death* (Philadelphia: Westminster Press, 1975), p. 42.

8. Wiesel, *Ani Maamin*, p. 105.

9. Elie Wiesel, *Five Biblical Portraits* (Notre Dame: University of Notre Dame Press, 1981), pp. 120–121.

10. Dietrich Bonhoeffer, *Letters and Papers from Prison* (New York: Macmillan, 1972), pp. 15–16.

11. Donald K. McKim, ed., *Encyclopedia of the Reformed Faith* (Louisville: Westminster/John Knox Press, 1992), p. 143.

12. Maimonides, *Mishneh Torah*, "Laws of Repentance," chap. 5, par. 1.

CHAPTER FIVE

1. Reinhold Niebuhr, *Moral Man and Immoral Society* (New York: Charles Scribner's Sons, 1960), p. 277.

2. Marion Pritchard, speaking in the video *The Courage to Care*, produced by Rob Gardner for the United Way of America, 1985.

3. Pope John Paul II, from an unpublished speech.

4. The Theological Declaration of Barmen, quoted in *The Constitution of the United Presbyterian Church in the United States of America, Part I, The Book of Confessions* (Philadelphia: Office of the General Assembly, 1967), 8.08.

5. "Memorandum to Chancellor Hitler," quoted in Arthur Cochrane, *The Church's Confession Under Hitler* (Pittsburgh: Pickwick Press, 1976), p. 277.

6. Theological Declaration of Barmen, 8.03.

7. Cochrane, *The Church's Confession*, p. 268.

8. Quoted in Hubert Locke, ed., *The Barmen Confession: Papers from the Seattle Assembly* (Lewiston: Edwin Mellen Press, 1986), p. 98.

9. Ibid., p. 99.

10. The Stuttgart Declaration of Guilt, quoted in Victoria Barnett, *For the Soul of the People: Protestant Protest Against Hitler* (New York: Oxford University Press, 1992), p. 209.

11. Dietrich Bonhoeffer, *Creation and Fall: A Theological Interpretation of Genesis 1–3* (London: SCM Press, 1960), p. 35.

12. Cited from "Hitler's Table Talk," in Rosemary Ruether, Faith and Fratricide: The Theological Roots of Anti-Semitism (New York: Seabury Press, 1974), pp. 223–224.

13. Dietrich Bonhoeffer, *Ethics* (New York: Macmillan, 1965), p. 35.

14. Václav Havel, *Summer Meditations* (New York: Alfred A. Knopf, 1992), pp. 19–20.

15. William Sloane Coffin, quote on a serigraph by Sister Corita.

16. Václav Havel, *Open Letters: Selected Writings 1965–1990* (New York: Alfred A. Knopf, 1991), pp. 57–58.

17. Albert Camus, *Resistance, Rebellion, and Death* (New York: Modern Library, 1960), pp. 208–209.

CHAPTER SIX

1. Albert Camus, *The Plague* (New York: Modern Library, 1948), p. 230.

2. Quoted in a review of Ralf Reuth, *Goebbels*, by Claudia Koonz, *New York Times Book Review*, January 16, 1994, p. 14.

3. Quoted in Douglas K. Huneke, *The Moses of Rovno* (New York: Dodd, Mead, 1985), pp. xii–xiii.

4. Samuel P. Oliner and Pearl M. Oliner, *The Altruistic Personality: Rescuers of Jews in Nazi Europe* (New York: Free Press, 1988).

5. Blaise Pascal, *Pensées* (1670), no. 277.

6. Philip Hallie, *Lest Innocent Blood Be Shed* (New York: Harper and Row, 1979), p. 172.

7. Ibid., p. 173.

8. Ibid., pp. 15, 24.

9. Stanley Milgram, *Obedience to Authority* (New York: Harper Colophon, 1974), p. 6.

10. Perry London, "The Rescuers: Motivational Hypotheses About Christians Who Saved Jews from the Nazis," in *Altruism and Helping Behavior*, ed. J. Macaulay and L. Berkowitz (New York: Academic Press, 1970), p. 244.

11. Peter L. Berger, *Invitation to Sociology: A Humanistic Perspective* (New York: Doubleday Anchor Books, 1963), p. 137.

12. William L. Shirer, *The Rise and Fall of the Third Reich: A History of Nazi Germany* (New York: Simon and Schuster, 1960), p. 961.

13. The verbatim sworn testimony is contained in two documents that are reprinted in their entirety in Huneke, *The Moses of Rovno*, pp. 189–195.

14. Magda Trocmé, speaking in the video *The Courage to Care,* produced by Rob Gardner for the United Way of America, 1985.

15. Elie Wiesel, *The Gates of the Forest* (New York: Avon Books, 1966), p. 91.

16. Yehuda Bauer, *The Holocaust in Historical Perspective* (Seattle: University of Washington Press, 1978), p. 74.

17. The Louis Harris Associates, "Attitudes Toward Racial and Religious Minorities and Toward Women," prepared for and quoted in The National Conference of Christians and Jews booklet "Familiarity Breeds Respect," 1979.

18. Henri J. M. Nouwen, *Reaching Out: Three Movements of the Spiritual Life* (New York: Doubleday, 1975), pp. 46–47.

19. Alexander Ramati, *The Assisi Underground: The Priests Who Rescued Jews* (New York: Stein and Day Publishers, 1978).

20. Martin Luther King, Jr., "I See the Promised Land" in *A Testament of Hope: The Essential Writings of Martin Luther King, Jr.,* ed. James Melvin Washington (San Francisco: Harper and Row, 1986), p. 285.

CHAPTER EIGHT

1. Gerald Green, *The Holocaust: A Novel of Survival and Triumph* (New York: Bantam Books, 1978).

CHAPTER TEN

1. Elie Wiesel, "Foreword" to Carol Rittner, R.S.M., and Sondra Myers, eds. *The Courage to Care: Rescuers of Jews During the Holocaust.* (New York and London: New York University Press, 1986), p. XI.

CHAPTER THIRTEEN

1. Quoted in Eberhard Bethge, *Dietrich Bonhoeffer* (New York: Harper and Row, 1977), p. 252.

2. Dietrich Bonhoeffer, *Letters and Papers from Prison* (New York: Macmillan, 1972), p. 17.

3. Bethge, *Dietrich Bonhoeffer*, p. 336.

4. Quoted in *A Testament to Freedom: The Essential Writings of Dietrich Bonhoeffer*, ed. Geffrey B. Kelly and F. Burton Nelson (San Francisco: Harper-Collins, 1990), p. 33.

5. Ibid., p. 46.

6. The following abbreviations identify texts by or about Dietrich Bonhoeffer. The numerical reference next to the initials in the text refers to the page number:

Letters and Papers from Prison	(LLP)
Ethics	(E)
The Cost of Discipleship	(CoD)
Prayers from Prison	(PFP)
Creation and Fall	(CaF)
Meditating on the Word	(MTW)
Kelly and Nelson, *A Testament of Freedom*	(ToF)
Bethge, *Dietrich Bonhoeffer*	(DB)
Bethge, *Bonhoeffer: Exile and Martyr*	(BEM)
Wind, *Dietrich Bonhoeffer: A Spoke in the Wheel*	(SiW)

Bibliography

This bibliography is divided by theme to make it a resource for those who will plan services, sermons, and classes based on the primary topics covered in the body of the book. Where it seemed useful, certain books are briefly annotated.

HISTORY OF THE SHOAH

Arad, Yitzhak, Shmuel Krakwoski, and Shmuel Spector. *The Einsatzgruppen Reports*. New York: Holocaust Library, 1989.

Dawidowicz, Lucy S. *The War Against the Jews: 1933–1945*. New York: Holt, Rinehart and Winston, 1975.

_____ . *The Holocaust Reader*. New York: Behrman House, 1976.

Gilbert, Martin. *Atlas of the Holocaust*. London: Michael Joseph Limited, 1982.

_____ . *The Holocaust: A History of the Jews of Europe During the Second World War*. New York: Holt, Rinehart and Winston, 1985.

Hilberg, Raul. *Documents of Destruction: Germany and Jewry, 1933–1945*. Chicago: Quadrangle Books, 1971.

_____ . *The Destruction of the European Jews*. New York: New Viewpoints, Franklin Watts, 1973.

Shirer, William L. *The Rise and Fall of the Third Reich: A History of Nazi Germany*. New York: Simon and Schuster, 1960.

VIDEO RESOURCES

Lanzman, Claude. *Shoah*. Nine-hour, five-part video, released by Paramount Home Video, with study guide, 1984.

HISTORY FOR CHILDREN AND YOUTH

Stadtler, Bea. *The Holocaust: A History of Courage and Resistance*. New York:
    Behrman House, 1974. This book is particularly useful for students in the
    sixth through the tenth grades. It offers a balanced introduction to the
    Shoah and is unique in its field.

BY ELIE WIESEL

It is important to read Wiesel's first five works (*Night, Dawn, Day, Town Beyond
The Wall*, and *Gates of the Forest*) together, in sequence. There is a progression of
thought, roles, and responses through these books. Wiesel writes and publishes in
French. The original titles are included. (Unless otherwise noted, the French texts
were printed in Paris by Editions du Seuil.)

Wiesel, Elie. *Night/Dawn/Day*. New York: Aronson-B'nai B'rith, 1985.
La Nuit, l'Aube, le Jour, 1969.
These single volumes contain the first three books: Wiesel's memoir and two novels.
        Day was originally titled *The Accident* in its English-language editions.
_____. *The Gates of the Forest*. New York: Avon Books, 1966.
Les portes de la forêt, 1964.
_____. *The Jews of Silence*. New York: Holt, Rinehart and Winston, 1966.
Les juifs du silence, 1966.
_____. *Legends of Our Time*. New York: Holt, Rinehart and Winston, 1968.
Les chant des morts, 1966.
_____. *The Town Beyond the Wall*. New York: Avon Books, 1969.
La ville de la chance, 1968.
_____. *A Beggar in Jerusalem*. New York: Random House, 1970.
Le mendiant de Jérusalem, 1968.
_____. *One Generation After*. New York: Random House, 1970.
Entre deux soleils, Textes, 1970.
_____. *Souls on Fire: Portraits and Legends of Hasidic Masters*. New York:
        Random House, 1972.
Célébration hassidique, 1972.
_____. *Ani Maamin: A Song Lost and Found Again*. New York: Random House,
        1973. The French text to this cantata is printed on opposite pages.
_____. *The Oath*. New York: Random House, 1973.
Le serment de Kolvillàg, 1973.
_____. *Zalmen, or the Madness of God, a Play*. New York: Random House, 1974.
Zalmen ou la folie de Dieu, Theatre, 1968.
_____. *Messengers of God: Biblical Portraits and Legends*. New York: Random
        House, 1976.
Célébration biblique: Portraits et legendes, 1975.
_____. *A Jew Today*. New York: Random House, 1978.

Un Juif, aujourdhui: Recits, essais, dialogues, 1977.

———. *Four Hasidic Masters and Their Struggle Against Melancholy*. Notre Dame: University of Notre Dame Press, 1979.

Contre la mélancolie: Celebration hassidique II, 1981.

———. *The Trial of God (As It Was Held on February 25, 1649, in Shamgorod). A Play in Three Acts*. New York: Random House, 1979.

Le procès de Shamgorod: tel qu'il se dercula le 25 février 1649, 1979.

———. *Images from the Bible*, with Shalom of Safed. Woodstock: Overlook Press, 1980.

———. *Five Biblical Portraits*, Notre Dame: University of Notre Dame Press, 1981.

———. *The Testament*. New York: Summit Books, 1981.

Le testament d'un poète juif assassiné, 1980.

———. *Somewhere a Master: Further Hasidic Portraits and Legends*. New York: Summit Books, 1982.

———. *The Golem*, with Mark Podwal. New York: Summit Books, 1983.

———. *The Fifth Son*. New York: Summit Books, 1985.

Le cinquième fils, Grasset, 1983.

———. *The Nobel Peace Prize*. New York: Summit Books, 1986.

Discours d'Oslo, Grasset, 1987.

———. *A Song for Hope*. New York: The 92nd Street Y, 1987.

———. *Twilight*. New York: Summit Books, 1987.

Le Crépuscule, au loin, Grasset, 1987.

Wiesel, Elie, and Albert Friedlander. *The Six Days of Destruction: Meditations Towards Hope*. New York: Paulist Press, 1988.

———. *From the Kingdom of Memory: Reminiscences*. New York: Summit Books, 1990.

Wiesel, Elie, and John Cardinal O'Connor. *A Journey of Faith*. New York: Donald I. Fine, 1990.

de Saint-Cheron, Philippe, and Elie Wiesel. *Evil and Exile*. Notre Dame: University of Notre Dame Press, 1990.

———. *Sages and Dreamers: Biblical, Talmudic, and Hasidic Portraits and Legends*. New York: Summit Books, 1991.

———. *The Forgotten*. New York: Summit Books, 1992.

L'oublié, 1989.

———, with Mark Podwal. *A Passover Haggadah*. New York: Touchstone, Simon and Schuster, 1993.

Abrahamson, Irving, ed. *Against Silence: The Voice and Vision of Elie Wiesel*. 3 vols. New York: Holocaust Library, 1985.

Cargas, Harry James. *Harry James Cargas in Conversation with Elie Wiesel*. New York: Paulist Press, 1976.

———. *Conversations with Elie Wiesel*. South Bend: Justice Books, Diamond Communications, 1992.

BOOKS REFLECTING ON THE WORKS OF ELIE WIESEL

Berenbaum, Michael. *The Vision of the Void: Theological Reflections on the Writings of Elie Wiesel*. Middletown: Wesleyan University Press, 1979.

Brown, Robert McAfee. *Elie Wiesel: Messenger to All Humanity*. Notre Dame: University of Notre Dame Press, 1983.

Cargas, Harry James, ed. *Responses to Elie Wiesel*. New York: Persea Books with the Anti-Defamation League of B'nai B'rith, 1978.

———, ed. *Telling the Tale: A Tribute to Elie Wiesel*. St. Louis: Time Being Press, 1993.

Fine, Ellen S. *Legacy of Night: The Literary Universe of Elie Wiesel*. Albany: State University of New York Press, 1982.

Friedman, Maurice. *Abraham Joshua Heschel and Elie Wiesel: You Are My Witnesses*. New York: Farrar Straus Giroux, 1987.

Rittner, Carol, ed. *Elie Wiesel: Between Memory and Hope*. New York: New York University Press, 1990.

Rosenfeld, Alvin H., and Irving Greenberg, eds. *Confronting the Holocaust: The Impact of Elie Wiesel*. Bloomington: Indiana University Press, 1978.

Roth, John K. *A Consuming Fire Encounters with Elie Wiesel and the Holocaust*. Atlanta: John Knox Press, 1979.

Stern, Ellen Norman. *Elie Wiesel: Witness for Life*. New York: KTAV Publishing House, 1982.

DIARIES

Anne Frank: The Diary of a Young Girl. New York: Modern Library, 1952.

Gollwitzer, Helmut, Kathe Kuhn, and Reinhold Schneider, eds. *Dying We Live: The Final Messages and Records of the Resistance*. New York: Pantheon Books, 1956.

Hillesum, Etty. *Letters from Westerbork*. New York: Pantheon Books, 1986.

———. *An Interrupted Life*: *The Diaries of Etty Hillesum, 1941–1943*. New York: Pantheon Books, 1983.

Levi, Primo. *Survival in Auschwitz*. New York: Collier Books, 1976.

Lilje, Hanns. *The Valley of the Shadow*. Philadelphia: Fortress Press, 1977.

Locke, Hubert G., ed. *Exile in the Fatherland: Martin Niemöller's Letters from Moabit Prison*. Grand Rapids: William B. Eerdmans, 1986.

INTERNATIONAL AWARENESS OF THE SHOAH

Gilbert, Martin. *Auschwitz and the Allies*. London: Michael Joseph, 1981.

Laqueur, Walter. *The Terrible Secret: Suppression of the Truth About Hitler's 'Final Solution.'* Boston: Little, Brown, 1980.

Laqueur, Walter, and Richard Breitman. *Breaking the Silence*. New York: Simon and Schuster, 1986.

Morse, Arthur D. *While Six Million Died: A Chronicle of American Apathy*. New York: Hart, 1968.

Ross, Robert W. *So It Was True: The American Protestant Press and the Nazi Persecution of the Jews*. Minneapolis: University of Minnesota Press, 1980.

Wyman, David S. *The Abandonment of the Jews: America and the Holocaust, 1941–1945*. New York: Pantheon Books, 1984.

GERMAN CHURCH STRUGGLE AND BARMEN

Barnett, Victoria. *For the Soul of the People: Protestant Protest Against Hitler*. New York: Oxford University Press, 1992.

Cochrane, Arthur C. *The Church's Confession Under Hitler*. Philadelphia: Westminster Press, 1962.

Dowey, Edward, Jr. *A Commentary on the Confession of 1967 and an Introduction to the Book of Confessions*. Philadelphia: Westminster Press, 1968.

Erickson, Robert P. *Theologians Under Hitler: Gerhard Kittel, Paul Althaus, and Emanuel Hirsch*. New Haven: Yale University Press, 1985.

Forstman, Jack. *Christian Faith in Dark Times: Theological Conflicts in the Shadow of Hitler*. Louisville: Westminster/John Knox Press, 1992.

Friedlander, Saul. *Pius XII and the Third Reich: A Documentation*. New York: Alfred A. Knopf, 1986.

Hochhuth, Rolf. *The Deputy*. New York: Grove Press, 1964.

Littell, Franklin H., and Hubert G. Locke, eds. *The German Church Struggle and the Holocaust*. Detroit: Wayne State University Press, 1974.

Locke, Hubert G., ed. *The Barmen Confession: Papers from the Seattle Assembly*. Vol. 26 of Toronto Studies in Theology. Lewiston: Edwin Mellon Press, 1986.

Morley, John F. *Vatican Diplomacy and the Jews During the Holocaust, 1939–1943*. New York: KTAV Publishing House, 1980.

Scholder, Klaus. *The Churches and the Third Reich, Vol. One: Preliminary History and the Time of Illusions, 1918–1934*. Philadelphia: Fortress Press, 1988.

_____ . *The Churches and the Third Reich, Vol. Two: The Year of Disillusionment: 1934 Barmen and Rome*. Philadelphia: Fortress Press, 1988.

RESCUE

Anger, Per. *With Raoul Wallenberg in Budapest: Memories of the War Years in Hungary*. New York: Holocaust Library, 1981.

Anne Frank in the World. Amsterdam: Anne Frank Foundation, 1985.

Anne Frank's Tales from the Secret Annex. New York: Washington Square Press, 1983.

Anne Frank: The Diary of a Young Girl. New York: The Modern Library, 1952.

Bauminger, Arieh L. *Roll of Honor*. Tel-Aviv: HaMenora Publishing House, 1971.

Bierman, John. *Righteous Gentile: The Story of Raoul Wallenberg, Missing Hero of the Holocaust.* New York: Viking Press, 1981.

Block, Gay, and Malka Drucker. *Rescuers: Portraits of Moral Courage in the Holocaust.* New York: Holmes and Meier Publishers, 1992. The Block and Drucker book is a superb collection of photographs of the rescuers and accompanying narratives about each person. The book is a companion to the traveling exhibit.

Carr, Joseph. *Christian Heroes of the Holocaust: The Righteous Gentiles.* South Plainfield: Bridge Publishing, 1984.

Fender, Harold. *Rescue in Denmark.* New York: Holocaust Library, 1963.

Fogelman, Eva. *Conscience & Courage: Rescuers of Jews During the Holocaust.* New York: Anchor Books, 1994.

Ford, Herbert. *Flee the Captor.* Nashville: Southern Publishing Association, 1966. This is the story of John Weidner, who was a hero of the Dutch-Paris underground.

Friedman, Philip. *Their Brothers' Keepers.* New York: Holocaust Library, 1978.

Gies, Miep, with Allison Leslie Gold. *Anne Frank Remembered: The Story of the Woman Who Helped to Hide the Frank Family.* New York: Simon and Schuster, 1987.

Goldberger, Leo, ed. *The Rescue of the Danish Jews: Moral Courage Under Stress.* New York: New York University Press, 1987.

Gushee, David P., *The Righteous Gentiles of the Holocaust: A Christian Interpretation.* Minneapolis: Fortress Press, 1994.

Hallie, Philip. *Lest Innocent Blood Be Shed: The Story of the Village of Le Chambon and How Goodness Happened There.* New York: Harper and Row, 1979.

Hellman, Peter. *Avenue of the Righteous.* New York: Atheneum, 1980.

Huneke, Douglas K. *The Moses of Rovno: The Stirring Story of Fritz Graebe, a German Christian Who Risked His Life to Lead Hundreds of Jews to Safety During the Holocaust.* New York: Dodd, Mead, 1985. Reissued in 1990 and available from the author, 240 Tiburon Boulevard, Tiburon, Calif. 94920.

Keneally, Thomas. *Schindler's List.* New York: Simon and Schuster, 1982.

Koblik, Steven. *The Stones Cry Out: Sweden's Response to the Persecution of the Jews, 1933–1945.* New York: Holocaust Library, 1988.

Oliner, Samuel P., and Pearl M. Oliner. *The Altruistic Personality: Rescuers of Jews in Nazi Europe.* New York: Free Press, 1988.

Opdyke, Irene Gut, with Jeffrey M. Elliot. *Into the Flames: The Life Story of a Righteous Gentile.* San Bernadino: Borgo Press, 1992.

Ramati, Alexander. *The Assisi Underground: The Priests Who Rescued Jews.* New York: Stein and Day Publishers, 1978.

Rittner, Carol, R.S.M., and Sondra Myers, eds. *The Courage to Care.* New York: New York University Press, 1986.

Stein, Andre. *Quiet Heroes: True Stories of the Rescue of Jews by Christians in Nazi-Occupied Holland.* New York: New York University Press, 1988.

Tec, Nechama. *When Light Pierced the Darkness: Christian Rescue of Jews in Nazi-Occupied Poland.* New York: Oxford University Press, 1986.

———. *In the Lion's Den: The Life of Oswald Rufeisen.* New York: Oxford University Press, 1990.

ten Boom, Corrie. *The Hiding Place.* Washington Depot: Chosen Books, 1971.

van der Rol, Ruud, and Rian Verhoeven. *Anne Frank: Beyond the Diary.* New York: Viking Press, 1993.

Yahil, Leni. *The Rescue of Danish Jewry.* Philadelphia: Jewish Publication Society of America, 1969.

Zuccotti, Susan. *The Italians and the Holocaust: Persecution, Rescue, Survival.* New York: Basic Books, 1987.

ADDITIONAL RESOURCES ON ALTRUISM

Coles, Robert. *The Call of Service: A Witness to Idealism.* Boston: Houghton Mifflin, 1993.

Date, Barbara, Boyd Lien, and George Parsons. *A Vision of a Caring Community* (Christian Education and Vacation Church School curriculum). Available from Boyd Lien, 11612 Memorial Drive, Houston, TX. 77024.

Latané, Bib, and John Darley. *The Unresponsive Bystander: Why Doesn't He Help?* New York: Appleton-Century-Crofts, 1970.

Mussen, Paul, and Nancy Eisenberg-Berg. *Roots of Caring, Sharing, and Helping.* New York: Freeman Books, 1977.

Wuthnow, Robert. *Acts of Compassion: Caring for Others and Helping Ourselves.* Princeton: Princeton University Press, 1991.

CHILDREN'S AND YOUTH BOOKS ON RESCUE

Anne Frank in the World. Amsterdam: Anne Frank Foundation, 1985.

Anne Frank's Tales from the Secret Annex. New York: Washington Square Press, 1983.

Anne Frank: The Diary of a Young Girl. New York: Modern Library, 1952.

The Anne Frank books will be of particular interest to mature youth who are reading *The Diary of a Young Girl*, *Anne Frank in the World*, and *Anne Frank, Beyond the Diary* (see van der Rol and Verhoeven below).

Bishop, Claire Huchet. *Twenty and Ten.* New York: Puffin Books, 1978. This book is suitable for young readers. The illustrations are enriching.

Daniel, Jamie, Michael Nicholson, and David Winner. *People Who Made a Difference: Raoul Wallenberg.* Milwaukee: Gareth Stevens Children's Books, 1992. This book is suitable for older youth. The drawings and pictures support the well-documented text.

Meltzer, Milton. *Rescue: The Story of How Gentiles Saved Jews in the Holocaust* New York: Harper and Row, 1988. This text should be used with older youth, middle and high school. It is a basic introduction to rescue narratives.

Pettit, Jayne. *A Place to Hide: True Stories of Holocaust Rescue*. New York: Scholastic, 1993. *A Place to Hide* is for use with students in the fifth through ninth grades. It ably retells the best-known stories of rescue.

Reiss, Johanna. *The Upstairs Room*. New York: Bantam Books, 1972.

_____ . *The Journey Back*. New York: Harper Keypoint, 1987.

In *Upstairs Room* and *Journey Back*, the author tells the moving story of her three-year experience hiding in Holland, and in the second text, she recounts the postwar years. Both books are for older youth.

Van der Rol, Ruud, and Rian Verhoeven. *Anne Frank: Beyond the Diary*. New York: Viking Press, 1993.

Vos, Ida. *Hide and Seek* Boston: Houghton Mifflin, 1991. The author recalls her years in hiding in Holland. The book is for high school students.

VIDEO RESOURCES ON RESCUE

Videos listed below that indicate availability from the Anti-Defamation League (ADL) may be secured by writing or calling the ADL-Braun Holocaust Study Center, 823 United Nations Plaza, New York, N.Y. 10017.

Avenue of the Just. This 57-minute video introduces the rescuers and their honors at *Yad Vashem*. Available from ADL.

The Boat Is Full. This 104-minute feature film video recounts the story of a family of Swiss rescuers. It was honored at the Berlin Film Festival and was nominated for an Academy Award as the Best Foreign Film.

The Courage to Care. Produced and directed by Robert Gardner for the United Way of America for the United States Holocaust Memorial Council. Based on the book of the same title, by Carol Rittner, R.S.M., and Sondra Myers. An exceptional series of interviews with rescuers and the rescued. 28 minutes with study guide. Available from ADL.

Joseph Schultz. A dramatic rendering of the story of a German soldier fighting in Yugoslavia who refused to take part in the execution of a group of villagers. 14 minutes with study guide. Available from ADL.

Weapons of the Spirit. Produced and directed by Pierre Sauvage, this video recounts the rescues in the French village of le Chambon and celebrates the compassion and courage of the Huguenot community led by Pastor André Trocmé. The video greatly enriches the narrative account by Philip Hallie, *Lest Innocent Blood Be Shed*. It is available from ADL in full-length and classroom-length (38 minute) versions.

The following videos are part of an ever-expanding collection of documentary films produced and directed by Sy Rotter of Documentaries International: Film and Video

Foundation (1800 K Street, NW, Suite 1120, Washington, D.C. 20006). They are available, with study guides, directly from Documentaries International and also from ADL.

The Other Side of Faith. 28 minutes. Featuring the story of two Polish teenagers who rescued thirteen Jewish refugees.
Rescue in Scandinavia. 55 minutes. Narrated by Liv Ullmann and featuring the rescues that occurred in Denmark, Finland, Norway, and Sweden.
Zegota—A Time to Remember. 52 minutes. Featuring the account of a clandestine Polish Underground effort to save the Jews of Warsaw.

OTHER RESCUE-RELATED RESOURCES

"The Miracle of Denmark." The National Conference of Christians and Jews (NCCJ). This booklet offers a service in the Christian tradition, remembering and celebrating the rescue of Danish Jews. Local offices of the NCCJ stock the booklet, or it may be ordered from NCCJ, 43 West 57th Street, New York, N.Y. 10019.
"Rescue & Goodness: Reflections on The Holocaust." The United States Holocaust Memorial Museum. Essays by The Rev. Dr. John Pawlikowski and Professor Philip Hallie reflect on the moral implications of the Shoah and on rescue. Copies are available from the Office of Church Relations at the museum, 100 Raoul Wallenberg Place, SW Washington, D.C. 20024–2150.

THE SHOAH AND ANTI-SEMITISM

Flannery, Edward H. *The Anguish of the Jews: Twenty Three Centuries of Anti-Semitism.* New York: Paulist Press, 1985.
Poliakov, Leon. *From the Time of Christ to the Court Jews: The History of Anti-Semitism.* New York: Schocken Books, 1976.
Ruether, Rosemary. *Faith and Fratricide: The Theological Roots of Anti-Semitism.* New York: Seabury Press, 1974.
Sandmel, Samuel. *Anti-Semitism in the New Testament?* Philadelphia: Fortress Press, 1978.

BIBLICAL TEXTS—SERMON INTERPRETATIONS

There are two practical, relatively current resources for dealing with texts that have traditionally contributed to an anti-Semitic animus and that adequately understand the relationship between Jesus and his Jewish faith.

Borg, Marcus. *Meeting Jesus AGAIN for the First Time: The Historical Jesus and the Heart of Contemporary Faith.* San Francisco: Harper San Francisco, 1994. See Chapter Two, the section entitled "The Jewishness of Jesus."

Williamson, Clark M., and Ronald Allen. *Interpreting Difficult Texts: Anti-Judaism and Christian Preaching*. Philadelphia: Trinity Press International, 1989.

BOOKS BY DIETRICH BONHOEFFER

Bonhoeffer, Dietrich. *Life Together: A Discussion of Christian Fellowship*. New York: Harper and Row, 1954.
_____ . *Creation and Fall: A Theological Interpretation of Genesis 1–3*. London: SCM Press, 1960.
_____ . *Ethics*. New York: Macmillan, 1965.
_____ . *No Rusty Swords: Letters, Lectures and Notes, 1928–1936*. New York: Harper and Row, 1965.
_____ . *Christ the Center*. New York: Harper and Row, 1966.
_____ . *Letters and Papers from Prison*. New York: Macmillan, 1972.
_____ . *The Cost of Discipleship*. New York: Macmillan, 1974.
_____ . *Prayers from Prison: Prayers and Poems*. Philadelphia: Fortress Press, 1977.
_____ . *Meditating on the Word*. Nashville: Cowley Publications for The Upper Room, 1986.
_____ . *A Testament to Freedom: The Essential Writings of Dietrich Bonhoeffer*. Edited by Geffrey B. Kelly and F. Burton Nelson. San Francisco: HarperCollins, 1990.

BONHOEFFER BIOGRAPHIES AND RESOURCES

Berryhill, Elizabeth. *The Cup of Trembling: A Play in Two Acts Derived from the Life of Dietrich Bonhoeffer*. New York: Seabury Press, 1958.
Bethge, Eberhard. *Bonhoeffer: Exile and Martyr*. New York: Seabury Press, 1975.
_____ . *Dietrich Bonhoeffer: Man of Vision, Man of Courage*. New York: Harper and Row, 1977.
Bethge, Eberhard, Renate Bethge, and Christian Gremmels. *Dietrich Bonhoeffer: A Life in Pictures*. Philadelphia: Fortress Press, 1986.
Reist, Benjamin A. *The Promise of Bonhoeffer*. Philadelphia: J.B. Lippincott, 1969.
Sorensen, David Allen. *Life Together: A Leader's Guide*. New York: HarperCollins, 1992.
Stauffer, Donald. *Study Guide to the Cup of Trembling*. New York: Seabury Press, 1963.
Wind, Renata. *Dietrich Bonhoeffer: A Spoke in the Wheel*. Grand Rapids: William B. Eerdmans, 1990.

VIDEO RESOURCE ON BONHOEFFER

Dietrich Bonhoeffer: Memories and Perspectives. 90-minute documentary with study guide. Black and white.

THEOLOGY AND THE SHOAH

Bennett, Gordon C. *God Is My Fuehrer: A Dramatic Interpretation of the Life of Martin Niemoeller*. New York: Friendship Press, 1970.

Berkovits, Eliezer. *Faith After the Holocaust*. New York: KTAV Publishing House, 1973.

Eckardt, Alice I., and A. Roy Eckardt. *Long Night's Journey into Day: A Revised Retrospective on the Holocaust*. Detroit: Wayne State University Press, 1982.

Ellis, Marc. *Ending Auschwitz: The Future of Jewish and Christian Life*. Louisville: Westminster/John Knox Press, 1994.

Fackenheim, Emil L. *God's Presence in History: Jewish Affirmations and Philosophical Reflections*. New York: Harper and Row, 1970.

———. *The Jewish Bible After the Holocaust: A Re-reading*. Bloomington: Indiana University Press, 1990.

Fasching, Darrell, Jr. *Narrative Theology After Auschwitz*. Minneapolis: Fortress Press, 1992.

Frankl, Viktor E. *Man's Search for Meaning: An Introduction to Logotherapy*. New York: Washington Square Press, 1965.

Harrelson, Walter, and Randall M. Falk. *Jews and Christians: A Troubled Family*. Nashville: Abingdon Press, 1990.

Jacobs, Steven L., ed. *Contemporary Jewish Religious Responses to the Shoah*. Vol. 5 of Studies in the Shoah. Lanham: University Press of America, 1993.

———. *Contemporary Christian Religious Responses to the Shoah*. Vol. 6 of Studies in the Shoah. Lanham: University Press of America, 1993.

Littell, Franklin. *The Crucifixion of the Jews: The Failure of Christians to Understand the Jewish Experience*. New York: Harper and Row, 1975.

McGarry, Michael B., C.S.P. *Christology After Auschwitz*. New York: Paulist Press, 1977.

Neusner, Jacob. *Telling Tales: Making Sense of Christian and Judaic Nonsense— the Urgency and Basis for Judeo-Christian Dialogue*. Louisville: Westminster/John Knox Press, 1993.

Roth, John K., and Michael Berenbaum, eds. *Holocaust: Religious and Philosophical Implications*. New York: Paragon House, 1989.

Rubenstein, Richard L. *After Auschwitz: Radical Theology and Contemporary Judaism*. Indianapolis: Bobbs-Merrill, 1966.

Wiesenthal, Simon. *The Sunflower (with a Symposium)*. New York: Schocken Books, 1969.

Williamson, Clark M. *A Guest in the House of Israel: Post-Holocaust Church Theology*. Louisville: Westminster/John Knox Press, 1993.

OTHER THEOLOGICAL RESOURCES

"Christians Confront the Holocaust: A Collection of Sermons." Published by the National Conference of Christians and Jews, 1979.

Pawlikowski, John T., O.S.M. "The Challenge of the Holocaust for Christian
Theology." Booklet published by the Anti-Defamation League of B'nai
B'rith, 1978.

THEOLOGY AND THE SHOAH: VIDEO RESOURCE

The Cross and the Star: Jews, Christians, and the Holocaust. 52-minute video
confronting the various responses to the Shoah.

THEODICY

Birnbaum, David. *God and Evil: A Jewish Perspective*. Hoboken: KTAV Publish-
ing House, 1989.
Blumenthal, David R. *Facing the Abusing God: A Theology of Protest*. Louisville:
Westminister/John Knox Press, 1993.
Buber, Martin. *Good and Evil*. New York: Charles Scribner's Sons, 1953.
Cooper, Burton Z. *Why, God?* Atlanta: John Knox Press, 1988.
Hick, John. *Evil and the God of Love*. London: Macmillan, 1977.
Irish, Jerry. *A Boy Thirteen: Reflections on Death*. Philadelphia: Westminster
Press, 1975.
Schulweis, Harold M. *Evil and the Morality of God*. Cincinnati: Hebrew Union
College Press, 1984.
Willimon, William H. *Sighing for Eden: Sin, Evil & the Christian Faith*. Nash-
ville: Abingdon Press, 1985.

LITURGICAL RESOURCES

Littell, Marcia Sachs. *Liturgies on the Holocaust*. Lewiston: Edwin Mellen Press,
for the Anne Frank Institute, 1986.
Wiesel, Elie, and Albert Friedlander. *The Six Days of Destruction: Meditations
Towards Hope*. New York: Pergamon Press, 1988.

THE ARMENIAN GENOCIDE

Hartunian, Abraham H. *Neither to Laugh nor to Weep: A Memoir of the Armenian
Genocide*. Boston: Beacon Press, 1968.
Hovannisian, Richard G. *The Armenian Genocide: History, Politics, Ethics*. New
York: St. Martin's Press, 1992.
Miller, Donald E., and Lorna Tourgan Miller. *Survivors: An Oral History of the
Armenian Genocide*. Berkeley: University of California Press, 1993.

Index

About the Author

DOUGLAS K. HUNEKE is currently Senior Minister at Westminster Presbyterian Church in Tiburon, California, and a visiting lecturer at San Francisco Theological Seminary. He has served as a university pastor, was an Honors College faculty member at the University of Oregon, and received the Faculty Research Award from the Oregon Committee for the Humanities. He is the author of numerous books, articles, and essays on the Holocaust, including *The Moses of Rovno: The True Story of a German Christian Who Rescued Jews* (1985), and *In the Darkness–Glimpses of Light: A Study of Nazi Era Rescuers.*